Critical Affinities

SUNY series, Philosophy and Race
Robert Bernasconi and
T. Denean Sharpley-Whiting, editors

Critical Affinities

Nietzsche and African American Thought

EDITED BY

Jacqueline Scott
and
A. Todd Franklin

———

FOREWORD BY

Robert Gooding-Williams

State University of New York Press

Published by
State University of New York Press

© 2006 State University of New York

For information, address State University of New York Press,
194 Washington Avenue, Suite 305, Albany, NY 12210-2384

Production by Diane Ganeles
Marketing by Michael Campochiaro

Library of Congress Cataloging-in-Publication Data

Critical affinities : Nietzsche and African American thought / edited by Jacqueline
Scott and A. Todd Franklin ; foreword by Robert Gooding-Williams.
    p.   cm. — (SUNY series, philisophy and race)
  Includes bibliographical references and index.
  ISBN-13: 978-0-7914-6861-6 (hardcover : alk. paper)
  ISBN-10: 0-7914-6861-5 (hardcover : alk. paper)
  ISBN-13: 978-0-7914-6862-3 (pbk. : alk. paper)
  ISBN-10: 0-7914-6862-3 (pbk. : alk. paper)
   1. Nietzsche, Friedrich Wilhelm, 1844–1900. 2. African Americans—Intellectual
life. 3. Race relations—United States. 4. Racism—United States. I. Scott,
Jacqueline. II. Franklin, A. Todd, 1968– III. Series.

B3317.C685 2006
193—dc22

2005029978

10   9   8   7   6   5   4   3   2   1

Contents

Foreword
  Robert Gooding-Williams   vii

Acknowledgments   xix

Note on Abbreviations   xxi

Introduction: The Art of the Cultural Physician   1

Part I: Diagnoses

1. Kindred Spirits: Nietzsche and Locke as Progenitors
   of Axiological Liberation
   A. Todd Franklin   17

2. Nietzsche, *Ressentiment*, Lynching
   John Pittman   33

3. Double Consciousness and Second Sight
   Kathleen Marie Higgins   51

4. Of Tragedy and the Blues in an Age of Decadence:
   Thoughts on Nietzsche and African America
   Lewis R. Gordon   75

Part II: Prescriptions

5. Ecce Negro: How To Become a Race Theorist
   Paul C. Taylor   101

6. Nietzsche's Proto-Phenomenological Approach
   to the Theoretical Problem of Race
   Daniel W. Conway   125

7. The Price of the Ticket: A Genealogy and
   Revaluation of Race
   Jacqueline Scott   149

Part III: Regimens of Recovery

8. Unlikely Illuminations: Nietzsche and Frederick Douglass
   on Power, Struggle, and the *Aisthesis* of Freedom
   Christa Davis Acampora   175

9. Masculinity and Existential Freedom:
   Wright, Ellison, Morrison, and Nietzsche
   Cynthia Willett   203

10. Why Nietzsche (Sometimes) Can't Sing the Blues,
    or Davis, Nietzsche, and the Social Embeddedness
    of Aesthetic Judgments
    James Winchester   225

List of Contributors   247

Index   251

Foreword:
Supposing Nietzsche to Be Black—
What Then?

ROBERT GOODING-WILLIAMS

The chapters here mark the advent of a new, new Nietzsche, a convergence of recurrence and singularity. They present not a German Nietzsche, a French Nietzsche, or an Anglo-American Nietzsche, but an African American Nietzsche, a black Nietzsche. Supposing Nietzsche to be black—what then? To suppose Nietzsche to be black is to suppose, with the editors of this anthology, that he may be interpreted with an eye to the typical concerns of African American thought; or, more generally, the typical concerns of black studies. If Nietzsche becomes French when read in the perspective of poststructuralism, or Anglo-American when read in the perspective of contemporary analytic philosophy, then he becomes black when read in the perspective of black studies.[1]

Consider too that these chapters complicate and perhaps disrupt common notions of the discursive options available to black studies. Rather than promote an Afrocentric, diasporic, queer, or feminist black studies (and here I make no judgment as to the comparative merits of these now-familiar approaches to the discipline), they tacitly envision a black studies charmed and unsettled by a seducer (*ein Versucher*), by Nietzsche—a black studies richer in itself, newer to itself than before, full of new will and currents, full of new dissatisfactions.[2] In Jacqueline Scott's and A. Todd Franklin's enticing volume of Nietzsche scholarship, a black new Nietzsche inspires new thoughts about black thought and black studies.

But we should not proceed too hastily. While new and still- newer Nietzsches continue to thrive, spectres of older Nietzsches remain, one of which is Nietzsche, the philosopher of aristocratic radicalism, likewise the brutally scathing critic of socialism, feminism, and liberalism—indeed, of all forms of modern egalitarianism. This, for example, is the figure Georg Lukács described when he wrote that Nietzsche's "whole life's work was a continuous polemic against Marxism and socialism."[3] Similarly, it is the figure William Preston evokes when, with hyperbole to match Lukács, he very recently insists that "Nietzsche's whole philosophy—and not just his view of blacks—is racist."[4] Preston's racially inflected revival of an older Nietzsche merits attention here, for it suggests that Nietzsche has precious little to offer African American thought, and that to hold otherwise, as do the editors of this collection, is absurd.

In a chapter meant for an anthology devoted to black existentialism, Preston asks "Can Nietzsche help black existentialists find answers to *their own* questions?"[5] "No" is Preston's clear response to this question, but a careful reading of his argument urges a still stronger conclusion: namely, that progressive philosophers given to a serious engagement with issues like white supremacy, colonialism, black politics, and black identity, whether or not they are existentialists, and whether or not they are black, have no use for Nietzsche. Preston tends toward this conclusion when he claims that Nietzsche saw suffering blacks as laboratory animals whom he wanted "*to make . . . suffer more.*"[6] In effect, Preston argues that black and other progressives have no use for Nietzsche, because Nietzsche was a "cruel racist" and a forward-looking, trans-European "man of the Right."[7]

Supposing Nietzsche to be black—what then? Specifically, what then can be said to support this philosophical gambit, this *supposing*, faced with considerations like the ones that Preston adduces? In the remainder of this foreword to *Critical Affinities*, I offer some answers to this question, giving the central thrust of Preston's argument its due and scouting a few of the topoi where, perhaps, the new, new Nietzsche may be found. I explore these topoi under the rubrics of two broad headings, each of which indicates some fruitful points of departure for African American thought that is tempted to consociate with Nietzsche. These are (1) Nietzsche, colonialist fantasy, and anti-racism, and (2) Nietzsche and German nationalism.

Nietzsche, Colonialist Fantasy, and Anti-Racism

In his excellent essay on Nietzsche and colonialism, Robert Holub remarks that events heralding Germany's emergence as a colonial power (Germany began to acquire colonies in Africa and the Pacific in 1884) "reached their height during the years that Nietzsche was composing his major works."[8] Holub also reminds his readers that Nietzsche became personally involved with colonialism through the adventures of his sister and brother-in-law, Elisabeth and Bernhard Förster, founders of the Paraguayan colony of *Nueva Germania*. Finally, and most important for my purposes, Holub recognizes that this personal involvement has "a philosophical counterpart in [Nietzsche's] writings."[9] More exactly, he acknowledges that Nietzsche's philosophical imagination becomes a colonialist imagination when it conjures the images of the "good European" and a "great politics" to envision a caste of "new philosophers" that would rule Europe and subjugate the entire earth.[10] A critic of the sort of nationalism the Försters embraced, Nietzsche endorsed a supranationalist imperialism:

> Nietzsche's untimeliness . . . involves his unusual way of approaching the problems posed by foreign affairs and world politics. Eschewing the nationalist, mercantile, and utopian/idealist approach to colonization, he developed . . . a conceptual framework that entailed a geopolitical perspective. In the "good European" he found a term for a future elite that could overcome the nation-state, create a superior cultural life, and achieve domination of the world. With "great politics" he offered an alternative to parliamentary life and actual colonial fantasies, as well as a vague blueprint for global conquest on a grand scale.[11]

Holub's description of Nietzsche's geopolitics helps put Preston's remarks into perspective. Thus, when Preston describes Nietzsche as a forward-looking, trans-European "man of the Right," he alludes to Nietzsche's colonialist fantasy of a future, European elite that would dominate the world beyond Europe. When he describes Nietzsche as a racist, he reminds us that this fantasy is, in part, the fantasy of a black Africa subjected to European rule, and that Nietzsche's anti-black racism (evident, for example, in his suggestion that the black race is less intelligent than the white race[12]), in tandem with his enthusiasm for breeding higher human beings, suggests that he imagined an "imperialism of the future" as involving the domination of racially inferior black Africans by racially superior white Europeans. In short, Preston exposes the white supremacist connotations of Nietzsche's colonialist imagination.

Let us assume that some of Nietzsche's writings express racialized colonialist fantasies. Does it follow from this assumption that black and other progressives have no use for Nietzsche's writings except to castigate them? I think not, but not because progressives should ignore these ideas and attend to some other features of Nietzsche's writing. On the contrary, progressives may find in Nietzsche's colonialist fantasies an Ariadne's thread leading them into a rich labyrinth of insight that can well serve African American thought.[13] And throughout Nietzsche's writings, they may discover philosophical resources for exposing imperialist and racist ideologies that he himself occasionally echoes.

Where, then, might the thread of Nietzsche's colonialist fantasies lead African American thinkers? My answer to this question has some affinity for Edward Said's discussion of the colonialist imagination of one of Nietzsche's contemporaries, Joseph Conrad. According to Said, Conrad's novels (e.g., *Nostromo* and *The Heart of Darkness*) do not "give us the sense that he could imagine a fully realized alternative to imperialism."[14] Still, and despite this limitation, "Conrad *dates* imperialism, shows its contingency, records its illusions and tremendous violence and waste . . . [thus] he permits his later readers to imagine something other than an Africa carved up into . . . colonies."[15] Nietzsche was not a student of the imperialist mind in a colonial setting, and so he did not date imperialism in the way Conrad did. But he did date *Europe*, showing *its* contingency, recording *its* illusions, violence, and waste. Because Nietzsche declines to flatter European culture but represents it as the contingent, overdetermined product of slave morality, cruelty, decadence, and nihilism, he remains a useful model for any thinker — indeed, for any African American thinker—who would puncture European or now Euro-American pieties in order to date and imagine alternatives to the Euro-cultural legacies of white supremacy. Nietzsche's colonialist fantasies can be a guide in this endeavor, for they repeatedly implicate his demystifying criticisms of European culture.[16]

I conclude the present section by noting some examples of anti-racist and/or anti-imperialist social thought that draw inspiration from Nietzsche. The first is Michel Foucault's use of a Nietzschean concept of genealogy to analyze the advent of modern racism (see volume 1 of *The History of Sexuality*, as well as Foucault's 1976 lectures at the Collège de France).[17] A second example is Ann Laura Stoler's attempt to expand the scope of Foucault's inquiry. Well aware that Foucault limits his focus to intra-European racial formations (specifically, he develops the claim that "the emergence of biopower inscribed modern racism in the mechanisms of the normalizing [European] state"), Stoler has begun to explore the implictions of his argument for the field of colonial studies.[18] In a similar vein, Cornel West also has invoked Nietzsche's and Foucault's notions of genealogy to lay a theoretical basis for his own account of modern racism (an account that differs from the one Foucault sketched).[19]

My final example is James Snead's valuable essay, "Repetition As a Figure of Black Culture," and the emphasis that Snead places there on Nietzsche's "revised metaphysics of rupture and opening."[20] For Snead, Nietzsche's "metaphysics" (which he interprets as prefiguring Derrida's critique of the metaphysics of presence) is important, because it provides him a conceptual tool for critically debunking a view of European culture—specifically, the view that European culture, in contrast to black African culture, is "ever developing"— that white supremacist, imperialist Europe has often advanced to distinguish itself from black Africa. Like Foucault, Stoler, and West, Snead productively deploys Nietzschean philosophical insights to analyze and expose racist ideology.[21]

Nietzsche and German Nationalism

I now turn to *The Birth of Tragedy* (1871), Nietzsche's most explicitly nationalist book, and a work that he presents as conflating "patriotic excitement and aesthetic enthusiasm" (*BT*, P).[22] Here I consider *Birth* in the perspective of African American thought, taking DuBois's masterpiece, *The Souls of Black Folk* (1903), as my point of departure.[23]

In the first chapter of *Souls*, DuBois famously attributes a double consciousness and a double self to African Americans. "One ever feels his two-ness," DuBois writes, "an American, a Negro." Additionally, DuBois describes "the history of the American Negro" as a struggle "to merge his double self into a better and truer self," but without losing either "older" self. Wanting neither to "Africanize America" nor to "bleach his Negro soul in a flood of white Americanism," the American Negro "wishes to make it possible for a man to be both a Negro and an American, without being cursed and spit upon by his fellows." DuBois's portrait of black duplicity summarizes his view of the African American experience of modernity. While African Americans aspire to assimilate—that is, to bring their American lives more fully into accord with the moral and economic norms of modern America—they remain collectively bound together by a distinctive *Volksgeist*, a unifying folk spirit that animates the lives of all African Americans. The African American's struggle "to merge his double self" is, in part, his effort to make manifest this unique spirituality, even as he embraces the norms of modernity.[24]

Considered from the perspective of DuBois's interpretation of the African American experience of modernity, *Birth* comes into view as a remarkably similar attempt to resolve the conflict between modernity and a putatively distinctive (German) *Volksgeist*; or, more exactly, as a like attempt to resolve that conflict with the idea of a "double self," an idea that Nietzsche figures with the image of an "artistic Socrates." We need only review the general argument of *Birth* to make clear its affinity for *Souls* in this respect.

In *Birth*, Nietzsche argues that, due to a dialectic immanent in modern, scientific, Socratic culture, a postmodern, Dionysian culture is soon to be born: a "sublime . . . illusion accompanies science . . . and leads science again and again to its limits at which it must turn into *art—which is really the aim of this mechanism*" (*BT* 15). Nietzsche describes the art he mentions, the art of Wagner's music, as German and Dionysian. Specifically, he claims that Wagner's music embodies the artistic self-reformation of a self-estranged German spirit. Expressing the German spirit's Dionysian "root" and essence, Wagner's music effects that spirit's "return to itself," bringing its "form" into harmony with its essence (*BT* 19).

According to Nietzsche, Wagner's musical re-formation of the German spirit is the culmination of a cultural movement that Luther began with the re-formation of German religion. Nietzsche also suggests that Luther's initiative had an essentially musical character that prefigured the development of German music from Bach to Beethoven to Wagner: it is from a primordial Dionysian abyss that "the German Reformation came forth; in its chorales the future tune of German music sounded for the first time . . . as the first Dionysian luring call breaking forth from dense thickets at the approach of spring"(*BT* 19, 23).

By representing Wagner's music as the cultural fulfillment of the German Reformation, Nietzsche identifies that music as the apex of a distinctively Germanic reaction to the Alexandrian-Romantic culture he associates with the figure of Socrates. Effecting a "return to itself of the German spirit," Wagner's music marks the final phase of the purification (*Läuterung*) of that spirit (*BT* 20). Purification, in this context, entails the "elimination of everything Romanic (*der Ausscheidung des Romanischen)*" from the German spirit, including the Socratic and secularizing tendencies that estranged it from its "sacred," Dionysian essence, leaving it rootless, exhausted, and prey to a "homeless roving" that seeks nourishment from "foreign tables"

(*BT* 23). In the modern world, the "abstract education; abstract morality; [and] abstract law" essential to Alexandrian-Romanic culture have subjected a Dionysian and distinctively German sensibility to a logic-driven, Socratic cast of mind that privileges no attachments to German (or to any) national culture (e.g., "native myth"). Thus German spiritual renewal requires that German culture purge itself of its "forcibly implanted" Alexandrian-Romanic elements (*BT* 23). Like Herder before him, Nietzsche relies on the chauvinistic language of German nationalism to advance German cultural autonomy. His high praise of German culture entails an aggressive antipathy to foreign cultures, precisely because he sees them as colonizing forces that have stifled the cultural self-expression of the German spirit.

It needs to be added, finally, that Nietzsche's nationalism does not lead him to abandon the Socratic ethos of modernity. That he declines to abandon this ethos is evident from his use of the figure of an "artistic" or "a music-practicing" Socrates to represent German spiritual renewal (*BT* 14, 15, 17). Nietzsche's appeal to this figure suggests that the postmodern culture he foresees is one that combines both Socratic and Dionysian elements, a culture that will come into being through an *Aufhebung* (in Hegel's sense) of modernity that, while preserving the Socratic ethos of modernity, will still emancipate the Dionysian, German spirit from the repressive strictures of that ethos. Nietzsche's image of a music-practicing Socrates, like DuBois's image of the African American who would be "both a Negro and an American," symbolizes a merged, double self that reconciles the ethical or otherwise normative demands of modernity with the spiritual demands of a unique *Volk*.

We know, of course, that Nietzsche later repudiates the German nationalism that the image of a music practicing Socrates presupposes. In 1886, for example, in the extended palinode he adds to a new edition of *Birth* (his "Attempt at a Self- Criticism"), he rejects his earlier contention that a renewed German spirit could invest modernity with Dionysian vigor, suggesting now that German culture has thoroughly succumbed to "levelling mediocrity . . . and 'modern ideas'"(*BT*, "Attempt" 6). For the Nietzsche of the mid-1880s and after—hence, for the Nietzsche who also has begun to produce "untimely" colonialist fantasies—supposing that the German *Volk* has an identity that is not a part of the (decadent) cultural repertoire of modernity, and that could supplement and vitalize that repertoire, is nonsense.

Considering *Birth* in connection to *Souls* lets us see the affinities between Nietzsche's and DuBois's attempts to imagine what contemporary scholars call "alternative modernities,"[25] in short, to imagine cultures that embrace modernity without wholly sacrificing their cultural or spiritual distinctiveness. Nietzsche's self-criticism, which suggests that modern decadence can all-too-easily nullify cultural distinctiveness, also raises doubts as to the validity of any attempt to conceptualize modern identities by appeal to figures of a double "self" or "consciousness" that assume the presence "outside" modernity of cultural orientations not available "inside" modernity. I leave open, for present purposes, the question as to whether such doubts threaten the argument of DuBois's *Souls*. It is clear, however, that they raise questions for certain *neoDuBoisian* views of black identity. I conclude the present section by examining one such view, namely, Paul Gilroy's treatment of black identity in *The Black Atlantic*.

Deliberately echoing DuBois, Gilroy argues that black identity involves a double consciousness of being inside and outside modernity. Corresponding to the inside/outside distinction, he identifies two kinds of politics. The first, a politics of fulfillment, proceeds by way of an immanent critique of modernity and aspires to complete the project of Enlightenment. The second, a politics of transfiguration, (putatively) proceeds from outside the cultural repertoire of modernity. As Gilroy describes it, the politics of transfiguration is an anti- and perhaps a pre-discursive politics that complements without repudiating the project of immanent critique. This politics is "played, danced and acted."[26] Its basic desire is "to conjure up and enact new modes of friendship, happiness, and solidarity."[27]

Arguing that the politics of transfiguration is based outside the cultural repertoire of modernity, Gilroy emphasizes the expressive power of Afro-Atlantic music. In particular, he holds that the modern music of the black diaspora transcends its modernity, showing that, contrary to "the conventions, assumptions, and rules that distinguish and periodise modernity," music has an expressive power not possessed by the "petty power of words."[28] Gilroy's assertion is questionable, for it depends on an attenuated view of the cultural repertoire of modernity. Specifically, it relies on the assumption that modern European aesthetics knows nothing of the proposition that music, in comparison to words, is privileged in its ability to express subjective states of experience. Counterexamples to this assumption include arguments espoused by Herder, the German *Frühromantiker*, and Kierkegaard. Gilroy can plausibly propose that, in seeking to express the ineffable, Afro-Atlantic music escapes the cultural repertoire of modernity, precisely because he ignores such counterexamples and reduces the aesthetic debates of modernity to Hegelian dictums regarding the relative value of art and philosophy.[29] It is ironic, moreover, that in defending his position he only slightly modifies Schopenhauer's anti-Hegelian but still modern view, which Nietzsche repeats in *Birth*, that music is a "direct image of the will (*unmittelbar Abbild des Willens*)" (*BT* 16). According to Gilroy, "music should enjoy the higher status because of its capacity to express a *direct image of the slave's will*."[30]

I can summarize my critique of Gilroy by noting its affinity for Nietzsche's self-criticism. As we have seen, this self-criticism questions the thesis that having a German identity is tantamount to having a (Dionysian) cultural orientation that is not part of the cultural repertoire of modernity. Similarly, I question the thesis that having a black diasporic identity (as interpreted by Gilroy) is tantamount to having a cultural orientation that is not part of the cultural repertoire of modernity. Because Nietzsche believes that Germany has thoroughly succumbed to modern decadence, he doubts his youthful claim that German identity has something distinctive to add to modern culture. And because Gilroy has a cramped view of modern culture, I doubt the particulars of his claim that black diasporic identities have something distinctive to add. While Gilroy echoes the early Nietzsche, a Nietzsche who praises the German spirit as a supplement to modernity, my critique echoes a later Nietzsche, who looks askance at the pretension to supply such a supplement. Perhaps this outcome will be exemplary for a black studies that has been unsettled by Nietzsche, for the essence of Nietzsche's rigor is his relentless if often stressful practice of thinking against himself.[31]

Conclusion

Supposing Nietzsche to be black—but who has the will to concern himself or herself with such a questionable conjecture? Surely for that we require a new species of philosopher (some of them black, no doubt, for philosophers begin to entertain such conjectures, just when black faces appear amongst them), imaginative, dare I say "original," thinkers who bridge the rift in academia between Nietzsche and black studies. Here I have explored two places where this rift permits some bridging, highlighting—perhaps counterintuitively—Nietzsche's colonialist fantasies and his nationalism. But where are the philosophers to explore other places, philosophers whose knowing will be a creating and whose creating will continue to forge the profile of a black Nietzsche? Do such philosophers exist?

By editing this anthology, A Todd Franklin and Jacqueline Scott have tellingly addressed these questions, inviting their readers to proclaim in all earnestness, "We see such new philosophers coming up!"[32]

Notes

1. Alan Schrift alludes to "the often contentious discussions of the 'French Nietzsche' and, more generally, of the work of the poststructuralists" in the introduction to his book, *Nietzsche's French Legacy: A Genealogy of Poststructuralism* (New York: Routledge, 1995), 2. The first, groundbreaking attempt to interpret Nietzsche from the perspective of Anglo-American analytic philosophy was Arthur Danto's now well-known *Nietzsche as Philosopher* (New York: Macmillan, 1965). For a detailed history of the "German Nietzsche," see Steven E. Aschheim, *The Nietzsche Legacy in Germany: 1890–1990* (Berkeley: University of California Press, 1992).

2. Cf. Nietzsche's description of Dionysus in *BGE*, 295.

3. See Georg Lukács, *The Destruction of Reason*, trans. Peter Palmer (Atlantic Highlands, NJ: Humanities Press, 1981), 313.

4. William A. Preston, "Nietzsche on Blacks," *Existence in Black: An Anthology of Black Existential Philosophy* (New York: Routledge, 1997), 170.

5. Preston, "Nietzsche on Blacks," 168.

6. Preston, "Nietzsche on Blacks," 168.

7. Preston, "Nietzsche on Blacks," 169, 171.

8. Robert Holub, "Nietzsche's Colonialist Imagination: Nueva Germania, Good Europeanism, and Great Politics," in *The Imperialist Imagination: German Colonialism and Its Legacy*, ed. Sara Friedrichsmeyer, Sara Lennox, and Susanne Zantop (Ann Arbor: The University of Michigan Press, 1998), 34.

9. Holub, "Nietzsche's Colonialist Imagination," 40.

10. Holub rightly suggests that among Nietzsche's published writings *Beyond Good and Evil* is the locus classicus for Nietzsche's colonialist imagining of the idea of a great politics (see Holub, "Nietzsche's Colonialist Imagination," 48). Moreover, *Beyond Good and Evil* makes explicit the links between that idea and those of the "good European" and the "new philosopher."

11. Holub, "Nietzsche's Colonialist Imagination," 49.

12. For Niezsche's suggestion to this effect, see *D* 241. To support his claim that Nietzsche saw blacks as racial inferiors, Preston cites this passage. He also cites *GM*: II 7, where Nietzsche takes blacks as representatives of prehistoric man. For an alternative interpretation of the latter passage, which interestingly interprets Nietzsche as revising Hegel's image of blacks, see Sander Gilman, *On Blackness without Blacks: Essays on the Image of the Black in Germany* (Boston: G. K. Hall, 1982), 113–118.

13. Nietzsche himself alludes to the idea of an Ariadne's thread leading into, rather than out of, the labyrinth. On this point, see Robert Gooding-Williams, *Zarathustra's Dionysian Modernism* (Stanford, CA: Stanford University Press, 2001), 264.

14. Edward Said, *Culture and Imperialism* (New York: Alfred A. Knopf, 1993), 25.

15. Said, *Culture and Imperialism*, 26.

16. For a discussion of the connections between Nietzsche's colonialist fantasy of a "great politics" and his critique of the culture of European modernity, see Gooding-Williams, *Zarathustra's Dionysian Modernism*, especially chapters 1 and 6.

17. The locus classicus of Foucault's analysis of the idea of genealogy that Nietzsche develops in *On the Genealogy of Morals* is "Nietzsche, Genealogy, and History," in *Language, Counter-memory, Practice*, ed. Donald F. Bouchard (Ithaca, NY: Cornell University Press), 139–164. My understanding of the arguments that Foucault develops in his 1976 Collège de France lectures derives from Ann Laura Stoler, *Race and the Education of Desire: Foucault's History of Sexuality and the Colonial Order of Things* (Durham, NC: Duke University Press, 1995), passim.

18. See Stoler, *Race and the Education of Desire*, 55 and passim.

19. See Cornel West, *Prophesy Deliverance* (Philadelphia: Westminster Press, 1982), 48, 160 fn.2

20. James A. Snead, "Repetition As a Figure of Black Culture," in *Black Literature and Literary Theory*, ed. Henry Louis Gates, Jr. (New York: Metheuen, 1984), 64, 76 fn.11, and passim.

21. Other authors who draw on Nietzsche for the purposes of anti-racist social critique and who deserve to be mentioned here include Frantz Fanon and, more recently, Cynthia Willett. See, for example, Frantz Fanon, *Black Skin, White Masks*, trans. Charles Markmann (New York: Grove, 1967), 36, 154, 222, and Cynthia Willett, *Maternal Ethics and Other Slave Moralities* (New York: Routledge, 1995), chap. 7. For a valuable, Nietzsche-inspired discussion of identity politics that has substantial bearing on questions relating to African American resistance to racism, see Wendy Brown, *States of Injury* (Princeton, NJ: Princeton University Press, 1995), chap. 3.

22. See Friedrich Nietzsche, *The Birth of Tragedy,* in *The Birth of Tragedy and the Case of Wagner*, ed. and trans. Walter Kaufmann (New York: Vintage, 1967).

23. Possibly the first attempts to consider *The Birth of Tragedy* in light of the concerns of African American or, more generally, African-diasporic thought may be found in Aimé Césaire's contributions to *Tropiques* (a journal that played a critical role in establishing the negritude movement) in the 1940s. For a brief, general discusssion of Nietzsche's influence on Césaire, see the introduction to *Aimé Césaire: The Collected Poetry*, trans. and ed. Clayton Eshleman and Annette Smith (Berkeley: University of California Press, 1983), 3. For a discussion of the almost contemporaneous Nazi appropriation of *Birth*, which preceded Césaire's reflections on the text by less than a decade, see Hans Sluga, *Heidegger's Crisis: Philosophy and Politics in Nazi Germany* (Cambridge, MA: Harvard University Press, 1993), chap. 2.

24. For all of the material quoted in the paragraph immediately preceding this footnote, see W. E. B. DuBois, *The Souls of Black Folk*, ed. David Blight and Robert Gooding-Williams (New York: Bedford Books, 1997), 38–39.

25. See, for example, *Public Culture* 2:1 (1999), especially the essays by Charles Taylor and Thomas McCarthy.

26. Paul Gilroy, *The Black Atlantic* (Cambridge, MA: Harvard University Press, 1993), 37.

27. Gilroy, *The Black Atlantic*, 38.

28. Gilroy, *The Black Atlantic*, 73, 76.

29. Gilroy, *The Black Atlantic*, 73–74.

30. Gilroy, *The Black Atlantic*, 74, emphasis added.

31. I develop this theme at length in *Zarathustra's Dionysian Modernism*.

32. Cf. *BGE* 2.

Acknowledgments

The idea for this volume originated with conversations that both of us had with P. J. Ivanhoe. Without his unending enthusiasm and encouragement, we doubt that this volume would exist. We also would like to thank the editors of the series, Robert Bernasconi and T. Denean Sharpley-Whiting, and Jane Bunker, editor-in-chief at State University of New York Press, for their guidance and patience.

Lastly, we also would like to express our gratitude to the contributors to this volume for their work and patience throughout the whole process.

Note on Abbreviations of Nietzsche's Texts

References to Nietzsche's writings will be given parenthetically in the body of the text using the italicized standard English title acronyms below. Roman numerals are used to denote the volume number of a set of collected works or a standard subdivision within a single work in which the sections are not numbered consecutively. Arabic numerals will be used to denote the section number rather than the page numbers, and "P" will be used to denote Nietzsche's Prefaces.

If a particular translation is used, the initial citation reference appears in an endnote to indicate the translation used. References to the *Kritische Gesamtausgabe* (*KGW*) or the *Kritische Studienausgabe* (*KSA*), edited by Colli and Montinari, will appear with the volume number followed by the fragment number. For example, the abbreviation "*KSA* 2:4[78]" refers to Volume 2, fragment 4[78]. References to *Thus Spoke Zarathustra* list the part number and chapter title, for example (*Z*:3 "The Convalescent"). References to *Twilight of the Idols* and *Ecce Homo* list the abbreviated chapter title and section number, for example (*TI* "Ancients" 3) or (*EH* "Books"). References to texts in which sections are too long to be cited helpfully by only section number cite the section number followed by a comma, then the page number, for example (*SE* 3, p. 142), with the translation/edition indicated in an endnote.

A	*The Antichrist / Antichristian*
AOM	*Assorted Opinions and Maxims*
BGE	*Beyond Good and Evil*
BT	*The Birth of Tragedy*
CW	*The Case of Wagner*
D	*Daybreak / Dawn*
DS	*David Strauss, the Writer and Confessor*

EH	*Ecce Homo* ["Wise," "Clever," "Books," "Destiny"]
GM	*On the Genealogy of Morals*
GOA	*Nietzsches Werke (Grossoktavausgabe)*
GS	*The Gay Science / Joyful Wisdom*
HC	"Homer's Contest"
HCP	"Homer and Classical Philology"
HH	*Human, All-Too-Human*
HL	*On the Use and Disadvantage of History for Life*
KGB	*Briefwechsel: Kritische Gesamtausgabe*
KGW	*Kritische Gesamtausgabe*
KSA	*Kritische Studienausgabe*
KSB	*Sämtliche Briefe: Kritische Studienausgabe*
MA	*Nietzsches Gesammelte Werke (Musarionausgabe)*
NCW	*Nietzsche Contra Wagner*
PCP	*Philosopher as Cultural Physician*
PTA	*Philosophy in the Tragic Age of the Greeks*
RWB	*Richard Wagner in Bayreuth*
SE	*Schopenhauer as Educator*
TI	*Twilight of the Idols* ["Maxims," "Socrates," "Reason," "World," "Morality," "Errors," "Improvers," "Germans," "Skirmishes," "Ancients," "Hammer"]
TL	"On Truth and Lie in an Extra-Moral Sense"
UM	*Untimely Meditations / Thoughts Out of Season*
WDB	*Werke in drei Bänden* (Ed. Karl Schlechta)
WP	*The Will to Power*
Z	*Thus Spoke Zarathustra*

Introduction:
The Art of the Cultural Physician

The chapters in this volume bring to light a number of ways in which the themes of cultural and human flourishing reveal a nexus of convergence between Nietzsche's philosophy and various expressions of African American thought. More specifically, however, these chapters articulate the ways in which the critical affinities they delineate serve as guides to new ways of conceptualizing, analyzing, and cultivating human and cultural well-being. In doing so, they simultaneously foster and exemplify a nuanced understanding of what both traditions regard and revere as the art of the cultural physician.

In general, much of Nietzsche's philosophy connotes an attempt to assume the role of the cultural physician. Troubled by what he considers the conspicuous decay and decline of modern culture, Nietzsche turns to the ancient Greeks for insights concerning ways to effectively promote and preserve the future health of Europe. Focusing more specifically on the pernicious potential of fixed cultural ideals, he concludes that at their height the Greeks skillfully availed themselves of philosophy as a powerful liberating and regulating tool of culture. Moreover, he surmises that for the Greeks, the ultimate significance of philosophy was predicated on the way it embodied a "*skeptical* impulse" that would strengthen "the sense of truth over [and] against free fiction," and in doing so bring about the destruction of all "barbarizing, immoral, and stultifying" forms of "rigid dogmatism."[1]

Thus viewed, Nietzsche considered the Greeks an early example of a people who deftly utilized philosophy as a means of curbing and controlling our very powerful and potentially dangerous "*mythical impulse.*" Burdened with a consciousness that beckons us to question the meaning of our own existence, Nietzsche finds that our mythical impulse, that is, our impulse to create our own narratives of meaning, saves us from falling prey to a life-threatening sense of nihilism (*GM*

1

III, 28) Unfortunately, however, grandiose efforts to avoid the Scylla of nihilism eventually plunged the Western descendants of the Greeks into the downward spiraling Charybdis of otherworldly idealizations of identity and value. Leery of the way modern Westerners dogmatically cling to such metaphysical contrivances, Nietzsche challenges all conscientious seekers of knowledge to take seriously the possibility that such sacred pillars of culture may actually connote "a danger, a seduction, a poison, a narcotic," through which human beings in the present are wantonly living at the expense of the vigor and health of human beings in the future (GM P, 6).

Convinced that this is indeed the case, Nietzsche chastises the purveyors and proponents of dogmatic ideals and values for arresting humanity's development. Moreover, inspired by the Greek ideal of the cultural physician, Nietzsche strives to counteract the root causes of Europe's insidious decadence by cultivating a powerful new generation of philosophers that embodies a revitalized skeptical impulse. Dedicating themselves to what Nietzsche foreordains as a new "aristocratic" vision of cultural health, these new philosophers initially focus on unmasking and undermining all of the ideologies and ideals that impede this vision from becoming a reality.[2]

Sadly, however, Nietzsche's highly touted new generation of philosophers is prone to exhibit more of the persona of dictatorial legislators than that of compassionate physicians. Consecrating themselves to the task of "[forcing] the will of millennia upon new tracks," Nietzsche's new philosophers are aptly described as embodying a willingness to sacrifice untold numbers of human beings for the sake of promoting the welfare of those he exalts as "higher types" (*BGE* 203).[3]

In contrast to Nietzsche's rather ominous aspirations for the future, African American thought has traditionally been preoccupied with promoting much more egalitarian and cosmopolitan agendas. Moreover, whereas Nietzsche frames and addresses existential and cultural issues in ways that are actually amenable to domination and exploitation, most expressions and exponents of African American thought exemplify an overarching commitment to subverting the institutional and ideological underpinnings of all forms of human oppression.

Ironically, notwithstanding this radical difference in social aim, the affinities between Nietzschean and African American engagements in the art of the cultural physician are both palpable and powerful. Deeply concerned about the prospects of those intellectuals, artists, and free spirits who lie at the margins of mainstream society, Nietzsche exposes and combats cultural constructs that undermine their flourishing. Similarly, many of the critical and creative aspects of African

American thought resolutely illuminate, resist, and contest the ideologies and discourses that threaten and undermine the flourishing of blacks.

Three of the most notable African American devotees of the art of the cultural physician are Frederick Douglass, W. E. B. DuBois and Ralph Ellison. In addition to tracing the historical arc of African American thought, these three figures also exemplify three of its main facets— the revelatory, the theoretical, and the aesthetic. Functioning in his capacity as a cultural physician, Douglass authors a riveting autobiographical text that simultaneously describes and deconstructs the odious institution of slavery. Emphasizing what was all too often elided, Douglass's narrative focuses squarely on the sinister ways in which slavery diminishes the humanity of the slave and thereby precipitates the very inhumanity it presupposes. More specifically, Douglass's narrative recounts his personal experience of systematically being mentally and physically reduced to virtually nothing more than a beast.[4]

Noting the fact that those most ardent in their attempts to dehumanize him and others were those who were most pious in the profession and practice of the Christian faith, Douglass castigates the prevailing religious discourse as "a mere covering for the most horrid crimes—a justifier of the most appalling barbarity—sanctifier of the most hateful frauds—and a dark shelter under, which the darkest, foulest, grossest, and most infernal deeds of slaveholders find the strongest protection."[5] Fixating on the biblical story of Ham, the American orthodoxy proclaimed all descendants of Ham, namely Negroes, morally corrupt and foreordained by God to be eternal subordinate and subservient to all other races.[6] Moreover, given God's decree, the practice of slavery was divinely sanctioned; and given the vile nature of the Negro race, violence and cruelty were deemed acceptable means of effecting subjugation and maintaining control. In contrast, however, Douglass proclaims that

> . . . between the Christianity of this land, and the Christianity of Christ, I recognize the widest possible difference—so wide, that to receive the one as good, pure, and holy, is of necessity to reject the other as bad, corrupt and wicked. To be the friend of one is of necessity to be the enemy of the other. I love the pure, peaceable, and impartial Christianity of Christ: I therefore hate the corrupt, slaveholding, women-whipping, cradle plundering, partial and hypocritical Christianity of this land. Indeed, I can see no reason, but the most deceitful one, for calling the religion of this land Christianity. I look upon it as the climax of all misnomers, the boldest of all frauds, and the grossest of all libels.[7]

Functioning as a cultural physician, Douglass deftly juxtaposes "the Christianity of this land" and true Christianity, that is, "the Christianity of Christ," in a way that challenges the propriety of the former and beckons all who would embrace the latter to resolutely renounce and denounce the invidious practice of slavery.

Shifting the locus of concern from deconstructing slavery to deciphering the virulent underpinnings of its persistent vestiges, one of the main theoretical currents of African American thought is the critical analysis of the psychological dimension of racial oppression. Widely hailed for his pioneering accounts and analyses of the impact of denigrating oppositional and essentialistic constructions of racial identity on both "the souls of black folk" and "the souls of white folk," DuBois aptly outlines the psychical consequences of dubious and divisive hierarchical conceptions of race by drawing upon the language and imagery of sight.

"Only in man does man know himself; life alone teaches each one what he is."[8] Reminiscent of this immortal line from Goethe's *Tasso*, DuBois's account of the development of self-conscious racial identity emphasizes the formative role of the Other. Focusing first and foremost on his Negro brethren, DuBois adumbrates and amends Hegel's enumeration of six world historical peoples by adding the Negro and describing him as "a sort of seventh son, born with a veil, and gifted with second-sight in this American world—a world which yields him no true self-consciousness, but only lets him see himself through the revelation of the other world.[9] In one sense, Du Bois's description emphasizes the fact that within the sociohistorical context of nineteenth century America, the Negro experiences the "peculiar sensation" of "always looking at one's self through the eyes of others, [and] of measuring one's soul by the tape of a world that looks on in amused contempt and pity.[10] Although the emphasis here is on the unmediated self-perception, and therewith, the true self-consciousness that is denied, DuBois's brief description also touts the view that within the context of this "American world," the Negro is also "gifted with second sight."[11]

When read against the backdrop of African American folklore, DuBois's characterization of the Negro as "a sort of seventh son" touts him as a cultural healer who has the potential for unique insight into the psychological effects of the American malady of racism and forces the nation to confront it.[12] Unlike their white counterparts, blacks, according to DuBois, maintain a dual identity or "two-ness" that distinguishes them as both American and other. Imbuing a number of them with what David Levering Lewis describes as a "unique angle of vision,"[13] those like DuBois—namely, those blacks who were versed in and enamored of the best and the brightest aspects of Western culture—were uniquely positioned to trenchantly perceive the ways in which modern manifestations of white racial identity were degenerate and delusive.

> High in the tower, where I sit above the loud complaining of the human sea, I know many souls that toss and whirl and pass, but none there are that intrigue me more than the Souls of White Folk.
>
> Of them, I am singularly clairvoyant. I see in and through them. I view them from unusual points of vantage. Not as a foreigner do I come, for I am a native, not foreign, bone of their thought and flesh of their language. Mine is not the knowledge of the traveler or the colonial composite of dear memories, words and wonder. Nor yet is my knowledge that which servants have of master, or mass of class, or capitalist of artisan. Rather I see these souls undressed from the back and side. I see the working of their entrails. I know their thoughts and they know that I know.[14]

In brief, because of the "gift of second sight," DuBois sees and exposes the monstrous and fallacious hubris of a white supremacist discourse that enthralls white folks within the socially pernicious "phantasy" that "every great soul the world ever saw was a white man's soul; that every great thought the world ever knew was a white man's thought; that every great deed the world ever did was a white man's deed; that every great dream the world ever sang was a white man's dream."[15] Moreover, his conclusion is that the white soul suffers from a crippling myopia and megalomania that has infected the American cultural soul (and by extension the black soul) with oppositional, unequal, and psychologically damaging racial identities.

Equally attuned to the malevolence of divisive hierarchical conceptions of racial identity, Ralph Ellison dutifully declares that artists like him must likewise "shoulder the burden of conscientiousness" and craft works of fiction in accordance with their "sense of responsibility for the health of the society."[16] Crafting a novel ostensibly about a young African American's experience, Ellison's intention was to use the experience of Negroes as a metaphor for the experience of other people and in so doing to create a "study in comparative humanity" that allowed for universal identifications while simultaneously demonstrating and encouraging a respect for the "specificity of the particular experience and the particular character."[17] In so doing, he hoped to heal society of the problematic racial identities diagnosed by DuBois. In short, his treatment is aimed at the myopia of both whites and blacks so that both groups can come to see one another in both their similarities and differences.

Responding to a question from a presumably white West Point cadet about the significance of the scene near the end of *Invisible Man* when the narrator is chased by two white men, falls down an open manhole, and yells up to these two white men, "I still have you in this briefcase," Ellison describes this exchange as an allegorical response to the fissure that plagues American society. Moreover, he states that,

> What I wanted him to be saying was that these men who were hurling racial epithets down at him were not aware that *their* fate was in this bag that he carried—this bag that he had hauled around with his various identifications, his diploma, with Clifton's doll, with Tarp's slavery chainlink, and so on; that this contained a very important part of their history and of their lives. And I was trying to say, also, that you [the reader] will have to become aware of the connection between what is in this bag. . . and the racist whites who looked upon [the Negro narrator] mainly as a buffoon and a victim.[18]

Insofar as this pervasive lack of awareness of the connections between blacks and whites fosters "inadequate conceptions of ourselves, both as individuals and as citizens of a nation of diverse peoples," Ellison discharges his duties as a cultural physician by imploring artists and others to continually explore and make manifest "the network of complex relationships which bind us together."[19]

Sharing Ellison's conscientious "sense of responsibility for the health of the society," the authors included in this volume juxtapose various aspects of Nietzsche's philosophy and African American thought in an effort to explore and explicate the critical, hermeneutical, and practical import of the connections and interplay between them.[20] Calling attention to a number of different ways in which the underlying affinities between Nietzsche and African American thought are both informative and instructive, their chapters collectively constitute a wide-ranging mix of philosophical reflections that exemplifies the art of the cultural physician. Remaining faithful to this art in both content and form, the volume is essentially comprised of three sections.

The first, *Diagnoses*, is devoted to unveiling the diseased aspects of culture that impeded the creation of healthy identities and values. Using the method Nietzsche formalizes and baptizes as "genealogy," the chapters in this group examine the origins and/or operations of various discourses of dominance and reveal the psychological implications of their hegemony for both those who are in the majority and those who are at the margins.[21] The second section, *Prescriptions*, contains chapters that critique, recast, and theoretically revalue the historically pernicious concept of race in hopes of serving as prolegomena for overcoming the racism that plagues the culture. In general, the goal of each of these revaluations is to foster the creation of a new theory of race or simply a new way of thinking about race that opens up the possibility of developing more liberating conceptions of African American racial identity. Finally, the third section, *Regimens for Recovery*, focuses on existential liberation and cultural transformation. In particular, the chapters contained in this section explore African American resistance, African American wisdom, and art in an effort to articulate the ways in which assertive and creative expressions of the will to power prove expedient in helping both the culture and individuals foster and embody new modes of libratory health and vitality.

Diagnoses

In keeping with the function of the cultural physician, the authors in this section assess the causes and/or consequences of a number of America's cultural maladies. A. Todd Franklin, in "Kindred Spirits: Nietzsche and Locke as Progenitors of Axiological Liberation," focuses on the similarities and convergences between the axiological theories of Nietzsche and Alain Locke. In this chapter, Franklin demonstrates how both philosophers call for a shift from an uncritical acceptance of value absolutism to an assiduous appreciation of the ways in which values are derivative expressions of human subjectivity. Having done so, Franklin goes on to contend that in calling for this shift, Nietzsche and Locke echo one another and emerge as kindred spirits whose insightful assessments set the stage for emancipatory critiques of cultural and racial forms of repression and subordination.

In "Nietzsche *Ressentiment* Lynching," John Pittman diagnoses the rise of lynching in post-Reconstruction America as a pernicious manifestation of Nietzschean *ressentiment*. In particular, he contextualizes and reconceptualizes the social practice of lynching by shifting from more conventional interpretations that focus on the racial dynamics between whites and blacks to one that focuses primarily on the psychological dynamics of social and economic relations between wealthy and poor whites. Analyzing these dynamics in terms of Nietzsche's concept of *ressentiment*, Pittman contends that the practice of lynching black men gave rise to a perverse community identity and value system that allowed them to see themselves and their place in society as valuable.

In "Double Consciousness and Second Sight," Kathleen Marie Higgins examines and assesses the psychological synergies between Nietzsche and DuBois as each strives to clarify the difficulties, dangers, and promise of the inner strife suffered by those relegated to stand outside of the mainstream of the social order. Detailing the ways in which Nietzsche's inner tension parallels that of African Americans, Higgins contends that although the former stems from Nietzsche's own personal sense of intellectual and axiological alienation, while the latter is the historical product of anti-black racism, both reveal the self-restorative and socially transformative power that lies nascent within the experience of marginalization.

Finally, in "Of Tragedy and the Blues in an Age of Decadence: Thoughts on Nietzsche and African America," Lewis R. Gordon draws upon Nietzsche's idea that health is something that is best understood in terms of one's ability to struggle against suffering. Noting the way Nietzsche characterizes the venerable health of the Greeks in terms of their ability to merge the Dionysian and Apollonian into an art form that abated suffering by beautifying it, Gordon describes the African American art forms of jazz and blues as functionally equivalent to ancient Greek tragedy and equally symbolic of cultural health. Having done so, however, Gordon then diagnoses the decadent decay of African American art and attributes it to the racial dynamics of a process of mass appropriation that perpetually devalues African American racial identity.

Prescriptions

Central within African American thought is the philosophical subfield of critical race theory. This subfield attempts to examine analytically the ways in which race has operated and continues to operate in cultures around the world but particularly in American contexts. Given that these traditional racial theories have led to various insidious forms of racism, and given that their supposed scientific foundations have been revealed to be sorely lacking, critical race theory endeavors to see what, if any, type of theory of race might allow for healthier individual identities and more liberated communities. It is argued in all three chapters in this part of the volume that, at least for now, health and liberation are aided by racialized identities. Moreover, each considers race a potent *Pharmakon* and avers that instead of doing away with it, we should reconstruct it and revalue it so as to facilitate its redeployment in the service of healthier lives. To this end, Paul C. Taylor, in his chapter, "Ecce Negro: How To Become a Race Theorist," describes his fervent attempts to reconstruct and revalue race as a personal journey that has traversed the theoretical work of both Molefi Asante and K. Anthony Appiah. Characterizing this journey as one that has been guided by both Deweyan pragmatism and Nietzschean perfectionism, Taylor's chapter charts his path to the realization that race is something that is best understood as a dynamic and an interactive phenomenon that is existentially relevant yet ontologically contingent. Daniel W. Conway, in "Nietzsche's Proto-Phenomenological Approach to the Theoretical Problem of Race," echoes Taylor's criticisms of Appiah but goes on to argue that Appiah's appeal to science is still in theory a promising strategy for deciphering and recasting the reality of race. Highlighting Nietzsche's very expansive and multidisciplinary conception of "Gay Science," Conway sketches a Nietzschean theory of race that draws upon the social sciences to develop a phenomenological account that downplays the role of biology and shifts our attention to the nature and significance of racial embodiment.

Lastly, as a commentary on the project of revaluing the concept of race, Jacqueline Scott's "The Price of the Ticket: A Genealogy and Revaluation of Race," explores the impact that such a revaluation would have on individual and cultural health. Reconstructing Nietzsche's genealogical "diagnosis" of the cultural dangers of traditional race purity, Scott urges contemporary race theorists to seriously consider a new concept of race—one that would reject all notions of racial purity and focus instead on "a multifariously thin" notion of racial impurity. Although radical in import, Scott ultimately contends that embracing and deploying such a concept would be well worth the "price of the ticket."

Regimens for Recovery

Encouraging the creation and affirmation of healthy racial identities, the chapters in this section address various actions, practices, and activities that foster mutually compatible forms of individual and collective self-realization. More specifically, the authors in these chapters celebrate and temper the existential implications of Nietzsche's call for the full recognition and exercise of our *"vis creativa"* [creative power][22] as they detail a variety of salutary African American expressions and conceptions of the Nietzschean will to power (*GS* 301). In "Unlikely Illuminations: Nietzsche and Frederick Douglass on Power, Struggle, and the *Aisthesis* of Freedom," Christa Davis Acampora argues that despite their broader differences, Nietzsche and Douglass "share a conception of human power and how it might seek or produce meaningful freedom." Highlighting the positive potential of an assertive will to power, Acampora details the way Douglass's struggle with Covey and Nietzsche's cultural analysis of Greek forms of *agon* both call attention to how the felt quality of the experience of actively engaging in struggle can make one conscious of the ways in which one's agency is full of creative and transformative possibilities. In the end, however, Acampora avers that in addition to an assertive will, the acquisition of meaningful freedom also involves a dynamic process of individual and social cooperation.

Building on this concept of "meaningful freedom," Cynthia Willett argues in "Masculinity and Existential Freedom: Wright, Ellison, Morrison, and Nietzsche" that one of the purposes of this freedom is to facilitate the healing of the psyche, and that such healing requires a healthy conception of the will to power. Drawing on Nietzsche's early work on the Greeks, Willett emphasizes the need for moderating cultural forces in order to avoid the dangers of unfettered and oppressive expressions of power. Juxtaposing Nietzsche's misguided views on power with those embodied within the writings of Richard Wright, Ralph Ellison, and Toni Morrison, Willett calls attention to the dangers of human hubris and highlights the way a will to power "with soul" connotes a more tenable conception of human flourishing.

Bringing the volume to a close, James Winchester's "Why Nietzsche (Sometimes) Can't Sing the Blues, or Davis, Nietzsche, and the Social Embeddedness of Aesthetic Judgments" analyzes the emancipatory possibilities of artistic endeavors. In this chapter, Winchester details the way Nietzsche's understanding of art vacillates between the view that artistic creation is enigmatic and the view that it is inextricably social. Drawing upon Angela Davis's compelling analysis of how the art form of the blues illustrates the intimate relationship between art and life, Winchester commends the so-called "bluesy-Nietzsche" for his recognition of the way artistic creation and aesthetic understanding are always relative to social contexts. More explicitly, however, Winchester stresses the fact that although art wells up from a social context, great art—like that of African American blues figures—connotes a great act of will that oftentimes beneficially transforms society by opening up new and challenging ways of reflecting upon and conceptualizing social realities. In the end, it remains abundantly clear that Nietzsche himself had no intention to develop or provide substantive solutions to the existential and cultural difficulties that plague African Americans as individuals and as members of a marginalized group. Nevertheless, we feel that it is extremely important for those dedicated to grappling with these difficulties to recognize the inadvertent ways in which Nietzsche's body of thought facilitates efforts to criticize and combat the ideological forces that continue to curtail African American prospects for individual and collective liberation.

Alternatively, we also believe that it is highly useful for those who wrestle with questions concerning the nature and significance of Nietzsche's thought to avail themselves of the many possible answers that can be obtained by observing Nietzsche through the "unique angles of vision" associated with African Americans and African American thought. Doubly significant, these unique angles of vision not only reveal the texture and nuance of many of the virtues of Nietzsche's thought, they also expose and make vivid its lamentable and unfortunate shortcomings. Reflecting these sentiments, the chapters in this volume collectively strive to shed light on the meaningful connections between Nietzsche's philosophy and the broad-ranging domain of African American thought by calling attention to the palpable ways in which each speaks to and enriches the other as both strive to deconstruct and transform the ontological and ideological obstacles that impede social and psychological flourishing. Although it is this endeavor that constitutes the overall aim of the volume, its greatest virtue derives from the hope and encouragement that such an effort provides to all who are similarly dedicated to the art of the cultural physician.

Notes

1. Friedrich Nietzsche, "Der Philosoph als Artzt der Kultur" ("The Philosopher as Cultural Physician"), in *Philosophy and Truth: Selections from Nietzsche's Notebooks of the Early 1870s*, trans. Daniel Breazeale (Atlantic Highlands, N.J.: Humanities International Press, 1979), 175.

2. For a brief account of Nietzsche's "aristocratic" vision, see A. Todd Franklin, "Nietzsche's Aristocratic Radicalism," *The Southern Journal of Philosophy* xxxvii (Supplement 1999): 143–50.

3. For more on Nietzsche's conception of those who are cultural "higher types," see Ofelia Schutte, "Nietzsche's Cultural Politics: A Critique," *The Southern Journal of Philosophy* 38 (Supplement 1999): 65–71.

4. Later in this volume, Christa Davis Acampora details Douglass's reclamation of his humanity and discusses it in conjunction with Nietzsche's account of Greek forms of *agon* as she explores the connections between power, struggle, and the *aesthesis* of freedom.

5. Frederick Douglass, *Narrative of the Life of Frederick Douglass, An American Slave* (New York: Penguin, 1986), ch. X, p. 117.

6. For more on this orthodoxy, see Josiah Priest's 1843 treatise, *Slavery as It Relates to the Negro, or African Race* (Albany, NY: C. Van Benthuysen & Co., 1843).

7. Douglass, *Narrative of the Life of Frederick Douglass, An American Slave*, Appendix, p. 153.

8. Johann Wolfgang Von Goethe, *Tasso*, trans. Charles E. Passage (New York: Frederick Unger, 1966), act 2, sc. 3.

9. W. E. B. DuBois, "Of Our Spiritual Strivings," in *The Souls of Black Folk,* ed. David W. Blight and Robert Gooding-Williams (Boston: Bedford Books, 1997), 38.

10. DuBois, *Souls*, 38.

11. DuBois, *Souls*, 38.

12. For more on the seventh son in African American folklore, see Yvonne Patricia Chireau, *Black Magic: Religion and the African American Conjuring Tradition* (Berkeley: University of California Press, 2003), and Newbell Niles Puckett, *Folk Beliefs of the Southern Negro* (New York: Dover, 1969).

13. David Levering Lewis, *W. E. B. DuBois: Biography of a Race, 1868–1919* (New York: Henry Holt, 1993), 280.

14. W. E. B. DuBois, "Souls of White Folk," *Darkwater* (New York: Dover, 1999), 18.

15. W. E. B. DuBois, "Souls of White Folk," 18. In the wake of DuBois's groundbreaking work, many recent scholars of African American thought, American studies, and ethnic studies are focusing on the history, psychology, and pathology of whiteness. Notably, John Pittman and Lewis Gordon both focus intently on the discourse of whiteness in their respective contributions to this volume. For a broad overview of whiteness and whiteness studies, see the proceedings from the 2002 Columbia University symposium, "Whither Whiteness?," in *Souls* 4: 4 (2002), and the wide ranging essays in *The Making and Unmaking of Whiteness*, ed. Birgit Brander Rasmussen, Irene J. Nexica, Eric Klinenberg, and Matt Wray (Durham, NC: Duke University Press, 2001).

16. Ralph Ellison, "On Initiation Rites and Power," *Going to the Territory* (New York: Vintage Books, 1986), 47.

17. Ellison, "On Initiation Rites and Power," 56.

18. Ellison, "On Initiation Rites and Power," 60–61.

19. Ellison, "On Initiation Rites and Power," 42.

20. Ellison, "On Initiation Rites and Power," 47.

21. In general, Nietzschean genealogy denotes a critical form of analysis that demystifies and de-essentializes various idealizations and reifications by calling attention to their "psychological genesis" (*KGW* VII, 1:7[35]). For more detailed accounts of the nature of Nietzschean genealogy, see chapter 7 of Alan Shrift's *Nietzsche and the Question of Interpretation* (New York: Routledge, 1990) and Eric Blondel's "The Question of Genealogy," 306–17, and Daniel Conway's "Genealogy and Critical Method," 318–33, in *Nietzsche, Genealogy, Morality*, ed. Richard Schact (Berkeley: University of California Press, 1994).

22. *GS* 301.

Part I

—

Diagnoses

1

Kindred Spirits:
Nietzsche and Locke
as Progenitors of Axiological Liberation

A. TODD FRANKLIN

Known primarily as one of the architects and fathers of the "New Negro Movement" of the 1920s, it is only as of late that Alain Locke has begun to be reckoned with as a serious and significant philosopher. Despite his own self-characterization as "more of a philosophical midwife to a generation of younger Negro poets, writers, and artists than a professional philosopher,"[1] African American scholars such as Ernest Mason, Leonard Harris, and Johnny Washington have been instrumental in bringing the content and character of his philosophical work to light.[2] As their efforts reveal, one of Locke's main philosophical concerns is the nature of values. Critical of all absolute conceptions of value and dismayed by philosophy's preoccupation with, or rather its fetishization of, a bloodless objectivity, Locke strives to unmask and lay bare the organic nature of values. More broadly, however, Locke's aim in doing so is to undermine the hegemonic force of a Western imperialism that denigrates diversity and perpetuates cultural and racial forms of subordination while proudly wrapping itself in the social and political ideals of democracy.

Forty-one years Locke's senior, Friedrich Nietzsche also stands out in the history of philosophy as a figure dedicated to issues pertaining to the character of values and the nature of culture. Troubled by what he sees as the stunting and stultifying effects of the Judeo-Christian moral values pervasive within modern European culture, Nietzsche makes it his mission to subvert their stranglehold on the future of humanity by encouraging those who possess a strong and independent spirit to recognize the plebeian origins of these values and ascend to their rightful station beyond what commonly passes for "good and evil."[3]

Although there are undoubtedly a number of differences between Locke the cultural pluralist and Nietzsche the cultural elitist, both figures distinguish themselves as talented intellectuals who challenge and contest the warrant of dogmatic systems of value by postulating that all values, norms, and standards are nothing more than human, all-too-human constructs that are indicative of various needs, dispositions, situations, and circumstances. Guided by a shared understanding of how such systems of value emerge and hold sway, Nietzsche and Locke both devise methodological strategies that encourage the development of a liberating critical consciousness.

Concentrating on the nuances of the critical affinities between Nietzsche and Locke, my goal in this chapter is to call attention to the ways in which the two prefigure the subversion of axiological forms of domination and oppression. In keeping with this aim, I have divided this chapter into two main sections. The first provides an overview of how Nietzsche and Locke both stand out as critics of axiological hegemony. Focusing on their shared account of the contingent nature of values, this section briefly notes how Nietzsche and Locke both trace the roots of axiological oppression to an overzealous and a tyrannical tendency for a people or group to envision its own way of life as universally ordained. The second section shifts the focus from their insights concerning the way axiological oppression emerges to a broader discussion of their differing accounts of its existential implications. Although one cannot help but be struck by the way Nietzsche and Locke differ widely in terms of their overall aims and concerns, in what follows, I will endeavor to show that in looking beyond these differences one finds two figures who both outline critical forms of analysis that undermine the hegemonic force of dogmatic systems of value by exposing them as nothing more than fallacious axiological idols of the mind.

Critics of Culture

Naturalized Conception of Values

In his self-styled autobiography, *Ecce Homo*, Nietzsche describes himself as one of the first to "stand in opposition to the mendaciousness of millennia," and prophesies that:

one day [his] name will be associated with the memory of something tremendous—a crisis without equal on earth, the most profound collision of conscience, a decision that was conjured up *against* everything that had been believed, demanded,[and] hallowed so far.[4] (*EH* "Why I am Destiny" 1)

In some sense I think that Nietzsche's words ring true, particularly in terms of the way his critical axiology serves as a strong impetus for challenging and deposing dogmatic systems of value. Calling into question the exalted status of all unassailable values, Nietzsche's axiological critique focuses on the conditions and circumstances that give rise to their emergence and evolution. In doing so, it reconceptualizes these so-called absolutes as idiosyncratic appraisals, standards, and ideals that are prefigured by the existential needs and interests of particular human beings. Similarly, Locke's critical axiology examines the way different values hold sway in different cultural contexts and proclaims that, "values are rooted in attitudes, not in reality, and pertain to ourselves, [and] not the world."[5]

Although the underlying aims of their critiques are quite different in nature, both figures contend that values are simply normative constructs that allow people to qualitatively discriminate between certain actions and objects in accordance with the attitudes, interests, dispositions, and desires that are constitutive of their particular way of life or mode of existence. In short, referring to various conglomerations of such constituents as horizons or perspectives, Nietzsche contends that the values espoused by various races, types, and individuals are merely relative or rather perspectival.[6] Collectively codified, these perspectival dictates constitute systems of value that justify particular beliefs and outlooks, and in doing so, serve as what Nietzsche metaphorically refers to as a life-sustaining sun that guides actions, bestows a sense of purpose, and provides a basis for determinations of human worth (*GS* 289).

Highlighting the way in which such values emerge as definitive, Nietzsche and Locke both claim that as we develop systems of value that are conducive to satisfying the existential demands of life, we tend to reify them into universally binding absolutes. Describing this process, Nietzsche writes:

Man has repeated the same mistake over and over again: he has made a means to life into a standard of life; instead of discovering the standard in the highest enhancement of life itself, in the problem of growth and exhaustion, he has employed the means to a quite distinct kind of life to exclude all other forms

of life, in short to criticize and select life. I.e., man finally loves
the means for their own sake and forgets that they are means:
so that they enter his consciousness as aims, as standards for
aims—i.e., a certain species of man treats the conditions of its
existence as conditions which ought to be imposed as a law, as
"truth," "good," "perfection": it tyrannizes—It is a form of faith,
of instinct, that a species of man fails to perceive its condi-
tionality, its relativity to other species. (*WP* 354)

In sum, Nietzsche holds that

a morality, a mode of living tried and proved by long experience and testing, at length enters consciousness as a law, as
dominating—And therewith the entire group of related values
and states enters into it: it becomes venerable, unassailable,
holy, true. (*WP* 514)

Similarly, Locke describes our value absolutes as the "rationalization of our preferred values and their imperatives" and claims that
their origin "stems more from the will to power than from the will to
know."[7] Drawing out the allusion to a will to power, Locke quotes Nicolai
Hartmann, who writes, "Every value, when once it has gained power
over a person, has a tendency to set itself up as a sole tyrant of the
whole human *ethos*, and indeed at the expense of other values, even
of such as are not inherently opposed to it."[8] Expressing much the
same view, Locke himself claims that "the common man," both as an
individual and as a member of a collective, "sets up personal and private
and group norms as standards and principles, and rightly or wrongly
hypostasizes them as universals for all conditions, all times and all men."[9]

Axiological Tyranny

Two of the most tyrannical consequences of ensuing forms of axiological dogmatism are repression and subordination. Once a system of
values establishes itself as universal and absolute, it becomes entrenched
as normative. Under its regime, almost everyone thinks and behaves
the same way. Ensconced within a world of abject conformity, all of
one's inclinations toward distinctive forms of self-expression and self-
determination are effectively repressed. Many of the most powerful

expressions of this sort of repression derive from dogmatic moral traditions like orthodox forms of religion. Staunchly conservative in bent, these traditions pride themselves on being resolute in their adherence to their respective system of values. In doing so, however, these traditions breed an unquestioning sense of allegiance that proves ideologically repressive.

In addition to being repressive, dogmatic systems of value also spawn demeaning forms of subordination. Under the auspices of its so-called norms, the worth and status of any particular group, way of life, or form of intellectual or aesthetic production is predicated on how well it accords with the dominant system of values. Dismissing the intellectual and cultural merits of Zulu literature, Saul Bellow is famously alleged to have quipped that "when the Zulus produce a Tolstoy we will read him." Bellow's troubling remark gives explicit voice to the arrogant idea that European values serve as the standard for determining what Mathew Arnold refers to as "the best that is known and thought in the world."[10] Implicitly, however, it also avers that since the Zulus have yet to produce a Tolstoy they are clearly culturally inferior and therewith rightly regarded as culturally subordinate.[11] Taking aim at that form of tyranny that each considers most troublesome, Nietzsche's critical focus centers on undermining a modern European morality that engenders repression, while Locke's centers on combating demeaning and dehumanizing forms of cultural imperialism that precipitate and perpetuate various kinds of subordination.

As Nietzsche describes it, modern European morality, that is, the prevailing morality of his day, connotes a conglomeration of selfless and communal values that he pejoratively refers to as a herd morality that is "merely *one* type of human morality beside which, before which, and after which" numerous other types of morality "are, or ought to be, possible" (*BGE* 202). Characterizing this morality as pervasive across Europe and throughout the countries dominated by its influence, Nietzsche laments the fact that it "resists such a 'possibility,' such an 'ought' with all its power" by saying "stubbornly and inexorably, 'I am morality itself, and nothing besides is morality'" (*BGE* 202).

Central to such a claim is the idea that there is only "one normal human type" and that the system of norms, standards, and values peculiar to this type is actually universal and absolute. Emphasizing the historical prevalence of such conceit, Nietzsche claims that the act of positing one's own system of values and deriving one's own "laws, joys, and rights . . . may well have been considered hitherto as the most outrageous aberration and as idolatry itself" (*GS* 143). Moreover, Nietzsche finds that the impulse that gives rise to such activity has typically been derided and dismissed as an impudent expression of "stubbornness, disobedience, and envy" (*GS* 143).

Exemplifying this hostility against the impulse to posit or create one's own system of values, Nietzsche finds that modern European morality effectively represses one's will "to create for [oneself one's] own new eyes," or rather one's own new outlooks on life and conceptions of self-worth. Given its ability to imprint a univocal conception of the whither and for what of humanity on the hearts and minds of its adherents, Nietzsche claims that it essentially transforms these people into faithfully compliant creatures whose "spirit," that is, their impulse or will to define their own sense of meaning, purpose, and self-worth in terms of new and different horizons and perspectives, is "imprisoned in," and hence repressed by, an ideological submissiveness that serves as the basis for their so-called "good conscience" (*Z*:3 "On Old and New Tablets" 26).[12]

In contrast to Nietzsche's focus on the problematic nature of modern European morality, Locke concentrates on the problematic nature of Western culture. Although the beginning of the twentieth century marks what Locke describes as the dawn of a pervasive philosophical rejection of a variety of different religious and scientific forms of absolutism, he emphasizes the fact that the ancient obsession with "absolutistic thinking" lingers on and remains entrenched as a fervent and pernicious belief in the idea that Western ideals and values delimit and denote the essence of culture. Highlighting the imperialistic and oppressive nature of this outlook, Locke quotes the great British historian Arnold J. Toynbee, who points out that as Westerners

> we are no longer conscious of the presence in the world of other societies of equal standing; and that we regard our society as being identical with "civilized" mankind and the peoples outside its pale as being mere "natives" of territories which they inhabit on sufferance, but which are morally as well as practically at our disposal, by the higher right of our assumed monopoly of civilization, whenever we choose to take possession. Conversely, we regard the internal divisions of our society—the national parts into which this society has come to be articulated—as the grand divisions of mankind, and classify the members of the human race as Frenchmen, Englishmen, Germans, and so on, without remembering that these are merely subdivisions of a single group within the human family.[13]

Although Locke quickly notes that the "ethnoracialized"[14] imperialism of Western culture is continually being challenged by the growing self-assertion of non-Western cultures, he laments the fact that a pervasive penchant for "absolutistic thinking" continues to undergird demeaning and dehumanizing forms of cultural and political subordination.

Given what Nietzsche and Locke hail as the conditional and perspectival nature of all systems of value, one would naturally expect that there would be no need for such demonstrative challenges or sorrowful laments. On the contrary, however, Nietzsche and Locke both stress the fact that although various forms of value absolutism prove philosophically untenable, they continue to hold sway as extraordinarily powerful idols of the mind. At base, Nietzsche attributes the lasting presence of all such idols to their fanatical unwillingness to concede the "highly conditional nature of [their] right to exist" (*TI* "Skirmishes" 5). Similarly, Locke points out that although cultural outlooks rooted in "inflated cultural bias and partisanship, or overweening national and racial chauvinism have been outflanked and outmoded by the developments of the present age," their philosophical demise simply compels them to "cling all the more tenaciously to . . . the mind-set of fundamentalism and orthodoxy."[15]

Pedagogues of Change

The Psychology of Axiological Oppression

Trapped within the throes of intractable forms of value absolutism, many people lose sight of the possibility of alternative moralities or cultures and therewith the possibility of alternative opportunities for self-actualization and self-affirmation. Outlining the way these provincial systems of value imprison the human spirit by enticing strict adherence, Nietzsche writes,

> Narrowness of views, through habit become instinct, [and] conducts to what is called strength of character. When someone acts from a few but always the same motives, his actions attain to a great degree of energy; if those actions are in accord with the principles held by the fettered spirits they receive recognition and produce in him who does them the sensation of the good conscience. (*HH* 228)

Enamored by the "sensation of the good conscience," people incessantly strive to adhere to prevailing views and revel in subsequent affirmations of their laudable character and worth. In doing so, however, these people become embedded in an environment that prevents them from realizing that there are many different possibilities of action and self-determination—an environment, moreover, that essentially renders their spirit or consciousness fettered and unfree.

In contrast to Nietzsche's focus on the moral habits and traditions that create and promote ideological totalitarianism, Locke concentrates on the way the "arrogant and long-standing bigotry of Western culture" proves psychologically oppressive.[16] Giving poignant expression to how the internalization of this vicious bigotry impedes the development of Negro art, Langston Hughes reflects as follows on a comment uttered by an aspiring young poet:

> ONE OF THE MOST PROMISING of the young Negro poets said to me once, "I want to write like a white poet"; meaning subconsciously, "I would like to be a white poet"; meaning behind that, "I would like to be white." And I was sorry the young man said that, for no great poet has ever been afraid of being himself. And I doubted then that, with his desire to run away spiritually from his race, this boy would ever be a great poet. But this is the mountain standing in the way of any true Negro art in America—this urge within the race toward whiteness, the desire to pour racial individuality into the mold of American standardization, and to be as little Negro and as much American as possible.[17]

Attributing the formation of this formidable mountain to the social context of one's upbringing and environment, Hughes goes on to describe the conditions that give rise to this young poet's tacit desire to be white:

> His family is of what I suppose one would call the Negro middle class: people who are by no means rich yet never uncomfortable nor hungry—smug, contented, respectable folk, members of the Baptist church. The father goes to work every morning. He is a chief steward at a large white club. The mother sometimes does fancy sewing or supervises parties for the rich families of the town. The children go to mixed school. In the home they read white papers and magazines. And the mother often says "Don't be like niggers" when the children are bad. A frequent phrase from the father is, "Look how well a white man does things." And so the word white comes to be unconsciously a

symbol of all virtues. It holds for the children beauty, morality, and money. The whisper of "I want to be white" runs silently through their minds. This young poet's home is, I believe, a fairly typical home of the colored middle class. One sees immediately how difficult it would be for an artist born in such a home to interest himself in interpreting the beauty of his own people. He is never taught to see that beauty. He is taught rather not to see it, or if he does, to be ashamed of it when it is not according to Caucasian patterns.[18]

Although Hughes here describes what he sees as the environmental forces that impede the development of Negro art, his account is in essence a very apt description of a Western—or in this case, white—ideology of supremacy whose pernicious psychological force stems from the way it is rooted in a dubious, yet uncontested, value absolutism.

The Counter-Hegemonic Force of Critical Consciousness

In spite of the differing natures of their cultural concerns, Nietzsche and Locke are both disturbed by the way people unreflectively acquiesce to the dictates and ideals of a prevailing system of values. In Nietzsche's case, this type of acquiescence is deemed emblematic of one's status as a herd animal or beast of burden and constitutes one's failure or inability to truly accept responsibility for one's own existence by reflectively choosing or constructing one's own system of values. In short, Nietzsche considers this type of unreflective acquiescence representative of those who fail to ascend to the ranks of "Good Europeans."[19] For Locke, however, the major concern is the problem of those who acquiesce to demeaning Western conceptions of their own racial or cultural identity. In this case, the danger of acquiescence is not so much the danger of failing to become what one might have the potential to be, but rather the danger of sadly denigrating and denying that which one is.

In both cases, one finds that people simply fail to understand how cultures or systems of value are inherently perspectival. Unfortunately, however, endeavoring to achieve such comprehension is no easy task. Dubbing those who exhibit the requisite concern as "seekers of knowledge," Nietzsche outlines the way in which their success will be predicated on their ability to consciously extricate themselves from the morays

of their environment and thereby rise above their accustomed systems
of value:

> "Thoughts about moral prejudices," if they are not meant to be
> prejudices about prejudices, presuppose a position *outside*
> morality, some point beyond good and evil to which one has to
> rise, climb, fly—and in the present case at least a point
> beyond our good and evil, a freedom from everything "Euro-
> pean," by which I mean the sum of imperious value judgments
> that have become part of our flesh and blood. That one *wants*
> to go precisely out there, up there, may be a minor madness,
> a peculiar and unreasonable "you must" . . . [but] the question
> is whether one really *can* get up there.
>
> This may depend on manifold conditions. In the main the
> question is how light or heavy [you] are—the problem of [one's]
> "specific gravity." One has to be *very light* to drive one's will
> to knowledge into such a distance and, as it were, beyond
> one's time, to create for oneself eyes to survey millennia and,
> moreover, clear skies in these eyes. . . . The human being of
> such a beyond who wants to behold the supreme measures of
> value of his time must first of all "overcome" this time in him-
> self. (*GS* 380)

Echoing Nietzsche's sentiments, Locke contextualizes the measures
involved in rising beyond the prejudicial values of one's time in terms
of the American Negro's struggle to escape from the tyranny of "social
intimidation" and shake off what he describes as "the psychology of
imitation and implied inferiority."[20] Characterizing the "inner objectives"
of this struggle as an effort to "repair a damaged group psychology and
reshape a warped social perspective," Locke highlights the fact that
the realization of these objectives hinges on the development of a "new
mentality" that rejects malicious stereotypes and actively endeavors
to establish a positive sense of racial self-worth.[21]

Fixating on the idea of transcending dogmatic systems of value,
Nietzsche and Locke both point to the importance of what is more
commonly referred to as critical consciousness. Coined by Brazilian Paulo
Freire and deployed regularly within the works of African American
intellectuals like bell hooks and Cornel West, the expression critical
consciousness denotes a nuanced recognition and understanding of
oppression that precipitates a concerted effort to effect human liberation.

Emphasizing the emancipatory significance of this type of enlightened perception, Freire fervently asserts that in order "to surmount the situation of oppression, people must first critically recognize its causes, so that through transforming action they can create a new situation, one which makes possible the pursuit of a fuller humanity."[22]

Pedagogies of Critical Consciousness

Although Nietzsche and Locke certainly differ with respect to their conceptions of what constitutes "the pursuit of a fuller humanity," both figures can be described as predicating the success of their pursuits on the development of critical consciousness. At base, the process that gives rise to the intellectual and axiological loftiness of critical consciousness is one that is best described as a process of demystification. Characterizing this process as an "illuminating mode of critical inquiry" that accents human agency, West praises it as a powerful form of analysis whose focus on the historicity and contingency of "the complex dynamics of institutional and other related power structures" is part and parcel of broader emancipatory efforts to "disclose options and alternatives for transformative praxis."[23] Animated by their distain for the real and potential tyranny of various unchecked forms of axiological dogmatism, Nietzsche and Locke distinguish themselves as early progenitors of this process by heralding critical methodologies that demystify and de-essentialize pernicious systems of value.

In the preface to *Daybreak*, whose subtitle is "Thoughts on the Prejudices of Morality," Nietzsche calls to our attention the pressing need for what he elsewhere describes as the task of painstakingly deciphering "the entire long hieroglyphic record . . . of the moral past of mankind" (*GM* P: 7). The urgency of this project stems from the belief that moral dogmatism has evolved into a psychological phenomenon that is so powerful that it threatens to completely undermine one's intellectual capacity for critical and independent thought. Noting the most obvious sense in which this is true, Nietzsche points out that "in the presence of morality, as in the face of any authority, one is not *allowed* to think, far less to express an opinion: here one has to *–obey!*"(*D* P 3). However, what Nietzsche finds far more troubling is that in addition to having recourse to "every kind of means of frightening off critical hands," virtually all forms of moral dogmatism—including modern European morality—also skillfully engage in the art of persuasion, and in doing so, succeed rather easily in enticing bright and intelligent people over to their side (*D* P 3).[24]

Endeavoring to free humanity from the seductive enchantments of dogmatic forms of morality and reinvigorate a sense of independence, Nietzsche boldly calls for the development of psychologically and historically sensitive genealogies that reveal the ways in which the emergence and evolution of each particular system of value is contextual. In this regard, Nietzsche's use of the term genealogy is strikingly apropos, for it evokes a reconceptualization of values that regards them as organic in nature. In contrast to traditional philosophical methodologies that focus on ideas and deal in abstractions, genealogy is much more anthropological in bent and much more focused on human particularity. Taking seriously the idea that it is our *vis creativa* that is responsible for "the whole eternally growing world of valuations, colors, accents, perspectives, scales, affirmations, and negations" (*GS* 301), Nietzsche's genealogical method examines the descent (*Herkunft*) of a system of values in terms of the contingent circumstances and conditions that highly influenced its creation and subsequent evolution.[25]

Equally concerned about the ways in which value absolutism promotes "authoritarian conformity and subordination,"[26] Locke follows Nietzsche in proposing a new critical methodology aimed at demystifying and delegitimizing tyrannical forms of culture. In its earliest formulation, Locke's critical methodology describes the development of a conscientious understanding of any given culture as predicated on

> first, its analytic and complete description in terms of its own culture-elements, [and] second, its organic interpretation in terms of its own intrinsic values as a vital mode of living, combined if possible with an historical account of its development and derivation.[27]

Basically speaking, Locke avers that in order to truly understand a culture one must first patiently and thoroughly compile a comprehensive catalogue of all of the values, standards, and ideals that uniquely define it. Once this is completed, one must then develop a psychologically and historically sensitive interpretation of the culture that contextualizes it in terms of the peculiar needs, interests, goals, and conditions that give rise to its emergence and evolution. Moreover, as Ernest Mason aptly points out, Locke's organic methodological approach holds that "we must undertake a functional and historical interpretation of values in order to gain some understanding of their validity or appropriateness in the context in which they are employed."[28]

Emphasizing the pedagogical merits of this organic, or integrative, approach to systems of value, Locke later baptizes it as "critical relativism" and touts its usefulness as a means of promoting a broader recognition and acceptance of diverse cultures and ways of life. Committed to the "humanist ideal and objective of the best possible human and self-understanding," Locke sees his critical relativism as a blueprint for "the concrete study of man in all of his infinite variety."[29] True to its name, Locke's critical relativism treats values as historically relative and strives to elucidate the various ways in which they change and develop while also subjecting them to comparative analyses in an effort to facilitate the development of a broader understanding and appreciation of cultural diversity.[30] Detailing the elements of critical relativism more specifically, Locke goes on to characterize it as a powerful methodology that would

1. implement an objective interpretation of values by referring them realistically to their social and cultural backgrounds;

2. interpret values concretely as functional adaptations to these backgrounds, and thus make clear their historical and functional relativity;

3. claim or impute no validity for values beyond this relativistic framework, and so counteract value dogmatism based on regarding them as universals good and true for all times and all places;

4. confine its consideration of ideology to the prime function and real status of being the adjunct rationalization of values and value interests; and

5. trace value development and change as a dynamic process instead of in terms of unrealistic analytic categories, and so eliminating the traditional illusions produced by generalized value terms—*viz.*, static values and fixed value concepts and "ideals."[31]

Thus constituted, Locke's critical relativism denotes a rigorous methodological strategy that bears a striking resemblance to Nietzsche's genealogy insofar as both endeavor to break the hegemony of recalcitrant expressions of value absolutism by fostering a critical consciousness that recognizes the dynamic, relativistic, and thereby human, all-too-human nature of all prevailing systems of value.

The Dawn of Critical Consciousness and the Promise of Axiological Liberation

Once enlightened by the dawn of critical consciousness, those who face social coercion and psychological debasement become cognizant of the open possibility of contesting their situation. Having developed a critical awareness of the contingent and dynamic nature of all systems of value, one realizes that one need not revere any particular culture or way of life as sacrosanct and definitive. Quite the contrary, for once one successfully comprehends the provincial and perspectival character of all systems of value, one also begins to realize that no particular system of values is unequivocally binding and absolute. For those whose eyes, "whose *suspicion* in whose eyes is strong and subtle enough" for such insight, the dawn of their critical consciousness marks the advent of the realization that alternative systems of value are indeed permissible and that this being the case, the horizon is once again free (*GS* 343).

In addition to recognizing the opportunity to chart new systems of value and sail proverbial new seas, those who become critically conscious also concomitantly become cognizant of the fact that they need no longer see themselves in terms of prejudicial and distortive racial perspectives that impugn their character and worth by denouncing their valued idioms, practices, and traditions as crude, shameful, and savage. Throwing off the psychological shackles of a false sense of abject inferiority, these newly freed spirits stand poised to self-confidently assume the task of cultivating and articulating what Locke aptly refers to as one's own racial sense, one's own racial consciousness, and one's own racial tradition.[32]

At base, what all of these new and liberating forms of enlightenment speak to is the fundamental significance of rigorous and circumspect forms of axiological critique. Looking beyond, or rather beneath, the more obvious ideological differences between Nietzsche and Locke, what one ultimately finds are two kindred spirits whose common aversion for absolute values propels them to develop potent methodological strategies that empower people to consciously reject the objective pretensions of insidious systems of value and in doing so free themselves from the psychological fetters of various forms of axiological oppression.

Notes

1. Quoted in Ernest Mason, "Alain Locke's Philosophy of Value," in *Alain Locke: Reflections on a Modern Renaissance Man*, ed. Russell J. Linnemann

(Baton Rouge: Louisiana State University Press, 1982), 1. Mason attributes the quote to the self-portrait that accompanies Locke's essay "Values and Imperatives," in *American Philosophy, Today and Tomorrow*, ed. Horace M. Kallen and Sidney Hook (New York: Lee Furman, 1935), 312.

2. Seminal works by these scholars include Ernest Mason's Alain Locke's *Philosophy of Value: An Introduction*. (Ph.D. dissertation, Philosophy Dept., Emory University, 1975), Leonard Harris's *The Philosophy of Alain Locke, Harlem Renaissance and Beyond* (Philadelphia: Temple University Press, 1989), and Johnny Washington's *Alain Locke and Philosophy: A Quest for Cultural Pluralism* (Westport, CT: Greenwood Press, 1986).

3. For an excellent account of Nietzsche's elitist cultural ideal, see Ofelia Schutte, "Nietzsche's Cultural Politics: A Critique," in *Nietzsche and Politics. The Southern Journal of Philosophy*, vol. XXXVII (Supplement), ed. Jacqueline Scott 65–71.

4. Friedrich Nietzsche, *Ecce Homo*, trans. Walter Kaufmann (New York: Random House, 1968). Unless otherwise noted, all of Nietzsche's texts will be quoted from the Kaufmann-Hollingdale translations and cited according to the standard abbreviations of their English titles, followed by the book and/or section number.

5. Alain Locke, "Values and Imperatives," in *The Philosophy of Alain Locke: Harlem Renaissance and Beyond,* ed. Leonard Harris (Philadelphia: Temple University Press, 1989), 46. Unless noted otherwise, all references to Locke's works are to those found in the aforementioned volume.

6. *WP* 259.

7. Locke, "Values and Imperatives," 46.

8. Nicolai Hartmann, *Ethics*, vol. II (London: G. Allen & Unwin, 1932), 423.

9. Locke, "Values and Imperatives," 35.

10. Mathew Arnold, "The Function of Criticism at the Present Time," in *Essays in Criticism*, vol. 1 ed. Mathew Arnold (New York: Macmillan & Co., 1864), 16.

11. Susan Wolf makes much the same point in her comments on Charles Taylor's "Politics of Recognition," in *Multiculturalism*, ed. Amy Gutmann, (Princeton, NJ: Princeton University Press, 1994), 75–85.

12. Nietzsche's "On the Three Metamorphoses," in his *Thus Spoke Zarathustra*, offers an allegorical depiction of this type of transformation as the metamorphosis of the human spirit into the form of a camel. For more on this allegory and the process of transformation, see Robert Gooding-Williams, "Zarathustra's Three Metamorphoses," in *Nietzsche as Postmodernist: Essays Pro and Con*, ed. Clayton Koelb (Albany: State University of New York Press, 1990), 231–45.

13. Arnold Toynbee, *The Study of History* (London: Oxford University Press, 1934), 31–32.

14. David Theo Goldberg coins this term on page 4 of the introduction to *Multiculturalism: A Critical Reader*, ed. David Goldberg (Malden, MA: Blackwell, 1995).

15. Locke, "Pluralism and Ideological Peace," 100–101.

16. Locke, "Pluralism," 99.

17. Langston Hughes, "The Negro Artist and the Racial Mountain," in *The Portable Harlem Renaissance Reader*, ed. David L. Lewis (New York: Penguin, 1994), 91.

18. Hughes, "Negro Artists," 91.

19. As Nietzsche describes them, "Good Europeans" are those who are the "heirs of Europe's longest and courageous self-overcoming" (*GS* 357). For more on Nietzsche's concept of the "Good European" see Ofelia Schutte, "Nietzsche's Cultural Politics: A Critique."

20. Alain Locke, *The New Negro* (New York: Simon & Schuster, 1997), 4.

21. Locke, *New Negro*, 10.

22. Paulo Freire, *Pedagogy of the Oppressed*, trans. Myra Bergman Ramos (New York: Continuum), 29.

23. Cornel West, *Keeping the Faith: Philosophy and Race in America* (New York: Routledge, 1993), 23.

24. As the rest of the Preface reveals, one of Nietzsche's favorite examples of one who falls prey to the forces of persuasion is undoubtedly Immanuel Kant.

25. For more on the critical function and organic nature of Nietzsche's genealogical method, see Eric Blondel's "The Question of Genealogy," in *Nietzsche, Genealogy, Morality*, ed. Richard Schacht (Berkeley: University of California Press, 1994), 306–17.

26. Locke, "Pluralism," 101.

27. Locke, "The Concept of Race as Applied to Social Culture," 198.

28. Mason, "Alain Locke's Philosophy of Value," 11.

29. Locke, "The Need for a New Organon in Education," 271.

30. Locke, "The Need," 273.

31. Locke, "The Need," 273–74.

32. Locke, "The Contribution of Race to Culture," 202.

2

—

Nietzsche, *Ressentiment*, Lynching

JOHN PITTMAN

Anyone even slightly familiar with the argument of Nietzsche's *Genealogy of Morality*, and especially the first and second essays of that lyric-philosophical triptych that may well be the summit of Nietzsche's work, cannot but be struck by the confluence of two interwoven themes.[1] The first of these, articulated in both essays but especially prominent in the first, is the conception of *ressentiment* as a fundamental component in what might be called the spiritual achievement of humanity, or what he himself calls "the meaning of all culture." (*GM*: I, 11; 23:24). The other theme, developed especially in the second essay, concerns the relation of practices of punishment to the phenomena of revenge, guilt, and bad conscience. Both themes yield up, in the course of Nietzsche's discursive dance of approach and deferral, formulations that have come to stand, in the main traditions of reception of his work, as crucial components of a distinctively Nietzschean manner of approach to "the problem of man"— the substantive claim of a slave revolt in morality and the methodological innovation of a genealogical type of analysis and/or critique.[2]

The *Genealogy*, published in 1887, appeared near the beginning of what was in the United States a period of bitter racial violence, particularly in the South, directed against black people. This period stretched, in its greatest intensity, from at least the early 1890s through the aftermath of the First World War, and it did not come to an end until the period of the Second World War. The racial violence was only one extreme expression of severe conflicts throughout American society. And one of the most striking expressions of that conflict and that violence was the growth of lynching, a social practice occupying the crossroads of moralized racial struggle, the practice of punishment, and the dynamic of *ressentiment*. In this chapter I will examine that crossroads using Nietzsche's conception of *ressentiment*. I will sketch his account of *ressentiment*, and then I will present some of the most salient facts about the history of lynching in the United States, focusing especially on the period from the end of Reconstruction in the South to the beginning of the civil rights movement there. Finally I will draw some conclusions about the conceptualization of lynching in relation to the issues surrounding the concept of *ressentiment*.

I.

Nietzsche first articulates his concept of *ressentiment* in the *Genealogy*, invoking the concept extensively throughout all three essays. The concept figures crucially both in Nietzsche's account of "slave morality" in the first essay and in his discussion of the functions of asceticism and the ascetic priest in the third essay. The word first appears in section 10 of the first essay, in the course of a discussion of the "slave revolt in morality," which is in turn introduced in section 7 of the same essay during a discussion of the Jews, who, Nietzsche claims,

> in the end were only able to obtain satisfaction from their enemies and conquerors through a radical revaluation of their values, that is, through an act of *spiritual revenge*. (*GM*: I, 7; 16: 27–29)

Ressentiment is in the first instance a psychic force, fundamentally reactive in nature, which seeks expression or externalization in hostile behavior aimed at another who is deemed the author of an original injury or humiliation. Characteristically, Nietzsche writes, "The slave revolt in morals begins when *ressentiment* itself becomes creative and gives birth to values: the *ressentiment* of beings denied the true reaction, that of the deed, who recover their losses only through an imaginary revenge" (*GM*: I, 10; 19: 3–6). Note that here ressentiment is identified first as a substantive, indeed, an agency, in itself; only secondarily is it related to "beings" placed in specific social circumstances. In both of these passages, the revenge is taken in a sublimated and/or an "ideological" form, manifested as ideas and attitudes toward the world and specific aspects of human reality, most especially the other—those whose instinctual life is fundamentally active and self-referential. It is perhaps not quite accurate to describe *ressentiment* as underwriting the master-slave dichotomy: it is rather articulated with that dichotomy as characteristic of the slave's mode of reaction to the master.

Nietzsche's notion of *ressentiment* has a further, metaphorical function to distinguish a kind of "personality structure" (not Nietzsche's terminology)—a developed character type grounded in the dominance of reactive feelings or impulses over the life and activity of the individual who exhibits it. This is indicated, I take it, by Nietzsche's comment that (he is referring to the priests—specifically of ancient Judaism): "It is on the soil of this *essentially dangerous* form of human existence . . . that man first became an *interesting animal*, that only here did the human soul acquire *depth* in a higher sense and become *evil*" (*GM*: I, 6; 15:38–16:2). Indeed, of the six uses of the term *ressentiment* in section 10 of the first essay, in which it is introduced, three occur in the phrase "beings of ressentiment," suggesting a constitutive role for the force in the very being of the 'humans' so characterized.

Nietzsche's conception of *ressentiment* as a psychic phenomenon thus seems to have several criterial marks:

First, it involves intentions and impulses whose full and open expression is thwarted and deferred in the context of their defining and original relation between the subject in whom they arise and an "other," the original object of the intention and/or impulse (the reactivity of *ressentiment*, essentially connected with the fact that the most immediate, direct expression of these intentions is thwarted);

Second, these intentions/impulses survive in something like their original form in the subject, specifically in relation to some content feature/s of their original object, pressing for and ultimately finding an object and a path of release different from yet similar in content to, its original or intended object (the content preservation of *ressentiment*);

Third, these reactive impulses are transformed in intensity, acquire "depth" or greater intensity and force, and so typically exhibit an increased strength of discharge when they ultimately reveal themselves in action (the deepening function of *ressentiment*);

Fourth, this "depth" or increased intensity necessarily involves what Nietzsche describes as cruelty, that is, a degree and an elaboration of psychic connotation not typically present in expressions that manifest the more original active rather than reactive impulses (the essential cruelty of *ressentiment*);

Fifth, and finally, *ressentiment* comes to define an entire "way of being," or, perhaps better, "way of seeing," rather than simply remaining a behavioral pattern of response or form of acting characteristic of slaves (the holistic tendency of *ressentiment*).

Nietzsche associates *ressentiment* distinctively with slave morality, on the one hand, and the priest and the priestly function, on the other hand. Slave morality is, itself, the unique creation of priests, a special cast of humans who are themselves clearly identified, by Nietzsche, with their original relation to and creation of slave morality. "Evil" as a category and form of valuation is the distinctive product of this priesthood, while not being unique to such priests as individuals. Indeed, as Nietzsche insinuates without actually saying, it is the adoption of this form of valuation by those identified as "slaves" as distinct from "priests" that comes to distinguish the slaves as such from their "others," the masters, and also marks the priests' first distinctive impact on human culture as such. So, while there can be no slave morality without priests, it is not however the case that there can be no slaves without the priesthood and their distinctive creation— slave morality. It is rather that slave morality, as the distinctive, organized expression of the way of seeing/being of the slave type as such, only arises as an explicit expression of the life of the slave through its articulation by the priest as the mode of valuation distinctive of the preexisting type of the slave.

But though the slave type preexists the "slave morality" brought into being by the priest's creative act, surely it is also true that the creation of slave morality itself represents a transformation of the slave/master social relation, most obviously in the sense that this "conceptual transformation" overthrows the overt political supremacy of the noble type. But at the very same time it creates a moralized and hypostatized opposition that works to entrench and consolidate the focus of reactive hatefulness and desire for revenge, for the displacement of the noble type from positions of power does not lessen the danger, the evil, that the powerful or noble figure at the focus of slave morality represents. The relationship is thus spiritualized, in two distinct senses: it becomes ideological in form— in which form the hegemony of the slaves is overtly expressed and achieved—and it is given a significance and "cosmic resonance" its pre-ideological form could not show.

In terms of the analysis presented so far, the priest is a hybrid, a type split between features of the slave type and those of the master type. On Nietzsche's account, the priest should be regarded as a kind of slave: what they have in common, or better, what they lack in common, is the fulsome physicality and strength that characterizes the noble type, the master. The initial specific difference, characterologically, between these two types of slave—the slave proper and the priest— is that the priest engages in specific practices of purification and abstinence in which the slave does not indulge. This characterological difference seems to be associated, in Nietzsche's text, with a sociological difference, namely, that the priests elevate and distinguish themselves as a distinct caste, one concerned not with manual labor but with its own distinctive social functions. Nietzsche explicitly identifies the priestly caste as derivative from what he calls the "knightly-aristocratic" caste (*GM*, 7; 16:5-9). Indeed, the priestly functions are themselves given meaning in the priests' own value-creative positing of "slave morality." But this very act, and related social function, of value creation points to the priests' affinity with the type of the master. The act of value creation is itself almost definitive characterologically of the master type, as well as bespeaking a strength of will that is distinctive of masters.

There also seems to be a distinction, but again one not clearly articulated by Nietzsche in the text itself, between the priest of the first essay and the "ascetic priest" of the third. While Nietzsche never uses "ascetic" to modify "priest" in the first essay, that modifier is ubiquitous in the third. Further, while the priest is all along distinguished from the "knightly-aristocratic" noble type by ascetic customs of *personal* hygiene, it might be argued that these remain only personal requirements in the early period of priesthood, that their ascendance and domination of priestliness as such is a later development.

Nietzsche claims at one point that *ressentiment* can on some occasions be attributed as the basis for action of a being of the noble type. (*GM*: I, 10; 21: 7-11). But in those instances, he is quick to point out, the desire for revenge is acted out quickly, and thereby discharged, without becoming "poisonous," collecting and turning dangerous. A further difference between the mode of action and evaluation that is fundamentally dictated by *ressentiment* and that which is only incidentally tinged with it is that while the latter is primarily self-referential, and so original and active, the former is wholly reactive, and has essential reference to the other type, and so is essentially contrastive and oppositional. In consequence, the being of *ressentiment* assumes an attitude that is generally contemptuous of the opposing other as enemy, while the noble type of antagonistic feeling is predicated on a relation to the antagonist that honors that enemy even as it opposes and fights him. Both are modes of opposition and antagonism, but in *ressentiment*, the opposition is rooted in a revulsion against or repulsion from the type of the opponent, while in the noble type of opposition, the opposition is grounded in an identification with the opposing other.

In Nietzsche's text *ressentiment* finds its expession and its most immediate outcome in the slave revolt that subordinates the noble natures to the moral ideology of the priests. A secondary result, which is unintentional in a way the slave morality is not, is the development of bad conscience as an expression of the persistent condition of interior humiliation that any "civilized" individual sustains in relation to the community. The third, more intense, and culturally distinct expression of this civilizing process is the domination of culture by ascetic ideals. These three "progressively" developed articulations of the basic force of *ressentiment* are recuperated successively in the themes of the three essays that constitute the *Genealogy*. Because and to the extent that culture and "civilization" come to be dominated to a greater extent by "guilt," "bad conscience," and the ascetic ideal, as ramified consequences of the original "slave revolt in morality," all creatures in such a civilized society become increasingly subject to *ressentiment*, become to a greater and greater extent, "beings of *ressentiment*." It is in this sense that Nietzsche can write, at the end of the first essay, that "today there is perhaps no more decisive mark of the *'higher nature,'* of the more spiritual nature, than to be conflicted in that sense and still a real battleground for those opposites [the noble and the slave manner of evaluation]" (*GM*: I, 16; 30:7-31:2) There are no longer, if there ever were, pure types.

What is implicit in this emerging paradigm of hybridity is the sociological correlate of the initial, psychic reference of the impurity of fundamental types in the Nietzschean schema. The social reality of power and powerlessness is relational and relative rather than biologically given and absolute. It is the hybridity of the value-creating priest that makes the slave revolt in morality possible: implicitly, the existence of other hybrid types should generate other forms of expression of *ressentiment*. Nietzsche's discussion of the criminal in the second essay may well be regarded as such a distinct hybrid type. What such types would have in common, as products and facilitators of distinct expressions of *ressentiment*, is an existence mediated through an imaginary or ideological field of valuation derivative from the basic structure of "spiritual revenge" established through the initial slave revolt. That basic structure is the site to which we will now direct our search for a key to the historical reality of lynching. We will consider what possibilities the basic structure of *ressentiment*, as a space of hybrid forms of social relation, offers for the understanding of American lynch law.

II.

The core content of the concept of lynch law is of the systematic practice of "punishment" of a perpetrator or suspect outside of or beyond the applicable legally authoritative procedures in place for such punishment: it is the idea of a group of citizens "taking the law into their own hands."[3] That having been said, there is a significant evolution in the practice of lynch law. There is a consensus among historians that the development of lynch law can be distinguished into three distinct stages or phases, and that the practices making up lynch law differed in important ways in these three stages. The three stages are demarcated, chronologically, as follows. The first stage extends from the earliest period of the formation of the nation during the Revolutionary War crisis up until about 1830; the second, briefest stage extends from the 1830s to the end of the crisis of the Union and the Reconstruction period; the third and final stage begins in the late 1870s with the fall of Reconstruction and extends to the very beginning of the civil rights era in the 1950s and 1960s.[4]

During the first period the institution took two distinct forms. First, the summary execution of perceived enemies during the Revolutionary War period, on the one hand—the practice is allegedly named after a colonel, Charles Lynch, who did just that to Royalist enemies of the colonists' cause in Bedford County, Virginia. Second, the institution of "frontier justice" developed in those territories that came to be populated and settled by Euro-Americans moving from the East, before the establishment of local legal authorities to make and enforce criminal law. This "Wild West" strand of lynch law, which came to be representative of the institution as such during the first two periods of its development, was characterized by punishments that stopped far short of execution, generally involving whiplashing and/or tar and feathering, after which the perpetrator was run out of town instead of being executed. The new feature added to this picture in the second period is that the victims of lynch law after 1830, during the gathering storm of the crisis of the Union, came increasingly to reflect national political struggles rather than local criminal justice requirements: the practice came to be used in the struggle over the fate of the slavocracy and specifically as a "punishment" of crusading abolitionists venturing into hostile communities.

Lynch law came into its own and acquired a fundamentally new quality during its third and last period of development: the features of lynch law during this period are largely definitive of the image of lynch law current today. The institution came to be *almost* completely racialized, the victims being overwhelmingly Afro-American men and the mobs generally exclusively white. The third-period institution of lynch law was largely, though not exclusively, a Southern phenomenon. Relatedly, lynching in the third period acquired a ritualistic and an extremely brutal character; the alleged crime perpetrated by the victim and the actual execution and death of the victim receded in importance relative to the ritualized torture and dismemberment that came to be the main point of the spectacle of lynch law. It is with this third-period form of lynch law that I will be concerned in what follows.

One of the things about the record of third-period lynchings noted almost universally is the enacted fury and the extreme cruelty displayed in these violent rituals. Indeed, "displays" is very much an apt word: lynchings came to be almost communal ceremonies of catharsis, as it were, of pent-up impulses of brutality. The severity of cruelty displayed in lynchings suggests that those involved in the "lynch mob" were animated by complexes of feeling and impulse that were latent and dynamic. This dynamic of cruelty in lynchings makes sense viewed in terms of the ideas of *ressentiment* and its relation to cruelty and violence, for the effect of *ressentiment*'s release in a directly physical or nonsublimated form would be to sweep before it all of the impulses of cruelty that have collected and intensified in the subject.

The lynch "mob," organized as it was around the prospect of "punishing" a violator of some community standard—and I shall return momentarily to the issues of punishment and of the nature of those alleged violations—was fundamentally animated by the prospect of witnessing and participating in the expected enactments of cruelty. Numerous accounts testify to the avidness with which spectators, given the chance, became participants, to the relish with which body parts were sought and collected as if prizes, to the feasts of mutilation and burning in which so many were so anxious to witness and participate. The lynching ritual, far removed from its original in the form of a rushed execution, became increasingly encrusted with more extensive and varied forms of atrocity perpetrated against the person and, after death, to the body of the victim. The grisly prologue to death became the main act, the payoff, for the participants as for the spectators.

The very fact that the lynching ceremonies were the work of a mob, a group composing itself for that express purpose, rather than the act of isolated individuals, also seems to support the suggestion that *ressentiment* was a decisive force in carrying out the atrocity. Nietzsche consistently associates *ressentiment* with what he calls the "herd instinct." Those who are weak-willed must need the solidarity of numbers to give expression to their cruel urges: only in the midst of the mob, where participation is encouraged, do these urges give rise to act.

But if the lynch mob is constituted in some sense, and in part, by these powerful reactive feelings, then what is the original stimulus and object of these feelings? What are the reactive feelings a reaction to? The Nietzschean account of *ressentiment* points to the deep-etched impact of humiliations sustained by the powerless at the hands of the powerful. My suggestion here is that we are dealing with the trace of class and power relations manifested in the lives of poor, disenfranchised Southern whites, these lowest social orders of Southern white society that provided the vast bulk of the members of lynch mobs. This is not to say that the social and political elite of the white South never participated in lynchings and never were spectators either. But the general pattern was for middle- and upper-class whites to condone lynchings or to "turn a blind eye" to them without actively participating, while the overwhelming participation and spectatorship came from among the lowest classes. Given this, we can surmise that the reactive feelings that fueled the lynchings were, at least in part, feelings and impulses within the poor whites rooted in their own oppression and poverty, feelings originally or logically directed against the ruling elite of wealthy whites who dominated southern society. That is to say, these feelings were in large degree, even in their bulk, class feelings that could not safely be directed against their proper objects—that is, the powerful and wealthy white plantocracy.

Another feature of the history of lynch law in the south that seems to strikingly confirm this Nietzschean interpretation I have constructed here is the role of fundamentalist Protestant ministers in Southern lynch parties. The Nietzschean account of *ressentiment* highlighted the role of priests as organizers and leaders of *ressentiment* as a social reality. At any rate, one of the most salient realities of Southern life from the 1890s to the 1950s, during the heyday of lynch law, was the role of fundamentalist Protestant ministers in the organization of that very lynch law. Fundamentalist ministers played an overwhelming role in the Ku Klux Klan, occupying prominent positions themselves or being closely allied with the leaders of what was almost certainly the single most important organizational force behind the lynch law reign of terror in the South during the seventy-year span just mentioned. The role of fundamentalist Christianity, in the persons of these ministers as well as in their speechifying and formulating of quasi-theological rationales justifying lynching, is so pervasive in the historical record that it led one writer to ask the following:

> How in heaven's name could Christianity, which worships as the one true living God a swarthy-skinned, working-class Semite from the sticks of ancient Roman Palestine who preached a doctrine of love and fellowship, end up as a sacrificial cult that

legitimized and celebrated the genocidal torturing and burning alive, by its most ardent believers, of helpless males from a wretchedly exploited ex-slave minority?[5]

I have so far pointed to some interesting parallels between Nietzsche's model of *ressentiment* as a fundamental type of psychic functioning and the known features of American lynch law in what I have characterized as its third-period phase. I have been suggesting that something that might seem not only profoundly disturbing but also inexplicable—the extent and regularity of third-period lynching as well as the degree of cruelty exhibited in it—can be made more intelligible by appeal to Nietzsche's notion of *ressentiment*. I now want to pursue a bit further the parallel, looking at several other comments Nietzsche makes in the second essay of the *Genealogy*, on "Guilt, Bad Conscience, and Related Matters."

III.

First I should mention Nietzsche's account of the criminal as a kind of debtor. Here Nietzsche, in effect, postulates a further fundamental contributor to the "civilization" of the human animal. He advances this notion in connection with his famous discussion of punishment, and in the course of his polemic against the idea that the practice of punishment always involves implicitly judgment of guilt and so is a normative practice that necessarily involves its own built-in justification in retributivist terms. Nietzsche's alternative conception appeals to the idea that punishment is rooted conceptually in the creditor-debtor relationship. Developing this case (in section 19 of the second essay), Nietzsche makes the speculative suggestion that this creditor-debtor relation has been "interpreted into . . . the relationship of *those presently living* to their *ancestors*. . . . Here the conviction holds sway that it is only through the sacrifices and achievements of the ancestors that the clan *exists* at all—and that one has to *repay* them through sacrifices and achievements: one thereby acknowledges *a debt* that is continually growing, since these ancestors, in their continued existence as powerful spirits, do not cease to use their strength to bestow on the clan new benefits and advances" (*GM*: II, 19; 60: 9–22).

A couple of points here related to the topic of lynching and lynch law: first, and fairly obviously, the cruelty and aggressiveness manifest in the rituals of third-period lynch law can be traced back to a specific kind of family dynamic, more specifically, the rough treatment, to put it euphemistically, of the child, and especially of the male child, at the hands of the father or the family patriarch. One of the peculiarities of Southern culture is the prominence of two related features: a fairly rigid militaristic ethos of public life focused on the male descendants of the familial bloodline and their relation to ancestral lands, and along with this an associated cult of nobility. This situation would seem to place a particular, and a particularly intense, kind of psychic pressure on the male children in their relation to the father figures. Of course, this situation has significant implications for the female children as well, also relevant to the distinctive features of third-period lynch law. But the main point is that here Nietzsche explicitly draws a connection between state practices of punishment and those characterizing the intergenerational relations within the family.

Nietzsche characterizes the criminal in relation to the community, again on the analogy of the debtor-creditor relation, and says this: "The criminal is the debtor who not only fails to repay the advantages and advances rendered him, but also even lays a hand on his creditor: he therefore not only forfeits all of these goods and advantages from now on, as is fair—he is also now reminded how much there is to these goods. The anger of the injured creditor, of the community, gives him back again to the wild and outlawed condition from which he was previously protected: it expels him from itself—and now every kind of hostility may vent itself on him" (*GM*: I, 9; 46:18–30).

In characterizing the community as the "aggrieved creditor," Nietzsche is postulating a collective or corporate subject as carrying out the act of punishment. This act of punishment *reconstitutes* the community precisely by and through ejecting the criminal from it. This process is both constitutively political, reaffirming as it does the identity of the political community of which it is the expression, as well as being a psychic mechanism through which the forces of cruelty are liberated and given expression and release. Rather than counterposing the structural to the psychological, Nietzsche sees their crucial and defining interpenetration: this is an extension of the earlier point, elaborated in relation to the "slave revolt in morality," concerning the way that the force of *ressentiment* tends to foster the stability and identity of "civilized society."

How does what Nietzsche says here fit the case of lynching? Let me suggest this answer: the very fury and force of the act of expulsion, the savagery with which it is effected, indicates the futility and desperation of the sought-for communal identity. Many commentators have remarked on the importance of third-period lynch law in the reassertion of the solidarity of the Southern white community in the face of its humiliation and defeat as a result of the Civil War crisis.[6] The enormity of the crime of lynching is a measure of the force and intensity of the contradictions that produce it. Of course, the former slave status of the Afro-American identified as criminal and lynched goes a long way toward explaining why he or she becomes a focus of the fury of the mob. Indeed, here the telltale mark of *ressentiment* reveals itself in the very process by which the mere fact of ex-slave status (or for that matter slave status itself) functions to make anyone branded with that status vulnerable to the charge of criminality. For the very physical strength of the African slaves could be taken as a sign of their (socially enforced) weakness, and that weakness then taken as a sign of their being debtors to the community whose social identity was so identified with slavocracy. Thus the slide from "Negro" to "criminal"— and from there to victim of lynch law—was made all the more slippery by the peculiar reversal of valuations that is almost definitive of *ressentiment*. What Nietzsche's account brings into focus is the "crude logic" of the community of those who dominate through violence—a community that is itself hostage to the reiterated violence and cruelty of its members.

Finally, I would like to make a more overtly political analogy or application of a comment of Nietzsche's to the problematic of lynching. This is a line of thought that he invokes in polemicizing against the social contract conception of the state. In putting forward his alternative, as it were, he begins with the claim that the

> fitting of a previously unrestrained and unformed population into a fixed form, given its beginning in an act of force, could be brought to its completion only by acts of force (*GM*: II, 17; 58: 6–8).

In relation to lynching, Nietzsche's remark here points to a fundamental issue—that of the functionality of lynching itself as a powerful force for the "management" of the subject populations, in the lynching case, specifically, of course the Southern African American ex-slaves. But we should not shrink from considering this insight also in relation to the white Southern (and to a lesser extent Northern) populations that perpetrated the lynchings—lynching practice as a reactive manifestation, as a reaction to the state-forming pressures and violence exerted upon them (having both local and national provenance), as well as the pressures to which they are subject as a result of broader, undirected social forces: modernization, industrialization, and most basically the adversities of wage labor and the competition constitutive of labor markets generally.[7]

IV.

We can perhaps draw the following conclusions from our—admittedly provisional and very incomplete—look at the phenomenon of lynching in the late nineteenth and early twentieth, "American" century through the lens of Nietzschean *ressentiment*. First, added to *ressentiment*'s drive toward the metaphysicalized hardening of its constructed moral distinctions and hierarchy— which hardening is precisely the content of the "slave revolt in morality," *ressentiment*'s most basic manifestation— is the tendency that, while initially appearing in a bipolar form, this hierarchy tends to ramify and expand such distinctions beyond that bipolar form. This tendency is inherent in the very dynamism of *ressentiment* and of the power relations that generate it. Indeed, the very figure of the priest embodies this generativity in conflict of *ressentiment*'s rank orderings. For, as discussed in the first section, the priest is, characterologically, both a slave type and a master type— a slave insofar as physically impotent, a master insofar as the priest is the one whose creative act brings slave morality into existence, and in so doing, does indeed overcome and "master" the master through the revaluation of values. The priest, is, therefore, a hybrid or mixed type already, although Nietzsche does not bring this out clearly in his discussion in the *Genealogy*. If it is true that at the very point of the slave revolt's creative act of overcoming there is such a differentiation or hybridization of type as embodied in the priest, then we might put it as a fundamental fact about *ressentiment* that it generates not only bipolar but more stratified and fragmented rank and type formations as well.

This claim—my basic conclusion—regarding the conception of *ressentiment*, while not explicitly worked out in Nietzsche's account, is not, I think, contradicted by anything he says there; indeed, it makes sense of the textual consequences of what he says, as well as of the phenomenon of lynching taken as an instance of *ressentiment*. But it does entail two consequences that require a realist understanding of Nietzsche's account of the social bases of *ressentiment*'s cultural dominance. These consequences are, first, that *ressentiment* in fact generates through its own dynamism a variegated and more-than-bipolar social structure, one in which in addition to a "master" and "slave" class, there are further intermediary classes as well. Second, for *ressentiment* to achieve what it does relative to the psychical requirements of the slaves by means of their ideological consciousness, that consciousness must be inherently split or contradictory—being both deceptive and involving the elements of veridical awareness as well.

If lynching is to be read as an effect of *ressentiment*, then this must be in terms very different from either the slave revolt or asceticism, its "classic" manifestations. For in the slave revolt the force of *ressentiment* is thrown back on the object—the master—whose power occasioned the humiliation that generated *ressentiment* in the first place. In the reign of ascetic ideals the force of *ressentiment* is turned inward against the very being whose mode of existence *ressentiment* is an expression of. Lynching, in contradistinction, is a phenomenon constituted by a *ressentiment* discharged neither against an object that is interior to the discharging subject— as "in the inwardly" turned aim of the ascetic ideal—nor in a sublimated form against the master race as the original source of injury or humiliation—as in the case of the slave revolt proper. The object must therefore be a vulnerable individual, a member of a social stratum distinct from both that of the slave-subjects themselves and from their masters, one that is relatively impotent—in relation to the "slaves," that is, the lynchers, themselves—and can serve as a proper object for the safe and satisfying discharge of the "spirit of revenge."

But at the same time, this object also must have two further identifying characteristics that are essential, I claim, to the proper discharge of *ressentiment*. The first is that the object must be, and be recognized to be, properly human, insofar as the "revenge" must be gotten out of the hide of a recognizably human being. For the essential content of *ressentiment* is to return the favor of a burning humiliation, of a stinging injury—here it seems crucial to add a "spiritual" injury that lingers and gets at the very integrity of the being of the object of revenge. Nietzsche is explicit that the injury that precipitates the operation of ressentiment must be felt as a humiliation, as the mark of a social powerlessness. This involves, I take it, something like social consciousness on the part of the one who serves as the object of such revenge. One cannot humiliate or oppress a nonhuman creature, only inflict pain of a dumb kind. Arguably the suffering and anguish produced by humiliation is much more inwardly damaging than "simple physical pain."

Thus I want to argue, first, that the function of *ressentiment* requires or presupposes a recognition of the humanity of the object of that reactive expression. To do so in the case of lynching is to affirm the self-deceptive component of racial hostility and oppression: for if to lynch a man requires that you acknowledge or accept, on some level, his humanity, then the ideology of the inferiority or subhumanity of 'the Negro,' which is generally taken to be at the core of the ideological justification of lynching (as well as other manifestations of domination and oppression generally), must be substantially or in some part self-deceptive.

The second is that the prospective object must appear in the guise of a dangerous and in some way powerful threatening other. This cannot, again, be merely a matter of projection or invention but rather must also in some sense correspond to the social reality. That is, while the constructed moral ideology of the relation will surely involve a fantastical and an exaggerated image of the other, the element of threat must, nonetheless, preexist and in some sense condition the moral ideology constructed "reactively" in relation to the original relation or pattern of interaction. Thus while the initial slave revolt generated the moral ideology—"slave morality"—through a moralized projection of "evil" as the original pole of the bipolar construct, the "evil one" of that ideology was, indeed, the powerful and commanding presence who overpowered, humiliated, and instilled fear and loathing in the slaves. That is, the revaluation of values affected by the slave revolt nonetheless retained a rightful reference to those who were indeed the powerful ones, the proper objects of the slaves' hate.

These last considerations relate to the case of lynching in the following sense. The institution of lynch law had a mechanism of self-justification, an entire ideology attendant to it. This ideology was essential to both the maintenance of the institution against pressures from the wider world for its demise, as well as a means of rationalization on the part of participants and spectators, a veil allowing them to hide from themselves the full extent of the inhumanity and cruelty in which they were immersed. The notorious myth of the black rapist was the occasioning and supportive narrative structure into which the event of a lynching was frequently put.[8] But this mythology should not be seen only as a cynical maneuver on the part of defenders of lynching but also as the manifest form of the unconscious structures of *ressentiment*. This manifest form expressed the fears and anxieties of the lynch party that in the third period faced a population of recently liberated ex-slaves. This population, reduced to peonage and a second slavery relatively quickly after the collapse of Reconstruction, represented a deep structural challenge to the security of the white wage worker. This population also existed to some degree outside of the rigid social ideology and customs that were increasingly felt to be a straightjacket in which the poor whites were trapped.[9] In addition, then, to the structural-economic danger that the ex-slave population posed for the white masses, they represented a further threat not to their economic well-being but to the very paternalist ideology of white womanhood that constituted part of the imaginary identity of interests shoring up the deeply divided white community itself. At the very same time, the very fact that the threat represented by black men, specifically, to

"Southern white womanhood," and correlatively to Southern white manhood, was rooted in a long history, partly acknowledged and partly submerged, of interracial sexual relations, brought with it the implicit recognition that consensual sexual activity between members of distinct racial groups implied the basic equality of all humans as such.

I have tried to bring out some of the implications of Nietzsche's account of *ressentiment* as a ground of the psychic repertoire constituting civilized society, out of the naturally given human stock. I have done so in part by presenting some elements for an interpretation of the phenomenon of American lynch law in the period from the collapse of Reconstruction in the South to the growth of the New Deal. These elements, points of contact between the conceptual resources derived from *ressentiment*, and some features of lynch law, point toward an understanding of lynch law as an expression of racial and class hostilities animating the most desperate and downtrodden of white Southerners. They asserted in their actions an allegiance to extreme forms of that barbarism, essential to the slavocracy, from which they had least to gain. I have tried to show how Nietzschean *ressentiment* might make more evident the source of those assertions as gestures of resistance. I can only conclude with a Nietzschean proviso that no such interpretive resource can singly account for the complex reality of lynch law.

Notes

1. I will be using the English translation of the *Genealogy* by Maudemarie Clark and Alan J. Swensen, published by Hackett Publishers (Indianapolis) in 1998 under the title *On the Genealogy of Morality*. Among its other virtues, this edition has line numbers running down each page of the text. In citing the text of the *Genealogy*, I will first identify the essay and section numbers of a passage and then provide the page and line numbers in Clark-Swensen. Thus my first citation, of a phrase Nietzsche uses toward the end of the eleventh section of the first essay, appears as *GM*:I, 11; 23:24, because the phrase occurs on the twenty-fourth line of the twenty-third page of their edition.

2. A number of articles discuss the reception of the *Genealogy* in the collection edited by Richard Schacht, *Nietzsche, Genealogy, Morality: Essays on Nietzsche's "Genealogy of Morals"* (Berkeley: University of California Press, 1984).

3. Stewart E. Tolnay and E. M. Beck, in their *A Festival of Violence: An Analysis of Southern Lynchings, 1882–1930* (Urbana: University of Illinois

Press, 1995), advert to the criterion used by the National Association for the Advancement of Colored People (NAACP) in compiling their historically important survey, *Thirty Years of Lynching in the United States, 1889–1918*. Documenting a lynching, for the NAACP's purposes, involved finding evidence that someone (a) was killed, (b) met death illegally, (c) had death inflicted by a group of three or more persons, or (d) acted under the pretext of serving justice or tradition.

4. But see the somewhat different chronology supplied by Walter White in his *Rope and Faggot: A Biography of Judge Lynch* (1928; 2d ed. New York: Arno Press, 1969).

5. Orlando Patterson, *Rituals of Blood: Consequences of Slavery in Two American Centuries* (Washington, DC: Civitas/Counterpoint, 1998), xiv–xv.

6. See White, *Rope and Faggot*, 15; Patterson, *Rituals of Blood*, 175; Tolnay and Beck, *Festival of Violence*, 25–29.

7. Tolnay and Beck, in *Festival of Violence*, discuss in detail the relation of the fluctuating fortunes of white Southern wage labor to the phenomenon of lynch law; see their chapter 5, "The Role of King Cotton." A classic discussion, from the inside, of the impact on postbellum Southern culture of the centripetal pressures of the modernizing national economy is *I'll Take My Stand: The South and the Agrarian Tradition, by Twelve Southerners*, ed. Louis D. Rubin Jr. (New York: Harper & Bros., 1930).

8. A myth discussed extensively by many writers on lynching; see especially White's *Rope and Faggot* chapter 4, as well as the writings of Ida B. Wells-Barnett, collected in *On Lynchings* (New York: Arno Press, 1969). For more recent treatments, see Angela Davis's "Rape, Racism, and the Myth of the Black Rapist," in her *Women, Race, and Class* (New York: Random House, 1981), 172–201, and Tommy L. Lott, "Frederick Douglass on the Myth of the Black Rapist," in *The Invention of Race: Black Culture and the Politics of Representation*, ed. Tommy L. Lott (London: Blackwell, 1999), 27–46.

9. W. E. B. DuBois, *The Souls of Black Folk* (New York: Washington Square Press, 1970), chapter VIII.

3

Double Consciousness and
Second Sight

KATHLEEN MARIE HIGGINS

Friedrich Nietzsche is not an obvious resource for thinking through the contemporary African American situation. He is hostile to egalitarianism, and indeed to political agendas of virtually any sort. Yet he frequently advocates liberation of the spirit and, at least implicitly, the changes to the status quo that would be necessary to support it. I will suggest that Nietzsche offers considerable insight of use to those concerned with African Americans' societal position, not through his ostensible political comments but through his psychological insight. I will offer what I hope is a prima facie case for this idea by considering some of the parallels and links between Nietzsche's ideas and those proposed by his near-contemporary W. E. B. DuBois, author of the "political Bible" of African American thought, *The Souls of Black Folk*.[1]

I will begin by describing DuBois's characterization of the dynamic but incoherent psychological state provoked by the African American's social circumstances which he terms "double consciousness." I will then suggest that Nietzsche makes a number of suggestions that resonate with this conception, and argue that Nietzsche's approach valuably complements that of Du Bois, both in terms of literary strategy and in the articulation of goals for the doubly conscious person.

DuBois describes double consciousness early in his book *The Souls of Black Folk*. Double consciousness, says DuBois, characterizes the American Negro, who is "born with a veil, and gifted with second sight."[2]

> It is a peculiar sensation, this double-consciousness, this sense of always looking at one's self through the eyes of others, of measuring one's soul by the tape of a world that looks on in

amused contempt and pity. One ever feels his twoness—an American, a Negro; two souls, two thoughts, two unreconciled strivings; two warring ideals in one dark body, whose dogged strength alone keeps it from being torn asunder.[3]

The term *double consciousness* is not original with DuBois. Keith Byerman observes that "In the psychological theory of the time, including that of DuBois's mentor, William James, 'double consciousness' was a form of mental illness in which the victim experienced self-alienation, an inability to maintain a coherent self-image."[4] Priscilla Wald describes the disorder as one that occurs when "two distinct personalities having no knowledge of each other 'coexist' in the same body."

Here . . . is the embodiment of the uncanny: the strange familiarity of the self in and as an other. . . . The disruptions in the narrative of identity of medical subjects suffering from double-consciousness become, in DuBois's formulation, the discontinued narrative of identity imposed on black Americans.[5]

As DuBois uses the term, double consciousness involves a number of aspects. First, it involves awareness that others see one in a manner that fails to confer genuine recognition. Sandra Adell argues that DuBois's notion of double consciousness has Hegelian roots, evident particularly in the suggestion that the soul with double consciousness seeks a higher synthesis that would integrate its two natures.[6] DuBois's portrait of double consciousness is Hegelian, however, in an even more basic sense. Like the parties in Hegel's parable of master and slave, the African American desires recognition from others and is frustrated in this aim. The single characteristic of dark complexion is typically taken to imply all other traits of the individual, according to DuBois. "We must not forget that most Americans answer all questions regarding the Negro a priori."[7] DuBois poignantly recalls his first discovery, that awareness of his race could obstruct recognition of his humanity:

I was a little thing, away up in the hills of New England, where the dark Housatonic winds between Hoosac and Teghkanic to the sea. In a wee wooden schoolhouse, something put it into the boys' and girls' heads to buy gorgeous visiting cards—ten cents a package—and exchange. The exchange was merry, till one girl, a tall newcomer, refused my card—refused it peremptorily, with a glance. Then it dawned upon me with a certain suddenness that I was different from the others; or like, mayhap, in heart and life and longing, but shut out from their world by a vast veil.[8]

The "veil" that DuBois indicates refers to the color line separating whites and blacks but also to a dimming of acuity. DuBois is aware that he is simultaneously seen by those on the other side of the veil but also obscured by the veil. While DuBois's double consciousness involves the awareness of being invisible as a distinct person, it also involves a sense of being under the white world's surveillance. This observation is predicated on the maintenance of the color divide.

The white world's identification of the African American in terms of the sole feature of skin color is not a mere oversight regarding other personal characteristics. It is accompanied by a threatening stance, maintained by the white world against any behavior deviating from acceptable deference to the status quo in which white privilege prevails. DuBois described the situation of blacks in the South: "The police system of the South was originally designed to keep track of all Negroes, not simply of criminals. Its police system was arranged to deal with blacks alone, and tacitly assumed that every white man was ipso facto a member of that police."[9]

The self-consciousness that such observation engenders is an internalization of external surveillance. One may choose to defy the pressures imposed by those watching, but one is well aware of them as one's audience. Indeed, one's self-conception comes to involve a sense that one is performing for others. Audience reaction becomes a test of one's success.[10] This reactive self-perception takes on a negative cast when the audience is predisposed to respond in a disparaging manner. This is certainly the situation of African Americans, according to DuBois:

> . . . the facing of so vast a prejudice could not but bring the inevitable self-questioning, self-disparagement, and lowering of ideals which ever accompany repression and breed in an atmosphere of contempt and hate.[11]

Thus far I have indicated three features of double consciousness: (1) the sense of being identified by virtue of a single trait (skin color), and thus being invisible in one's particularity, (2) the sense of being under the surveillance of parties predisposed to be unsympathetic, and (3) the internalization of the mechanisms of surveillance and the adoption of associated self-disparaging judgments. Double consciousness also involves an awareness of oneself as a mixed being. DuBois emphasized the unreconciled character of one's aspirations, the "two warring ideals in one dark body." This condition obstructs fulfillment of one's human potential and one's participation in societal life. DuBois says of the African American:

> This, then, is the end of his striving: to be a co-worker in the kingdom of culture, to escape both death and isolation, to husband and use his best powers and his latent genius. These powers of body and mind have in the past been strangely wasted, dispersed, or forgotten. And yet it is not weakness—it is the contradiction of double aims. The double-aimed struggle of the black artisan—on the one hand to escape white contempt for a nation of mere hewers of wood and drawers of water, and on the other hand to plough and nail and dig for a poverty-stricken horde — could only result in making him a poor craftsman, for he had but half a heart in either cause.[12]

Double consciousness easily drains one's energies while this tension remains unresolved. But the inner tension it creates also motivates one to aim at a new synthesis, which Du Bois describes as the African American's "longing to attain self-conscious manhood, to merge his double self into a better and truer self."[13] Although painful, the tension wrought by double consciousness provokes the desire for a more integrated self and instigates the self-questioning that might bring it about. The tension within the soul is thus ambivalent. One's duality provides ample resources for the development of a transfigured, comprehensive self, not just the potential for self-interference. In DuBois's characterization, as Byerman observes, "Blacks . . . are not nothing, but two things, both of which are coherent and meaningful; the difficulty is in successfully joining them for a greater self and, by implication, a greater culture."[14]

Although hopeful, DuBois sees the project of forging a synthetic self as inherently difficult. This difficulty is exacerbated by the temptation to be co-opted.

> In the Black World, the Preacher and Teacher embodied once the ideals of this people—the strife for another and a juster world, the vague dream of righteousness, the mystery of knowing; but to-day the danger is that these ideals, with their simple beauty and weird inspiration, will suddenly sink to a question of cash and a lust for gold."[15]

The allure of wealth is particularly dangerous, because riches are a clearer goal than that of forging an integrated self. The quest for gold cultivates the illusion that the deficiencies of one's position can be rectified through fulfilled material ambition. DuBois sees the promise of wealth as a false promise. Even if the aim is achieved, wealth does not eliminate the veil. Although wealth might be envied by individuals on both sides of the color divide, with accommodations from both sides to the person possessing it, wealth cannot resolve the psychological problem of developing a sense of one's own identity. To put it in Hegelian terms, wealth does not compel others to bestow human recognition on its possessor.

Moreover, as we observed earlier, DuBois believes that the divided mind that has been cultivated in African Americans interferes with whole-hearted pursuit of any dream. They are therefore at a disadvantage from the start in any effort as competitive as that of amassing wealth. Worst of all, money distracts attention from the goal of self-realization in a higher sense, which involves the construction of oneself as a harmonious being and self-assertion as a full participant in political and cultural life.

The danger that goals of self-development and a sense of dignity will be abandoned is particularly acute at the time DuBois is writing, when Booker T. Washington's "Atlanta Compromise" has become the doctrine of many on both sides of the veil. This compromise is the concession that "In all things purely social we can be as separate as five fingers, and yet one as the hand in all things essential to mutual progress."[16] DuBois sees Washington's compromise as capitulation, as a blatant abdication of spiritual and cultural aspirations to secure the satisfaction of African Americans' physical needs. Of Washington he comments,

> ... so thoroughly did he learn the speech and thought of triumphant commercialism, and the ideals of material prosperity, that the picture of a lone black boy pouring over a French grammar amid the weeds and dirt of a neglected home soon seemed to him the acme of absurdities. One wonders what Socrates and St. Francis of Assisi would say to this.[17]

Explicitly abandoned in Washington's program are political power, civil rights, and higher education for African Americans. According to DuBois, the disappearance of these aims from the agenda of black leaders such as Washington risks the permanent consignment of African Americans to a subordinate role within American society and the endless prolongation of unfulfilled inner conflict. Indeed, the abandonment of these goals reinforces the inferiority that African Americans have been taught to feel. DuBois comments:

Mr. Washington's programme practically accepts the alleged inferiority of the Negro races. Again, in our own land, the reaction from the sentiment of war times has given impetus to race-prejudice against Negroes, and Mr. Washington withdraws many of the high demands of Negroes as men and American citizens. . . . In the history of nearly all other races and peoples the doctrine preached at such crises has been that manly self-respect is worth more than lands and houses, and that a people who voluntarily surrender such respect, or cease striving for it, are not worth civilizing.[18]

DuBois's own view is that the resolution of the inner turmoil of African Americans can only be achieved through self-respect and self-assertion, and any policy that interferes with either should be resisted by all legitimate means.

The growing spirit of kindliness and reconciliation between the North and South after the frightful differences of a generation ago ought to be a source of deep congratulation to all, and especially to those whose mistreatment caused the war; but if that reconciliation is to be marked by the industrial slavery and civic death of those same black men, with permanent legislation into a position of inferiority, then those black men, if they are really men, are called upon by every consideration of patriotism and loyalty to oppose such a course by all civilized methods. . . . We have no right to sit silently by while the inevitable seeds are sown for a harvest of disaster to our children, black and white.[19]

Although the pain of inner turmoil makes the temptation to co-option a real danger, the turmoil within the African American's soul nevertheless yields a spiritual advantage, according to DuBois. This is the power of discernment that he calls "second sight." Wald describes DuBois's notion as "a rift between experience and evaluation,"[20] and she emphasizes the positive potential of this ability to refrain from giving whole hearted assent to unevaluated surface appearances. "DuBois describes not only the pain of measuring oneself by a contemptuous and pitying world, but also the empowerment that comes with knowing one is doing so."[21] Second sight, for DuBois, involves the ability to see through the debilitating judgments that one has absorbed and to recognize their dubious origins.

The second sight that DuBois describes is a function of having a perspective on everyday experience that differs from the majority's.

Even if one soul within the African American takes the majority's outlook on most experiences, the second soul provides alternative, modifying insights that are equally part of one's perception. For the person with double consciousness, common opinion cannot be naively accepted. The second sight that DuBois indicates is the multidimensional awareness that emerges from double consciousness, a deeper perspective than that of less complex contemporaries.

The ideal is to utilize this more penetrating perception to enhance one's effectiveness in the world. For the African American, awareness of how the white world views things can be useful knowledge, as long as one does not accept this outlook as something to which one should give deference. Moreover, double consciousness can provide the basis for distancing oneself from the contemptuous judgments of others, in that it prevents its possessor from giving simple assent to any judgment encountered. The gap between disparaging judgments that one has absorbed and the assent of one's entire consciousness is a starting point for refusing those judgments.

Unfortunately, all too often, the African American's double awareness does not develop into a deeper perspective that is enriched by this duality but instead nurtures feelings of incapacity or inspires self-deception. DuBois reflects:

> From the double life every American Negro must live, as a Negro and as an American as swept on by the current of the nineteenth while yet struggling in the eddies of the fifteenth century—from this must arise a painful self-consciousness, an almost morbid sense of personality and a moral hesitancy which is fatal to self-confidence. The worlds within and without the Veil of color are changing, and changing rapidly, but not at the same rate, not in the same way; and this must produce a peculiar wrenching of the soul, a peculiar sense of doubt and bewilderment. Such a double life, with double thoughts, double duties, and double social classes, must give rise to double words and double ideals, and tempt the mind to pretence or to revolt, to hypocrisy or to radicalism.[22]

DuBois's book illustrates with examples the extreme difficulty of this situation and the tragic consequences to which it has led many. It serves as a stirring call to conscience for his readers on either side of the veil.

DuBois directs the attention of all of his readers to their obligation to assist the reconstruction of social policies in a way that grants full social and cultural participation to all citizens. He is unswerving in his efforts to reveal the mechanisms by which African Americans are oppressed and the psychological toll that this has taken. At the same time, he rejects stances of submission and victimization, insisting that African Americans must assert their own dignity in order to successfully rectify the situation. He emphasizes the political goals that should be sought and the specific attitudes African Americans should cultivate, as well as some they should shun.

DuBois offers hints as to how African Americans' inner distress might be navigated, but these hints remain more suggestive than explicit. The Hegelian goal of the black man "merging his double self into a better and truer self"[23] is held out as the ideal. Some of Nietzsche's insights consider similar psychological territory, and I think that they can help clarify both the challenges, the temptations, and the positive potential of double consciousness. Accordingly, at this juncture I will direct the discussion to Nietzsche.

In Nietzsche's writings we find a parallel with DuBois's account in his frequent discussions of inner tensions and self-conceptions in conflict. Like DuBois, he describes conditions of being seen in a manner that fails to recognize who he is. Although we can only infer which particular experiences were most crucial to Nietzsche's sense of being an outsider, his works reveal that he did consider himself disconnected from many aspects of the way of life that those around him took for granted. He speaks of himself as "untimely" or "unfashionable" even in early works. The "free spirits" that he often mentions represent his assertion of a positive attitude toward his inability to fit his time and place; his letters, on the other hand, often reveal his disturbance with the same situation. Seemingly, he had ambivalent attitudes toward his sense of distance from the cultural mainstream. His autobiography, *Ecce Homo*, provides further evidence that Nietzsche considered himself marginalized. He comments that he is not read, that one cannot communicate where there are no ears for what one says, and that it is possible to be born posthumously. *The Gay Science* also abounds in suggestions that Nietzsche considers himself a member of a misunderstood minority. "There is a time for us, too!" he claims exuberantly at the end of the book's first section.[24] Elsewhere he insists, "The moral earth, too, has its antipodes. The antipodes, too, have the right to exist" (*GS* 289).

Nietzsche was quite conscious of the discrepancy between his multidimensional sense of himself and the reactions he provoked from other people. In the following passage, he uses humor to express this awareness.

> We are too prone to forget that in the eyes of people who are seeing us for the first time we are something quite different

from what we consider ourselves to be: usually we are nothing more than a single individual trait which leaps to the eye and determines the whole impression we make. Thus the gentlest and most reasonable of men can, if he wears a large moustache, sit as it were in its shade and feel safe there—he will usually be seen as no more than the appurtenance of a large moustache, that is to say a military type, easily angered and occasionally violent—and as such he will be treated.[25]

A mustache hardly seems to distinguish a person enough to be taken seriously, and Nietzsche seems to be playing with the cliché of using a mustache to go incognito. Nevertheless, Nietzsche draws attention here to his perception of distance from other people. Although he is the outsider, we readers are insiders—we know that Nietzsche is a sensitive philosophical person and what others miss when they see him merely as a man with a mustache.

Nietzsche's claims that his ideas (particularly those about morality) marginalize him indicate a difference between his sense of not fitting and that experienced by African Americans. One's ideas are not so obvious to others as one's skin color, and one might think that ideas are somewhat under one's voluntary control. Nietzsche would deny the latter. (He claims, "A thought comes when it wishes, not when 'I' wish."[26]) Nevertheless, reports of his almost excessive politeness toward acquaintances suggest that Nietzsche aimed to prevent others from noticing what he perceived as a gap between himself and them. In this respect, he was able to stave off to some extent the impact of other people's surveillance in a way that is not available to someone who is judged as suspect on the basis of pigmentation.

Nietzsche's comment about the mustache also indicates a major difference between the trait for which he is mistaken and that for which African Americans are mistaken. It was a matter of Nietzsche's own choice that he grew and groomed his mustache as he did (at least until he went mad). Skin color, in contrast, is not selected or varied by the person whose skin it is (except rather trivially through cosmetics and tanning, or more eccentrically through certain extreme forms of surgery); it is assigned, one might say, whether one likes it or not. As for the mustache, Nietzsche apparently wanted to seem a bit eccentric (though one might ask whether his desire to seem eccentric does not reveal a sense of inferiority disguising itself as pride in being nonstandard).

Nietzsche seems to have been able to limit or manipulate other's reactions to some degree. Nevertheless, he was aware of the internalization of a sense of being seen and judged by others, and the difficulty of asserting oneself in opposition to the observer's evaluations. For example, he reflects:

> The reproaches of conscience are weak even in the most con-
> scientious people compared to the feeling: "This or that is against
> the morals of your society." A cold look or a sneer on the face
> of those among whom and for whom one has been educated is
> feared even by the strongest. What is it that they are really
> afraid of? Growing solitude! This is the argument that rebuts
> even the best arguments for a person or cause. Thus the herd
> instinct speaks up in us. (*GS* 50)

Besides the pain of feeling the denigrating judgments of others amplified within one's own psyche, these internalized judgments are obstacles
to the development of a mature self, the achievement that Nietzsche
often describes, in a formula from Pindar, as "becoming what one is."
He comments in *Ecce Homo*, "To become what one is, one must not
have the faintest notion what one is."[27] Other's negative judgments
obstruct this effort. They assault one with hostile assertions of what
one is, and it is difficult for an individual to keep from absorbing them.

The features of Nietzsche's self-analysis that we have just
considered resonate with those of double consciousness as DuBois
characterizes it. Nietzsche draws attention to being identified in a
distorted manner on the basis of a single trait, sensing that one is seen
and judged by others, internalizing others' mechanisms of surveillance,
and adopting self-disparaging attitudes on the basis of others' contemptuous judgments. However, Nietzsche may appear idiosyncratic—
out of tune with his times, perhaps, but not obstructed by a veil that
is anything more than his own projection. Nietzsche realizes that his
self-reports (even indirect ones) might strike his readers as applying
only to himself. He imagines his reader asking after one of his accounts
of spiritual disturbance, "What is it to us that Herr Nietzsche has
become well again?" (*GS* P 2).

Nietzsche's answer is that he is presenting himself as a case in
point of someone who has traversed many states of soul, something
he takes to be critical to philosophy. Moreover, and more to the point
here, he takes the kind of inner conflict that he experiences as characteristic of any sensitive person in the modern era. The modern world
has lost belief in the vision that the human world is the centerpiece
of God's creation, and that it is well ordered in accordance with God's
plan. In the modern world, most people, whether theists or not, have
abandoned that vision—and yet their expectations and values are still

premised on such ideas. The sensitive person is torn between an awareness that the world is not designed as he or she imagines it should be and an inability to let go of demands it cannot fulfill.

Such a person, moreover, consciously torn in this way, is the exception in modern society. Most modern individuals either ignore the fact that their professed religious beliefs do not really inform their lives, or they abandon religious faith externally without changing their habits. The latter merely subordinate themselves to what Nietzsche calls "shadows of God," such as science or supposedly secular morality. Although both sorts of people might be commonly viewed as religious, Nietzsche sees both as spiritually deficient. He sees the sensitive person's inner conflict as a mark of spiritual distinction. At the same time, it is unavoidably connected to the condition of being marginalized.

Like DuBois, Nietzsche describes an awareness of himself as a being in tension with himself. Both similarly see this experience of inner tension as more than a personal characteristic. Both take themselves to be typical of a whole population in a given place and time. While not an exact parallel, the double consciousness of the spiritual person within modernity resembles the double consciousness that DuBois describes. In both cases, the person with double consciousness judges by a standard that neither fits one's own case nor ceases to structure one's longings. One wants a sense of a place in the world that accords with one's conception of oneself and reflects one's human dignity, but society acknowledges a person in this manner on a basis (having the "right" ideas, or being a member of the "right" race) that does not apply to oneself. The inner tension generated is tremendous, and the potential is great for either devastation or transfiguration.

What is the value of noting these parallels between DuBois's and Nietzsche's analyses of those who are inwardly conflicted by virtue of their uneasy relationship to the dominant culture? I think there are several benefits. First, Nietzsche's discussions complement DuBois's approach to the analysis of power and its impact. The character of Nietzsche's discussions is relatively nonspecific, as opposed to DuBois's more situated account of African Americans' inner life. In this way, each of the two accounts can supplement the perspective presented by the other. Second, the nonspecific character of Nietzsche's analyses makes it less likely that a reader will assess their plausibility on the basis of his or her sense of location on the map of social identities. Nietzsche's approach can help make readers more sensitive to the painfulness of certain positions on that map without making them defensive about their own status and prone to evade insight. Third, Nietzsche and DuBois can serve as foils for each other, because they use complementary literary devices to enhance the reader's sensitivity to those with perspectives not their own.

The complementarity of the two approaches becomes evident when we observe the different levels of specificity in the two thinkers' writing. DuBois uses his analysis of double consciousness to illuminate concrete situations in the experience of African Americans. Nietzsche, in contrast, theorizes in a more generalized fashion about the difficulties involved in translating multifaceted perceptions into an integrated vision. Nietzsche's speculations about psychological perspectives of the oppressed and of oppressors, in *On the Genealogy of Morals*, for example, are abstracted from concrete historical particulars of any sort, and his psychological sketches are often similarly abstracted from actual circumstances. Nietzsche may have witnessed interpersonal power ploys that would have provided a novelist with ample material for description,[28] but he distills from such observations formal analyses of ways that human beings sometimes interact. Even his discussions of Wagner, by far his most extensive analyses of a particular person, are presented most often in abstract form. Wagner becomes the representative of "the artist," "the problem of the actor," and so on (*GS* 87, 361).

I read Nietzsche as being an heir to the Enlightenment in his efforts to resonate with his readers' spiritual and psychological states regardless of their particular backgrounds. His "slaves" are not particular slaves—they are any slaves wrestling with the psychological impact of oppression. Indeed, this might strike some as a reason to think Nietzsche's discussion of slavery is bound to be out of touch with the African American experience. His accounts, rhetorically universalistic in seeming to apply to anyone, may actually apply to no one in particular.[29]

Nietzsche's universalistic stance might be objectionable if he took his claims to provide "the truth" on these topics. But he himself is the great teacher of the provisionality of all of our formulations of insights.[30] His own assertions about psychological possibilities, unqualified by concrete details in most cases, are powerful in their way because of this lack, for they offer the reader no distancing specifics. This is one way in which Nietzsche's analyses complement DuBois's more specific accounts. Nietzsche's analyses are offered as paradigm scenarios, story lines from humankind that one sees again and again. For example, "He cannot control himself, and from that a poor woman infers that it will be easy to control him and casts her net for him. Soon she will be his slave" (*GS* 227).

The more abstract focus that Nietzsche offers, besides broadening one's picture of power relations, has a second benefit as well. Although

Nietzsche lacks DuBois's gift for portraying the particular human story in its immediacy, his work yields penetrating abstract insights. He offers scenarios that are open-ended enough to prompt the reader to assent to their acuity, if they are apt, regardless of his or her sense of social identity. Nietzsche's insights, presented in this way, may bypass defense mechanisms that might be invoked if the reader were made more aware of his or her own political position.

While DuBois is explicitly concerned with particular power dynamics in historically specific terms, Nietzsche indicates the diverse and surprising forms that power dynamics can take, often in small-scale interpersonal interactions, leaving it to the present-day reader to determine where they apply in contemporary life. Because of this difference, Nietzsche's and DuBois's respective efforts to alert the reader to unfamiliar perspectives can be seen as mutually supporting. DuBois's attempt in this connection is most evident in relation to his white reader. Wald observes that he crafts *The Souls of Black Folk* in a way that makes the white reader aware of the veil.

> Moving unpredictably between past and present tenses, the narrator alternatively includes the reader on his journey and excludes him from an experience that has already transpired. The reader moves—or is moved—arbitrarily into and out of a shared perspective.[31]

DuBois's text conveys to the white reader an awareness of a social world from which he or she is excluded and of the veil that has obscured one's vision of those on the other side. DuBois's achievement in this respect may be to provoke an essential step in the consciousness-raising of the oblivious white reader. Nevertheless, this accomplishment risks a defensive reaction unless supplemented with other approaches. Nietzsche and DuBois each use a further literary strategy that can help the reader on the far side of the veil from black folk to overcome defensiveness and to mobilize moral imagination.

DuBois's further technique is the presentation of vivid anecdotes that give the reader a focus for sympathetic emotion. After being made aware of a whole social world behind the veil, a reader might be overwhelmed by its scope and the range of problems that afflict it unless given more manageable particular cases on which to focus. DuBois penetrates the defenses of the reader and incites specific sympathetic response by storytelling. I imagine that even a reader who maintains a fairly distant sense of self-identification feels great sympathy when

DuBois describes the death of his first child. I would expect that most readers empathetically experience something of the inner turmoil and horror of double consciousness when they read the following:

> All that day and all that night there sat an awful gladness in my heart,—nay, blame me not if I see the world thus darkly through the Veil,—and my soul whispers ever to me, saying, "Not dead, not dead, but escaped; not bound but free."[32]

By inviting the reader inside his or her own experiences in this fashion, DuBois helps him or her to imaginatively cross the gulf between the veil's two sides. At the very least, this motivates the reader's sympathy to cross through the veil. The focus on a particular case counteracts the danger that the reader will only feel numb and impotent in the face of social structures so deeply systematized as American racism. Sympathy itself involves the conferral of Hegelian recognition, and perhaps the first glimmer of respect for those on the other side of the veil and a refusal of the contemptuous perception on which the structures of racism depend.

Nietzsche's technique for provoking empathetic moral imagination is to provide more abstract cases that are sufficiently familiar to remind the reader of comparable experiences. The abstract character of the possibilities described encourages the reader to fill in the outline with concrete particulars drawn, at least in part, from memory. Not infrequently, the shapes that Nietzsche provides for analyzing types of situations bring particulars to the foreground that one has not previously noticed in the same way. When Nietzsche's examples draw attention to circumstances that one recognizes to some extent from one's experience, one finds it easier to recognize that certain seemingly alien experiences are not entirely unfamiliar. One may discover that one's consciousness has already experienced both sides of certain experiential divides.

Or I may realize through reading Nietzsche that even if I lack direct acquaintance with the other side of the veils he describes, the experience of those living there is not really so foreign to me. For example, he compares the lover's denial that his beloved is a mere biological specimen, subject to repulsive physiological processes, to the religious person's rejection of natural laws in previous centuries:

> . . . as lovers still feel about nature and natural functions, every worshiper of God and his "holy omnipotence" formerly felt. Every "natural law" sounded to him like a slander against God.

Oh, these men of former times knew how to dream and did not find it necessary to go to sleep first. And we men of today still master this art all too well. We artists! We ignore what is natural. We are moonstruck and God-struck. (*GS* 59)

Addressing himself mainly to contemporary "men of science," Nietzsche urges them to recall their own attitudes toward the women they love. This familiar attitude, he contends, should enable his readers to understand a perspective that seems entirely foreign, that of religious people opposed to science. Nietzsche goes on to suggest that some other contemporary viewpoints are not dissimilar, implying that those who pride themselves on their hardheaded scientific realism are not so different in their motivations from their very differently thinking forbears.

Other clear illustrations of this Nietzschean technique are evident, as I have argued elsewhere, in Nietzsche's passages on women in *The Gay Science*. These passages force his male readers to reconsider their own stereotypes about female behavior by inducing them to consider women's perspectives empathetically.[33] For example, Nietzsche urges men to consider the horrendous inner tension produced by the "amazing and monstrous . . . education of upper-class women."

All the world is agreed that they are to be brought up as ignorant as possible of erotic matters, and that one has to imbue their souls with a profound sense of shame in such matters until the merest suggestion of such things triggers the most extreme impatience and flight. And then to be hurled, as by a gruesome lightning bolt, into reality and knowledge, by marriage—precisely by the man they love and esteem most! . . .

Thus a psychic knot has been tied that may have no equal. Women easily experience their husbands as a question mark concerning their honor, and their children as an apology or atonement. In sum one cannot be too kind about women. (*GS* 71)

This strategy of inducing his readers to imaginatively penetrate perspectival veils is a third way in which Nietzsche's approach concurs with and supports DuBois's efforts to make the experience of being a member of a racial minority group clearer to the range of his readers. Nietzsche offers his readers practice in passing through experiential divides of exactly the sort that DuBois describes.

There is yet a further way in which Nietzsche's writing may be valuable for furthering DuBois's project, this time with respect to the psychological situation of African Americans themselves. Nietzsche offers guidance for those suffering from double consciousness from the standpoint of one who has been there. He makes suggestions relevant to self-reevaluation that might counter the pressures toward self-hatred arising from those who control the status quo. He also warns against some of the same dangers that DuBois sees for those afflicted by the conflict born of double consciousness, elaborating on the psychological mechanisms involved.

Nietzsche offers several strategies for overcoming self-disparagement motivated by the hostile attitudes of those who are comfortably ensconced within mainstream society. First, Nietzsche encourages the marginalized to recognize the limitations of the majority's viewpoint. Like all perspectives, the hegemonic viewpoint is incomplete. "We cannot look around our own corner," Nietzsche tells us (*GS* 374). No one is entitled to claim, as those in the majority are prone to do, that their own outlook is the objective view of things.

> There is only a perspectival seeing, only a perspectival "knowing"; and the more affects we allow to speak about a matter, the more eyes, different eyes, we know how to bring to bear on one and the same matter, that much more complete will our "concept" of this matter, our "objectivity" be.[34]

Those who claim objectivity have less of the only "objectivity" available than those who recognize other perspectives.

The perspective of those unfairly advantaged by the status quo is in fact far from dispassionate. Those who are particularly respected within a reigning social structure are easily moved to brutal reactions toward those who would question the legitimacy of the social support they receive. Nietzsche's character Zarathustra challenges the grounds for such individuals' "good" reputations.

> ... beware of the good and the just! They like to crucify those who invent their own virtue for themselves — they hate the lonely one. Beware also of holy simplicity! Everything that is not simple it considers unholy; it also likes to play with fire — the stake. And beware also of the attacks of your love! The lonely one offers his hand too quickly to whomever he encounters. To some people you may not give your hand, only a paw: and I desire that your paw should also have claws.[35]

Zarathustra goes on, however, to point out that the person who would transform society's current ways of valuing should not be surprised to feel inner conflict. While this conflict itself may be unavoidable, Nietzsche urges the individual tormented in this way to resist the temptation to use this as a basis for self-flagellation. Zarathustra proclaims, "I say unto you: One must still have chaos in oneself to be able to give birth to a dancing star" (Z P 5). He cautions against too much caution, and he indicates that the solution to this inner tension is self-transformation along the lines that DuBois also suggests.

> But the worst enemy you can encounter will always be you, yourself; you lie in wait for yourself in caves and woods.

> Lonely, you are going the way to yourself. And your way leads past yourself and your seven devils. You must wish to consume yourself in your own flame: how could you wish to become new unless you had first become ashes! (Z: 1 "The Creator")

Instead of viewing tension as a sign that one is doing something wrong, those suffering from marginalization and the inner strife that it occasions should reassess their situation, Nietzsche contends. As he comments in *Beyond Good and Evil*, "The great epochs of our life come when we gain the courage to rechristen our evil as what is best in us" (*BGE* 116). Instead of viewing oneself as deficient for not fitting in, one can view oneself as occupying a particularly valuable role. One might see oneself as a pioneer, an adventurer, or a legislator of new values. The last of these is particularly relevant to African Americans who seek a transformation of society's values. Seeing oneself in this manner, one is in a position to heal the self-doubt that typically arises in those who are exceptions to the communal norm. Nietzsche points out that the innovator is necessarily marginalized. Thus one's sense of being outside the mainstream, even of being cast outside it, may be an unavoidable feature of being a cultural pioneer.

One also can attempt to interpret one's own position as central to the unfolding development of humanity, even if this centrality is not recognized by those comfortable with their positions within the status quo. Nietzsche argues that each individual's perceptions are limited by virtue of being perspectival but are simultaneously real contributions to human understanding for exactly the same reason. This suggests that individual and minority outlooks represent an enhancement to society generally, the more so because they are not viewpoints taken for granted by the majority. Marginalization, on this view, is a precondition for assuming a particularly significant cultural role.

Nietzsche also suggests the possibility of the marginalized person's reversing the sense of separation from others by absorbing what one can from other perspectives. This is a way of developing second sight through double consciousness. Because one is aware that multiple perspectives exist and command one's attention in certain ways, one has an access to their implicit insights that is foreclosed to the literally more simpleminded.

The experience of enjoying literature illustrates the way that one can absorb understandings of value from the perspectives of others. Through literature we imaginatively project ourselves into other characters whose experiences and personalities may diverge significantly from one's own, and ideally we feel enriched by this process. Drawing on the perspectives of others is more complicated in the case of real people with whom one interacts in real power relations. But the case of literature offers a demonstration of the possibility of the ideal of absorbing multiple viewpoints into a richer sense of oneself. The person with double-consciousness, unable to restrict himself or herself to one outlook or another, might take comfort from the awareness of having an enlarged sense of self-understanding that draws from both sides of one's currently warring inner state. Nietzsche characterizes the extreme case of absorbing and integrating partial viewpoints as a condition of deep happiness, a state in which the sense of being a soul rent into pieces has been healed.

> Anyone who manages to experience the history of humanity as a whole as his own history will feel in an enormously generalized way all the grief of an invalid who thinks of health, of an old man who thinks of the dreams of his youth, of a lover deprived of his beloved, of the martyr whose ideal is perishing, of the hero on the evening after a battle that has decided nothing but brought him wounds and the loss of his friend. But if one endured, if one could endure this immense sum of grief of all kinds while yet being the hero who, as the second day of battle breaks, welcomes the dawn and his fortune, being a person whose horizon encompasses thousands of years past and future, being the heir of all the nobility of all past spirit—an heir with a sense of obligation . . . ; if one could burden one's soul with all of this—the oldest, the newest, losses, hopes, conquests, and the victories of humanity; if one could finally contain all this in one soul and crowd it into a single feeling—this would surely have to result in a happiness that humanity has not known so far; the happiness of a god full of power and love, full of tears and laughter, a happiness that, like the sun in the evening, continually bestows its inexhaustible riches, pouring them into

the sea, feeling richest, as the sun does, only when even the
poorest fisherman is still rowing with golden oars! This godlike feeling would then be called humaneness. (*GS* 337)

Of course, this condition is not easily achieved, particularly when
aspects of the history of humanity have been directed against oneself,
or at the whole side of the veil one inhabits. The natural tendency is to
respond with anger and hatred. If one is suffering, one wants to blame
someone. In *On the Genealogy of Morals*, Nietzsche characterizes the
outlook typically inspired by any condition of distress: "'I am suffering:
for this someone must be to blame'" (*GM* III: 15).

One of the most fascinating features of Nietzsche, and one that is
often overlooked, is the extent to which he thinks that blaming others
is harmful, not so much to them but to oneself. His whole case against
slave morality, articulated in *On the Genealogy of Morals*, amounts to
an analysis of the temptation to respond to oppression and contempt
from one's oppressors by asserting their guilt. Although the assertion
of oneself as judge, if only in one's own eyes, does indicate that one is
at least healthy enough to defend oneself, the effect of maintaining one's
self-esteem through this strategy is a poisoning strategy, according to
Nietzsche.[36] Resentment becomes one's fundamental project. This strategy enables one to bolster self-esteem by judging those who disdain
one with contempt, but because it makes self-esteem contingent on one's
attitude toward others, it precludes the attitude that the oppressed
most deeply desire, healthy self-regard. Nietzsche goes so far as to suggest that this strategy makes one's positive self-assessment contingent
on the very situation that challenged it in the first place.

With this in mind, we can see why Nietzsche describes his aim
in this manner: "I do not want to accuse; I do not even want to accuse
those who accuse. Looking away shall be my only negation. And all in
all and on the whole: some day I wish to be only a Yes-sayer" (*GS* 276).
Nietzsche's character Zarathustra similarly cautions that reacting to
hostility with hostility interferes with one's higher aspirations. "Injustice and filth they throw after the lonely one; but, my brother, if you
would be a star, you must not shine less for them because of that" (*Z*: 1
"The Creator").

Nietzsche's proposed strategy for overcoming the poisoning effects
of long resentment is to shift one's attention away from the past
toward the future-directed present.

"It was"—that is the name of the will's gnashing to teeth and
most secret melancholy. Powerless against what has been done,

he is an angry spectator of all that is past. The will cannot will backwards; and that he cannot break time and time's covetousness, that is the will's loneliest melancholy.

. . . This, indeed this alone, is what revenge is: the will's ill will against time and its "it was." (*Z:* 1 "The Creator")

The great danger for any frustrated individual is the tendency to rage against the past that has treated one unfairly. Even when one's grievances are justified, the stance of angry victim is a disease, certainly not a cure for anything.

In order to heal the wounds of the past (whether past ill treatment or guilt over one's own actions or inaction) one must resist the temptation to dwell on them. One compounds their damage if one takes them as evidence that one is pathetic and powerless. One can heal such inner wounds by learning to see oneself as having a will, with real power to affect change. One need not and in fact should not repress the fact that one's experiences have been what they were. But the aim is to recognize one's own will and dignity as having operated in these previous experiences, even if this was not what others chose to recognize. One needs to summon one's will to act, to make deliberate choices as to how to respond to the present situation, while recognizing the past as a source of insight, not just of affliction. To summarize Nietzsche's advice in a slogan, one must act, not react. As Zarathustra puts it, "All 'it was' is a fragment, a riddle, a dreadful accident—until the creative will says to it, 'But thus I willed it.' Until the creative will says to it, 'But thus I will it; thus shall I will it'"[37] (*Z:* 2 "On Redemption").

Nietzsche offers support for African Americans afflicted by double consciousness through his accounts of his own experiences and the psychological processes they involved. He has written about the inner difficulties of proposing new values, particularly when these challenge the dominant views of one's contemporaries. He saw his own inner tension as a source of insight, if a painful one. Through his discussions of these matters, Nietzsche maintains spiritual solidarity with those, such as African Americans, whose political position may be different from his, but with whom he shares a divided consciousness. Like them, he seeks a resolution to inner conflict. To them, he suggests that this resolution may be accomplished by directing one's attention away from the past to the present moment and one's ability to assert one's will. One can move beyond the impasse of being unable to assent wholeheartedly to anything by summoning one's will to bequeath something of value to the future. Nietzsche leaves it to his readers to determine, for themselves, what this legacy might be.

Notes

1. This expression is a coinage of William Ferris in 1913. See David W. Blight and Robert Gooding-Williams, "Introduction—The Strange Meaning of Being Black: DuBois's American Tragedy," in W. E. B. Du Bois, *The Souls of Black Folk*, ed. with and introduction by David W. Blight and Robert Gooding-Williams (Boston: Bedford Books, 1997), 21.

2. DuBois, *Souls*, 38.

3. DuBois, *Souls*, 38.

4. Keith E. Byerman, *Seizing the Word: History, Art, and Self in the Work of W. E. B. DuBois* (Athens: University of Georgia Press, 1994), 15.

5. Priscilla Wald, *Constituting Americans: Cultural Anxiety and Narrative Form* (Durham, NC: Duke University Press, 1995), p. 177.

6. Sandra Adell, *Double Consciousness: Theoretical Issues in Twentieth-Century Black Literature* (Urbana: University of Illinois Press, 1994), 19. Posnock also emphasizes the German idealistic roots as well as the pragmatic aspect of DuBois's thought. See Ross Posnock, *Color and Culture: Black Writers and the Making of the Modern Intellectual* (Cambridge, MA: Harvard University Press, 1998) 113–14, 119–21. Posnock adds, "Because scholarly work on DuBois's relation to James has largely been confined to the latter's possible influence on the notion of double consciousness, what has been missed is that DuBois seems to have internalized pragmatism as a method and style of thinking" (114).

7. DuBois, *Souls*, 81.

8. DuBois, *Souls*, 38.

9. DuBois, *Souls*, 141–42.

10. Feminists and others have described a similar psychological mechanism that develops on the part of women, who are aware of being under "the male gaze." For a particularly accessible account, see John Berger, *Ways of Seeing* (New York: Penguin, 1972), essay 3.

11. DuBois, *Souls*, 42.

12. DuBois, *Souls*, 39.

13. DuBois, *Souls*, 39. Wald goes on to point out the Emersonian roots of DuBois's reflections, noting that Emerson saw the "uncomfortable tension between 'the two lives, of the understanding and of the soul', which remain irreconcilable" as leading to a self-questioning that ultimately blossoms "into an advantage born of insight" (Wald, *Constituting Americans*, 177).

14. Byerman, *Seizing the Word*, 15.

15. DuBois, *Souls*, 85.

16. DuBois, *Souls*, 63.

17. DuBois, *Souls*, 63.

18. DuBois, *Souls*, 67.

19. DuBois, *Souls*, 70.

20. Wald, *Constituting Americans*, 178.

21. Wald, *Constituting Americans*, 176.

22. DuBois, *Souls*, 155–56.

23. DuBois, *Souls*, 39. Although DuBois adopts the convention of referring to a group by reference solely to its male members, I assume that his psychological observations are for the most part applicable to women as well.

24. Friedrich Nietzsche, *The Gay Science, With a Prelude in Rhymes and an Appendix of Songs*, trans. Walter Kaufmann (New York: Random House, 1974), *GS* 1.

25. Friedrich Nietzsche, *Daybreak: Thoughts on the Prejudices of Morality*, trans. R. J. Hollingdale (Cambridge: Cambridge University Press, 1982), 381. My thanks to Laurence Lampert for drawing my attention to the evident self-reference in this comment.

26. Friedrich Nietzsche, *Beyond Good and Evil: Prelude to the Philosophy of the Future*, trans. Walter Kaufmann (New York: Random House, 1966), 17.

27. Friedrich Nietzsche, *Ecce Homo*, trans. Walter Kaufmann [together with *On the Genealogy of Morals*, trans. Walter Kaufmann and R. J. Hollingdale] (New York: Random House, 1967), "Clever" 9.

28. There is reason to believe that Nietzsche may have engaged in observations of interpersonal political machinations early in his life. His classmates at the secondary school that he attended on scholarship, Schulforta, were in large measure the children of politicians and other social elites. Nietzsche may well have become aware of being from the other side of the proverbial tracks in this context. My thanks to Thomas Brobjer for this information about Schulforta.

29. This is a real possibility, of course, regarding any of his claims, as Nietzsche himself seems to have realized when he subtitled his *Thus Spoke Zarathustra* "a book for all and none."

30. See Kathleen Marie Higgins, *Comic Relief: Nietzsche's Gay Science* (New York: Oxford University Press, 2000), chapter 3.

31. Wald, *Constituting Americans*, 226.

32. DuBois, *Souls*, 162.

33. See Kathleen Marie Higgins, "Gender in the Gay Science," *Philosophy and Literature* 19:2 (October 1995): 227–47.

34. Friedrich Nietzsche, *On the Genealogy of Morality*, trans. and ed. Maudemarie Clark and Alan J. Swensen (Indianapolis: Hackett, 1998), III: 15.

35. Friedrich Nietzsche, *Thus Spoke Zarathustra*, in *The Portable Nietzsche*, trans. and ed. Walter Kaufmann (New York: Viking/Penguin, 1968), I: "The Creator."

36. Much could be said on this topic. I have discussed it at greater length in "On the Genealogy of Morals—Nietzsche's Gift," in *Nietzsche, Genealogy, Morality: Essays on Nietzsche's Genealogy of Morals*, ed. Richard Schacht (Berkeley: University of California Press, 1994), 49–62.

37. The primary example of past failure that Nietzsche appears to have in mind would be the self-initiated errors that the Judeao-Christian tradition calls "sins." "Thus I willed it" hardly seems the obvious response to make toward a past in which one has been treated unjustly by others. However, Nietzsche's basic point remains applicable: one can only overcome rancor against the past if one avoids seeing oneself as the passive recipient of harm and envisions oneself as an agent with dignity and the power to will creative responses to one's situation.

4

—

Of Tragedy and the Blues in an Age of Decadence: Thoughts on Nietzsche and African America

LEWIS R. GORDON

If you could imagine dissonance assuming human form—and what else is man?—this dissonance would need, to be able to live, a magnificent illusion which would spread a veil of beauty over its own nature. This is the true artistic aim of Apollo. At the same time, only as much of that foundation of all existence, that Dionysiac underground of the world, can be permitted to enter an individual's consciousness as can be overcome, in its turn, by the Apolline power of transfiguration, so that both these artistic drives are required to unfold their energies in strict, reciprocal proportion, according to the law of eternal justice. . . . That there is a need for this effect is a feeling which each of us would grasp intuitively, if he were ever to feel himself translated, even just in a dream, back into the life of ancient Hellene. As he wandered beneath rows of high, Ionic columns, gazing upwards to a horizon cut off by pure and noble lines, seeing beside him reflections of his own, transfigured form in luminous marble, surrounded by human beings who walk solemnly or move delicately, with harmonious sounds and a rhythmical language of gestures—would such a person, with all this beauty streaming in on him from all sides, not be bound to call out, as he raised a hand to Apollo: "Blessed people of Hellas! How great must Dionysos be amongst you, if the God of Delos considers such acts of magic are needed to heal your dithyrambic madness!" It is likely, however, that an aged Athenian would reply to a visitor in this mood, looking up at him with the sublime eye of Aeschylus: "But say also this, curious stranger: how much did this people have to suffer in order that it might become so beautiful! But now follow me to the tragedy and sacrifice along with me in the temple of both deities!"[1]

So Nietzsche concluded his first book, *Die Geburt der Tragödie aus dem Geiste der Musik* (*The Birth of Tragedy from the Spirit of Music*). Although his remarks exemplify nostalgic valorization of the ancient Greeks, they can be applied, ironically, to African Americans. I say "ironically" because of the familiar motif of pitting ancient Greek history against black history in modern racist scholarship, as found in Comte Arthur de Gobineau's remark, wrongly attributed to Léopold Sedar Senghor, that "Reason is Greek as emotion is Negro."[2] The criticism that Senghor made of that remark is in stream with the homage to the two gods in Nietzsche's final sentence: It is not to rely on one of these gods over the other—the rational, ordered, beautiful Apollo versus the passionate, ecstatic, dramatic Dionysos—but to develop a higher synthesis of both[3] (*BT* 1 and *BT* 8). For Senghor, a man or woman without passion was not a human being, and one locked solely in ecstatic revelry similarly falls short.

These reflections from the dialectical period in Nietzsche's thought resound the contradictions between African Americans and American (that is, "white") society.[4] In whiteness is presumed the Apolline rationalization of spirit. From modern technological achievements to the world of twentieth-century art, the role of whiteness has been consistently articulated by its major proponents as that of domestication of once chaotic forces. George Gershwin, we must remember, supposedly "made a lady out of jazz," African American classical music. In contrast, African Americans have been consigned the Dionysiac world of debauchery, passion, ecstasy; intoxication; sex; and music. Yet this dichotomy misrepresents much of the story, for, as is well known, the suffering whose purpose was to break the spirit of African Americans has also been the condition through which African Americans have created syntheses that have been the hallmarks of American aesthetic achievements: spirituals, ragtime, blues, jazz, rhythm and blues, soul, and hip-hop, as well as their many offshoots, which include reggae, samba, and salsa. This achievement is more than musical performance. It is the leitmotif of African American expression. The blues and jazz thus emerge through writings ranging from those of Langston Hughes to Richard Wright and James Baldwin and, today, Toni Morrison. They emerge on the level of theoretical reflection as well. Just read and feel it in W. E. B. DuBois's *Souls of Black Folk* through to Richard Wright's *Black Boy* and on to James Baldwin's *The Fire Next Time* and Amiri Baraka's *Blues People*. Often misunderstood as an art form of lamentation, the blues is much more: It is life-affirming testimonies in the face of misery and the threat of despair. As Ralph Ellison reflects in his poignant essay, "Richard Wright's Blues":

> The blues is an impulse to keep the painful details and episodes of a brutal experience alive in one's aching consciousness, to finger its jagged grain, and to transcend it, not by the consolation of philosophy but by squeezing from it a near-tragic, near-comic lyricism. As a form, the blues is an autobiographical chronicle of personal catastrophe expressed lyrically.[5]

The legendary jazz pianist Mary Lou Williams brings Ellison's reflections to the collective level when she adds that the blues and

> jazz—this derogatory title has been given to a great spiritual music . . . is healing to the soul. . . . [They] came out of the suffering of an entire race of people—not of just one person or one artist—making it a special music—the only true art in the world. Through the suffering and experiences of the early black slaves . . . this music was born. This beautiful music has special healing power—because of the nature of its origin and contents— for those who listen with the ears of the heart. The healing power comes from the deep feeling that is in jazz—the feeling of the blues which is characteristic of all good jazz no matter what form it takes.[6]

That the blues exemplifies an Apolline-Dionysiac synthesis (albeit through African quarter-tonal exemplifications of mediation— the "blue note," the musical note between half tones) raises an important challenge to the prevailing assessment of African Americans in American society. As Du Bois pointed out in his presentation to the American Academy of Political and Social Science, and then subsequently in his foreword to *The Souls of Black Folk*, African Americans are always presumed by the prevailing norms of American society "to be" a problem, to be unhealthy.[7] More recently, this query takes the form of the so-called "culture of poverty" or pathological culture motif. In each instance, African Americans are treated, even by some eminent

African American social critics, as problems, as unhealthy exemplars of "death, disease, and despair."[9] Looking at African Americans from the standpoint of Nietzsche's thought, however, suggests a different story.[9]

Health, for Nietzsche, should not be understood as the absence of disease.[10] It should be understood as what emerges in the struggle with disease, as Walter Kaufman observes in his influential study of Nietzsche's life and thought: "In terms of health: Nietzsche—though he does not use exactly these expressions—defines health not as an accidental lack of infection but as the ability to overcome disease; and unlike Lessing and Kant's conceptions of providence and nature, this idea of health is not unempirical. Even physiologically one might measure health in terms of the amount of sickness, infection, and disease with which an organism can deal successfully."[11] Nietzsche considered the ancient Greeks healthy because they confronted their suffering by creating life-affirming practices, the most notable of which was tragic drama (*BT* 8).[12] Reading the history of African Americans through the lens of such a theory, it is easy to see that African Americans should not be interpreted simply as a "surviving" people. Many people can, and have, survived in the face of suffering. What is significant about African Americans is the creativity of their form of survival. Theirs has not been at the price of assimilation, which, in principle, is a form of eradication of group survival for the sake of individual survival. In assimilation, descendants of Africans would live in North America as people who have been ingested into the American system both politically and culturally. A thorn in this narrative, African Americans have been the embodied criticism of melting-pot ideology. That ideology demands absorption into the American Body Politic as a white body politic. Because of their creativity as a black creolized people—that is, as black-inflected mixture with other racial and cultural formations—they have been fundamentally an indigestible people.[13] The metaphor of feces comes to mind: the demands of the system are for ingestion for the sake of emerging as the same excrement, but there are those who always come out of the system as they had gone in.[14]

African Americans have been so creative that they are a source of constant distress for much of white America. As Ellison revealed in *Going to the Territory*, for white America to destroy things black from American society requires destroying much that is original and culturally positive in their identity—including their way of speaking, and these days, even their ways of expressing joy and sorrow:

> For one thing, the American nation is in a sense the product of the American language, a colloquial speech that began emerging long before the British colonials and Africans were transformed

into Americans. It is a language that evolved from the king's English but, basing itself upon the realities of the American land and colonial institutions—or lack of institutions, began quite early as a vernacular revolt against the signs, symbols, manners, and authority of the mother country. It is a language that began by merging the sounds of many tongues, brought together in the struggle of diverse regions. And whether it is admitted or not, much of the sound of that language is derived from the timbre of the African voice and the listening habits of the African ear. So there is a de'z and do'z of slave speech sounding beneath our most polished Harvard accents, and if there is such a thing as a Yale accent, there is a Negro wail in it—doubtlessly introduced there by Old Yalie John C. Calhoun, who probably got it from his mammy.[15]

The Nietzschean query suggests a flipping over of the question of health from the standard American discourse of black pathology to the question of white inadequacy. Instead of asking whether African Americans are healthy, we should ask whether white Americans are so, especially since it is white, not black, America that dominates the institutions that dominate the image and values of American civilization.[16] The image of America as white, where even so-called value-neutral terms ultimately appeal to whiteness, creates a false reality that masquerades as a primordial feature of personhood in American civilization. The image of white versus black hides the truth that all Americans—and all human beings, for that matter—are, underneath, ultimately members of the same species. Moving from the level of group or "race" to individual, the situation of living through the weight of historical advantages poses the question of whether most white Americans could pass the test of double standards—at times even quadruple standards—that most African Americans faced and continue to face on a daily basis. An insight into this matter emerges in an old debate touched upon by Frantz Fanon in the 1950s:

> Why have black suicide rates been historically low? Some racists confess that just the thought of being black brings suicide to their mind. This is because they do not see anything life affirming in blackness. For them, the "rational" response to being black is to prefer death over living in such a hell.[17]

American society does not want to look truly at African Americans. To do so often requires a truth too painful to bear. That is why preference is made to the bad-faith activity of elevating the negative as a positive standard for blacks. As Fanon pointed out in chapter 6 of *Black Skin, White Masks*, there is no such thing as "normal" psychology for black people in societies like America. There is the "catch-22" situation of being abnormal if well adjusted, which makes abnormality the supposedly "normal" state for blacks. This means that the language of pathology dominates discourses on blackness, which makes black failures block out black achievements. Because of the absence of a systemic critique in such logic, American society invests failure in blacks at an abnormal level and becomes an ontological mode of being—at least through the eyes of the anti-black racist.

Much of American society is not, however, life affirming. The overflowing opulence and safeguards created by white supremacy have, if Nietzsche's argument is advanced to its dialectical conclusion, made many (if not most) white Americans patently unhealthy. They are unhealthy because these safeguards have created the nihilistic conclusion of leveling out all white people to afford the luxury of white mediocrity.[18] That the price of black achievements is often death threats from whites exemplifies this conclusion. Think of the death threats that Hank Aaron received for breaking Babe Ruth's home-run record; Tiger Woods for his achievements in golf; and even the conservative General Colin Powell when he was considering running for the presidency of the United States. Famed scholar and public intellectual Cornel West received similar ire as he emerged in the majority-white "public" eye.[19]

Another variation of such safeguards is the notion of "standardized exams." A standard is meant to identify an average. There are, however, activities that cannot be exemplified by averages nor by even the notion of being "above" average. Those activities, often marked by genius, simply "are." It might be that standardized tests, such as IQ tests, exemplify what the most refined average person can achieve. The results are life-inhibiting activities, such as the effort to configure the absolute rationalization of human life. Think of the absurdity of women today who purchase sperm to produce children from men toward whom they have no passionate attachment. A child born from a man one would not sleep with carries a greater probability of lacking features that will excite one's admiration beyond one's own, which would make one's attachment to that child firmly rooted in the self-reflecting waters of one's self, which is a sure indication of narcissism. The same applies, no doubt, to fathers who seek an impersonal birthmother.

African Americans live with a reality that most white Americans despise. They (African Americans) have been tested. The violence against blacks that emerged, and continues, in American society is guided by that anxiety. White men scurrying about in camouflage on weekend militia retreats; victimological discourses of "reverse discrimination" and "white pride" are rehearsals of this need to be tested. This urge transcends nearly all aspects of white American cultures and political spectra. On the Right it is often couched in American patriotism: Protect the (white) Constitution of the United States against its colored enemies. On the Left, it is usually advanced through the vagueness of class. I say "vagueness" because "class" in the United States is often conflated with income instead of the ownership or lack of capital. Class is often used for the sake of the evasion of race, and it is done so through attributing to whites an affliction through which to produce a heroic narrative of triumph in the face of adversity. But as Joe Feagin has shown so well in *Racist America*, whiteness is a very powerful commodity. It is what affirms American identity. One becomes an American when one becomes white, and one becomes white by demonstrating one's dialectical opposition to blacks. Each "white ethnic" has done so in the past few hundred years, and now Asian immigrants, too, have followed suit.[20]

The price of much modern whiteness is a sacrifice of the soul to the god of technocratic reason.[21] I say "much" because not all whiteness was such. The Romantic movement that succeeded eighteenth-century rationalism in Continental Europe was an example of an effort to construct an alternative route for, at least, European humanity, and Nietzsche's thought was on the heels of that effort. Technocratic whiteness is a world governed by the predictable and the secure. It is a world of a rationality that, as Nietzsche observed in *The Will to Power*, seeks method over the art of inquiry.[22] By art of inquiry, I mean the poetics of the imagination exemplified not only by musicians and painters but also by the understanding as we find it in the best of scientists. The predictable and the secure are not, however, healthy attributes of human existence, and to some extent this realization haunts the daily lives of many white Americans. Many are bored with what they are, and this boredom at times is so overwhelming that it implodes and becomes so self-destructive that it drags others in like the gravitational pull of a heavy star: think of how the phenomenon of young white men who "snap" has become a mundane feature of American society. Think of how this phenomenon works its way through the fantasy life of popular culture, where to be a white man is to be, in effect, a legitimate killer.[23] The great white hunter, whether as the fictional Tarzan or the charismatic Theodore Roosevelt and Ernest Hemingway, recurs as a theme of legitimate carnage. His "affliction" emerges as a consequence of unleashed nature. His "health" is to fight off those who are the system's disease. A white man, it seems, does not properly feel white until he has conquered something—whether it be another group of people, an animal, or one of nature's puzzles.[24] A problem emerges, however, in the question of the body's relation to mind in such regard. For this dualism of Apolline forces versus Dionysiac ones creates a schizophrenic relationship of the self's relation to itself as flesh. The flesh is the site to be conquered, which means that letting the flesh "go" is a rather difficult ideal for such a man. In Apolline clarity one gives; in Dionysiac revelry, one "gives up," one is enthused and ecstatic. Thus although Europeans once danced and, as we saw as recently as in the compositions of Ludwig Van Beethoven, danced passionately, today only few of their descendants are willing to let themselves "go with the rhythm."[26]

The semiotic order that locates blacks with music and dance (activities that Nietzsche advocated for whites, in his early valorization of Richard Wagner, to let loose of their yokes and partake in) paradoxically affords a freedom for blacks in the face of bondage. Ellison's parable of the Invisible Man's admission of loving soul food (which, here, literally becomes food for the soul) sets the stage as well for the moment of critical engagement with African American aesthetic production. As Ellison's Invisible Man describes tasting but a piece of this form of liberation,

> I took a bite, finding [the yam] as sweet and hot as any I'd ever had, and was overcome with such a surge of homesickness that I turned away to keep my control. I walked along, munching the yam, just as suddenly overcome by an intense feeling of freedom—simply because I was eating while walking along the street. It was exhilarating. I no longer had to worry about who saw me or about what was proper. To hell with all that, and as sweet as the yam actually was, it became like nectar with the thought. If only someone who had known me at school or at home would come along and see me now. How shocked they'd be! I'd push them into a side street and smear their faces with the peel. What a group of people we were, I thought. Why, you could cause us the greatest humiliation simply by confronting us with something we liked. Not all of us, but so many. Simply by walking up and shaking a set of chitterlings, or a well-boiled hog maw at them during the clear light of day![26]

The realm of music affords many manifestations of such insight. Perhaps the best fusions of the dual gods were such classic and broad-ranged performances as Billie Holiday's performance of Lewis Allan's "Strange Fruit" (1940), Max Roach's and Abbey Lincoln's protest album *We*

Insist: The Freedom Now Suite (1958), Marvin Gaye's *What's Going On* (1971), and Public Enemy's *Fear of a Black Planet* (1988), to name but a few. They exemplify a balance the tipping of which produces purely Dionysian abandonment. Gangsta rap's valorization of intoxication and sexuality—no doubt Maenads as female sex reduced purely to the plenitude of unreflective female bodies—plays out each classic motif.

Yet there are limitations. A fault in Nietzsche's thought is the amount of stock he placed in aesthetic resistance to life's vicissitudes, particularly by way of music. It is a problem whose legacy continues in contemporary valorizations of aesthetic or semiotic resistance to social and political injustice. Revolution or the effort at radical social transformation that remains on those levels tends often to change fashion more than the infrastructures of society and the travails of those who are institutionally locked at the bottom. This is not to say that such activities are not necessary for projects of social change. It is just that they are insufficient, and as a consequence their champions almost always promise more than they can deliver. White rebellion through the resources of black music has never, for instance, done more than either eradicate black competition in the performance of black aesthetic production or offer occasional black participation in popularized (read "white") versions. It is a pessimistic dialectic: black creativity, white capitalization (by virtue of owning both the means of production and cultural capital for the preferred "image" of its dissemination). Think of the losing situation that black management has in the record industry, where music remains black the extent to which it does not sell enough to "cross over" and become "pop." Perhaps hip-hop music's achievement in this regard is that even where white artists participate, it still keeps its meaning as a black creolized art form. An absurdity of rock 'n' roll is the legions of white devotees who claim to detest black music.

Frantz Fanon offered some insight into the question of the relation of the aesthetic/semiotics to the problem of achieving radical social change. Without a semiotic intervention, mere material reconstruction or redistribution leads to a grammar of the same. A disruption of the grammar and its significations is necessary for a radically different world or radically different way of life. By itself, however, such an effort leads to stoic resentment. Changing one's language, performing one's art, may help one get through the day, but the consequence of having more will than power is implosive. The self becomes the overwhelming project. It is thus no accident that American racism is wrought with demands for blacks to fix themselves. And fix themselves they do, constantly, through the continual offering up of creative expressions of social misery and defiant hope, often beautiful, sometimes ugly, and always ironic.

The content, however, of these modes of resistance is not always for the sake of resistance. A demanding feature of the American racial landscape is that it militates against black people living an everyday or a mundane existence. Because their existence is peremptorily treated as illegitimate, it means, ipso facto, that such activities are causes for correction. "Rest" is not afforded black people, only "laziness." A black person cannot be "average," for being so in the dialectics of anti-black racism means being "unqualified," which means being "below average." For black people to "play," then, represents a transgression of social norms, whether they intend it to be so or not. Functional play is by definition too serious for play. It is work. Black people thus paradoxically challenge many American social norms most when they have absolutely no intention of doing so. They do so when they simply play, because this society demands that they are only legitimate when they are locked in the mechanics of labor. In play, which suspends the seriousness of many institutions, they commit an illicit act. This is a peculiarly Nietzschean reading of African American society. One need only think of the contrast between black "house parties" and the many variations of white ones. Whether it be such depictions as Fats Waller's "The Joint Is Jumpin'" (1937) or Reggie Hudlin's *House Party* (1990), play is a ritual guided by a circular pattern of dance until the cops intervene. Many African American celebrations and playful get-togethers have the veneer of a secret meeting of joy beyond the overseers' eyes. White functions, as is well known, tend to have two forms. There is the gathering, dominated by speech (e.g., cocktail or dinner parties or suburbia backyard barbecues—Apolline-dominated leisure events), and the destructive, youthful (e.g., white rock 'n' roll and fraternity house) parties of drugs and destruction. Although both "parties" are moments in which ultimately Dionysos is to be celebrated (with alcohol and sometimes with dance and sex), the "meaning" is distinguished by the simple fact that even rabble-rousing whites know that they have the "right" to enjoy themselves. That is why to this day, white teenagers and white adults enjoy "wild parties" and "wild nights" that would be, if they were black, simply "criminal."

What African Americans bring to their leisure time that can be correlated with while being entirely distinct from tragedy for the Greeks is the blues. The blues, as we have seen, is the beautiful transformation of sorrow.[27] Although Frantz Fanon was a critic of the blues, he himself exemplified the blues well in his work.[28] In *Black Skin, White Masks*, he portrayed the failures of intrasystemic resistance by writing the autobiography of a protagonist whose cathartic tears afforded psychotherapeutic clarity that enabled him to face Negrophobia.[29] In true blues fashion, Fanon told a story in repeated instances of growing clarity. An admirer of Nietzsche's writings, he charted the dialectical path from language to sex to introspective stoicism to demonstrate that a healthy position would be to wage a struggle on both social and individual levels because "... society," he reminds us, "unlike biochemical processes, cannot escape human influences. Man is what brings society into being."[31] For him, the important thing is that blacks become actional.

Nietzsche's interpretation of the ancient Greek situation provides a chilling correlate to African Americans'. Those Greeks, as he sees them, faced Apolline statism versus Dionysiac resistance (liberation of the oppressed). Aeschylean tragedy, marked by a balance between the chorus and music, gave way to Sophoclean tragedy, where the hero (and dialogue) began to take the place of the chorus through to Euripedian tragedy, where women and sexual revelry (Dionysos) came to the fore. The African American situation is one of negotiating one's way between a racist state (the United States) and nationalistic hopes. This challenge dates back to the Booker T. Washington-W. E. B. DuBois debates over economic and political strategies and the magnificent critical theoretical work on double consciousness that emerged through DuBois's continued explorations of the African American condition. DuBois drew constantly on the potential of African American spirituals and subsequently African American music in general. He hoped for a fusion of formal and energetic forces in the creative synthesis of sustained improvisation. That the blues and jazz exemplified that ideal is without question. But within jazz, the role of the soloist grew and grew, and the art form, as is well known, eventually achieved a level of the esoteric that seemed more Apollonian than Bacchic. The reassertions of Bacchus/Dionysos were in the "birth" periods of the many offshoots of jazz and the blues. One of them was rhythm and blues (R&B), which focused on dancing to music marked by short, repetitive melodies and brief solos. By the time the blues achieved its specialized zenith of long, esoteric solos, rock 'n' roll emerged, and it too followed similar paths. When R&B and rock 'n' roll were getting too "polished," soul came about in North America, and in the Caribbean there appeared first ska and rock steady and then reggae. Within reggae, one could chart a history from chorus singing to a single lead, stating social criticism to the irreverent response through a new (and very sexual) form known as "dance hall." In North America, funk and then disco played their roles through their focus on dance, and from the same sites of social suffering, from the same inner-city regions from which the "funky chicken" and "the hustle" were born, came early break dancing and rap recordings and subsequently hip-hop. In hip-hop, a chart was paved from the initial focus on dancing to the realm of social commentary and then, eerily in stream with the dialectic that marks the early Nietzschean analysis, to ecstatic sexual release as "club" hip-hop returns, as evidenced by both the images and artists that dominate popular hip-hop by the middle 1990s and the early twenty-first century.[31]

The dialectical movement of a declining set of values in the expression of aesthetic production raises the question of decadence.[32] It is clear that African American art faces processes of decay that have a peculiar "interracial" quality to it. One need not speak long on black aesthetic production with African Americans before the thesis of white appropriation is brought up. For many blacks, the moment of decay in their cultural production begins with white involvement. This moment of white participation has two levels of decadence. The first is the unjust appropriation of wealth. Whites, in a nutshell, receive more rewards for performing black art forms than do blacks.[33] Few white artists, for instance, faced paying what Louis Armstrong and Duke Ellington had to pay their white managers (that is, more than 50 percent of their earnings), and it is rarely the case that black performers, writers, and athletes are paid on a par with their white counterparts. Yes, there are "exceptions," but that is the point: those are the exceptions. The "rule" is that average whites receive above-average rewards as performers of black aesthetic and intellectual production. The second criticism is, however, more at the heart of aesthetic evaluation. Most whites simply perform black aesthetic productions at either a lower level of quality or, at least in the case of music, without the blues. Even white blues artists, interesting though they may be, sound more like imitation than exemplification. Their participation often creates a different form, a "white" one. How is this possible, and why is it so?

The first thing to reject straight out is the notion of any biological inhibition for their performance. What makes the difference is the absence of the kind of group suffering, as Mary Lou Williams pointed out, that stimulates the blues.[34] This is true as well for blacks, who have been sheltered away from that suffering. For such blacks, the production is more anxiety ridden and often neurotic than blue. The underlying blues experience of being an unjustified existent in modernity is shared by those who have felt the weight of anti-black racism across the African diaspora. Cultural inflections from Africa in the forms of tone and execution of meters provided the syntax for this suffering. In premodern terms, the sources of such suffering were expressed in the existential struggles with predestination and life's travails that called for shouting out a resounding "why?"[35] But the modern semantics, the onomato-poeia of modernity, are constructed out of this ongoing realization, as Ellison's Invisible Man lamented, echoing Louis Armstrong, of being so "black and blue."[36]

So why do whites bring decay to black aesthetic productions? The answer is that whiteness affords a luxury that is paradoxically healthy for whiteness but unhealthy for blackness. It is a luxury that stimulates activities that are part of the process of a decaying society. For Nietzsche, a society that collapses into complacency and leveled equality for its ruling group is an unhealthy one. A Manichaean dualism emerges between white health and black health. White health is the moment of conquest. Although it is not the picture that contemporary America prefers, the many monuments to conquerors, the heroic cele-bration of killers and slave masters, found on everything from money to popular cultural celebrations in cinema and literature, reveal a legacy of a whiteness that begins to decay the moment it ceases to be imperial, racist, and narcissistic (holding a godlike self-image). The health of black people is exemplified by their struggle against that white world and their ability to transcend it. As that white world cedes, however, and the black world grows, the future becomes one in which whites are not so much eradicated as transformed into a relation-ship of obsolescence or irrelevance as whites.[37] Thus at the moment of convergence, in the art forms, what inhibits whites is the baggage of whiteness. Whites do not offer innovation but mass appropriation. Although political writers may use the phrase "the masses" to refer to the common folk, including those of color and those in the Third World, in practice, "mass" is a peculiarly white phenomenon. There is nowhere more "mass," for instance, than the white, middle-class societies of Europe and North America.[38] Black productions are not mass productions, although "massification" is a constant aim of those who seek their com-modification. They speak to the peculiarity of a condition that is prima facie not easy to assimilate. The transformation of black productions into mass items often requires reducing the elements of the production that are difficult for white assimilation—particularly those that are carried in black bodies. If a black body is inadequate for a white mass (often referred to as "the public"), then either an aesthetics of domes-tication is needed or simply a nonblack exemplar. The white exemplar brings with him or her the decadence of whiteness and the absence of communal suffering—that is, the suffering of a people as a problem people. Yes, there are whites who were and continue to be poor, and there are whites who have faced political persecution, but those indivi-duals and ethnic groups have never faced these forces on a historical level as whites. As whites, they face the history of other groups encroaching on that for which whites consider themselves entitled.

Is it possible for whites to participate in black cultural productions without ushering in the leechlike forces of decay? It should be clear that they can do so, but not as whites. They must do so as participants in a project that transcends white hegemony. Such a white has to come out of, learn through, and manifest the respect for the expressive resources of a world that is not white.

We have, then, two forms of nihilism linked to the question of white-black dynamics.[39] The first type of nihilism is passive nihilism: "I am white, and that's the way it is." The other is active nihilism: "I am white; that's the way it is; and I have no faith in the continued preservation of whiteness, so I fight for a world beyond this one." The former affirms white supremacy and struggles against its decay as a threat to reality: "If I cease to be white, all is lost." "If white supremacy falls, it will be the end of the world." Here there is a failure to imagine the end of this stage of empire. There is a failure, as in what Nietzsche calls "Socratic" culture, to realize that literally nothing lasts forever: "We should not now disguise from ourselves what lies hidden in the womb of this Socratic culture: an optimism which imagines itself to be limitless!" (*BT* 18). In his later years, he reminds us that "A society is not free to remain young" (*WP*, Book I, chap. 1, par. 40, p. 25). There are many manifestations of evading this reality. The query, for instance, on what causes the fall of the many empires of the past carries with it the mistaken notion that but for such and such a factor, those empires would have lasted forever. Such a feat is not only unnatural but also not desirable. It militates against the birth of the new, an insight revealed by many myths from antiquity, as in the case of Ouranos, god of sky, who attempted to prevent subsequent generations of gods from emerging from Gaia, mother earth, or Egyptian Horus/Osiris myths of rebirth.[40] The active nihilist wants to hasten the collapse of the decaying process: "We're at a moment of decline so a new world can emerge." "Let us build an alternative future since there is no hope in this present." Renewal is part of the natural order of things, which makes doom the constant tale on the horizon of every empire.

In the end, there is, however, an odd flaw that emerges both in Nietzsche's analysis of healthy individuals and healthy people. The former exemplifies the individualistic tendencies of an Overman. He emerges as healthy in spite of living among unhealthy people. His health is literally an overcoming of forces that militated against such an achievement. The latter represents a general achievement between the dialectic of individual genius and community values. The language of tragedy as an accomplishment of "the Greeks" is in stream with much European identification with those southeastern Mediterranean sets of people, but is this an appropriate position for Nietzsche to take? Is the blessing of the ancient Greeks simply a matter of their willingness to participate in festivals that culminated in the appreciation of excellent portrayals of their contradictions and anxieties? Or is it ancient Greek culture that is the source of great admiration the consequence of which is a disregard for its mundane dimensions? We know of Aeschylus, Sophocles, and Euripides, men who won various prizes for their productions, but a culture that is so admired receives the blessing of invisible mediocrity: the losers are as if they were more exceptions than the rule at best and at worst—as if they had never existed.

African American achievements reveal a different relationship. They are the stuff of a nation within a nation. Although African American athletes may receive cheers from white Americans while they wave the U.S. flag during moments of triumph, the reality is that many white Americans would prefer to have been represented in such moments of glory by another hue. There is always a racial subtext that demands willful blindness in the face of triumph. Although African Americans definitely fail as African Americans, and they sometimes succeed as "Americans," the contentious thesis of Americanization through antipathy to blackness often calls upon them to commit a second act of allegiance. That is why blacks who "make it" often do so through openly distancing themselves from blackness as much as possible.[41] Each act of black distancing garners a little more Americanization. The consequence is that African Americans rarely, if ever, succeed as African Americans, which makes the thesis of excellence elusive. Since failure is the rule instead of the exception, "America," an America sterilized of black achievement, always wins, while "black America" loses.

Notes

Special thanks to Jane Anna Gordon and Rowan Ricardo Phillips for discussion of an early draft of this chapter.

1. The text will hereafter simply be referred to as *The Birth of Tragedy*. I have opted for Ronald Speirs's translation, which appears in Friedrich Nietzsche, *"The Birth of Tragedy" and Other Writings*, ed. Raymond Geuss and Ronald Speirs, *Cambridge Texts in the History of Philosophy* (Cambridge: Cambridge University Press, 1999). The opening quotation is from section 25, pp. 115–16.

2. See Comte Arthur de Gobineau, *Essai sur l'inegalité des races humaines*, présentation de Hubert Juin (Paris: P. Belfond, 1967), volume 2, chapter 7.

3. See Léopold Senghor, *Liberté: I* (Paris: Seuil 1964), 24. For discussion, see Jacques Louis Hymans's excellent study, *Léopold Sédar Senghor: An Intellectual Biography* (Edinburgh, Scotland: Edinburgh University Press, 1971), 66.

4. Nietzsche's early thought was dialectical, that is, under the immense shadow of Hegel albeit with the influence of Arthur Schopenhauer's dissatisfaction with Hegelianism, but the impact of his genealogical approach, which marked his subsequent approach, is more known. For discussion, see the collection of essays in *Nietzsche, Genealogy, Morality: Essays on Nietzsche's "On the Genealogy of Morals,"* ed. Richard Schacht (Berkeley: University of California Press, 1994), part II, "Genealogy and Philosophy." The influence of this later approach on African American thought is quite clear in the Foucauldian wing of African American thought. Particularly noteworthy is Cornel West's *Prophesy, Deliverance!: An Afro-American Revolutionary Christianity* (Philadelphia: Westminster Press, 1982), chapter 2, "A Genealogy of Modern Racism." The importance of this aspect of Nietzsche's thought in African American academic struggles with intellectual history warrants a chapter of its own.

5. In Ralph Ellison, *Shadow and Act* (New York: Vintage, 1964), 78–79.

6. This quote is from the liner notes to the album *Mary Lou Williams and Cecil Taylor: Embraced.* Pablo Records, 2620 108 (1978). It also appears in Josiah Ulysses Young III, *A Pan-African Theology: Providence and the Legacies of the Ancestors* (Trenton, NJ: Africa World Press, 1992), 119.

7. For discussion, see "The Study of African American Problems: W. E. B. DuBois's Agenda, Then and Now," ed. Elijah Anderson and Tukufu Zuberi, special issue of *The Annals of the American Academy of Political and Social Science* 568 (March 2000): 7–316.

8. See, for example, Cornel West, *Keeping Faith: Philosophy and Race in America* (New York: Routledge), x, and Orlando Patterson, *Rituals of Blood: Consequences of Slavery in Two Centuries* (Washington, DC: Civitas, 1998), passim. A logical conclusion of Patterson's argument, for instance, is that the ultimate problem with black families is that they are not white nuclear ones. And the travails that black families face receive no systemic critique but are instead located in the moral depravity of black men. The scapegoat dimension of this form of argument is obvious. We also may be suspicious of the kind of wisdom that would replace black extended families (through which vibrant African-inflected cultures have been developed under the hostile conditions of modern slavery, colonialism, and racism) with a white structure—the bourgeois nuclear family, a wonderful breeding ground for neurosis. Another more recent and very popular exemplar of this trend is John McWhorter's *Losing the Race: Self-Sabotage in Black America* (New York: The Free Press, 2000).

McWhorter argues that blacks are their own worst enemies through their allegiance to values embedded in a logic of victimization, separatism, and anti-intellectualism. Unlike Patterson, whose arguments can be addressed analytically, McWhorter's arguments defy empirical evidence. The first claim requires denying the existence of racism and the history of racial violence. The second claim presumes that blacks control the conditions of their economic and social mobility on a par with whites; that, for instance, there has not been any study demonstrating that blacks have moved out of neighborhoods to more expensive or distant ones because too many whites have moved in basically contradicts such a claim. And the third examines at least black Americans outside of the context of the society in which they live. After all, the charge of anti-intellectualism could be, and often has been, made about American society in general. The fame of black intellectuals hardly suggests that black people are *intrinsically* anti-intellectual. But McWhorter's point is about a set of values, so we must ask, how does one *show* that black people *value* being victims—through a questionnaire on whether one would rather be the victim in many situations than not? It has been my experience that there *are* blacks who masochistically cling to the identity of victim and others who do *not*. In the world of race publishing, however, much depends, as in national polls, on what people are likely to *believe*, and since pathology is often treated by such writers as an intrinsic feature of blacks, the popularity of McWhorter's text (it went into a second edition in one year) exemplifies a continued, bad-faith (because of many people believing what they want to believe even in the face of contradictory evidence) tradition.

9. By looking from the standpoint of Nietzsche's thought, I do not mean his thought *on* blacks. There the material is not pretty. As William Preston remarks, "Nietzsche, to be sure, does not mention blacks that much. When he does, of course, they are described as inferior. All in all, blacks simply do not figure that much to Nietzsche's writings, and with good reason: the feeling of distinction derived from a sense of superiority towards blacks is not worth much. A man of distinction, on Nietzsche's account, could not feel ecstasy in his pathos of distance from blacks. In Nietzsche's scheme of things, the value to life of black people is so negligible it is absurd to try to acquire a rise by oppressing them." See "Nietzsche on Blacks," in *Existence in Black: An Anthology of Black Existential Philosophy*, ed. Lewis R. Gordon (New York: Routledge, 1997), 169–70. Still, this is a charge that could be made against most thinkers in the European canon since the Middle Ages. The usefulness of their thought, beyond their particular vices, is another matter.

10. See, for example, Friedrich Nietzsche, *On the Genealogy of Morals*, trans. W. Kaufmann and R. J. Hollingdale, intro. by W. Kaufmann (New York: Vintage, 1989), 1–4. This view is consistent with, although not reducible to, the Darwinian view of health. From the Darwinian perspective, disease is only consequential if it leads to the extinction of a species. Where extinction does not occur, disease could at times paradoxically be interpreted as what facilitates

survival. In some instances, disease leads to adaptation, and the most adaptable species to disease is the most likely to survive. This view has no bearing, however, on the individual organism. An organism could succumb to disease and yet be healthy from a Darwinian point of view because it has passed on its genes, which paradoxically could mean the survival of suffering and disease on the species level.

11. Walter Kaufmann, *Nietzsche: Philosopher, Psychologist, Antichrist*, 4th ed. (Princeton, NJ: Princeton University Press, 1974), 131. Although Kaufmann's discussion is more known in the English-speaking world, his point is supported by Karl Jaspers's classic, early study: *Nietzsche: An Introduction to the Understanding of His Philosophical Activity*, trans. Charles F. Wallraff and Frederick J. Schmitz (Baltimore, MD: Johns Hopkins University Press, 1997), 111–15. In the main, this early study (originally published in 1936) supports Kaufmann's view: "Nietzsche's concepts of illness and health possess a peculiar ambiguity: Illness which derives from and serves true health—the health of *Existenz* [authentic existence] which comes from within—is actually an indication of this health. Health in the medical sense, which typically belongs to a being without substance, becomes a sign of true illness" (111). Jaspers's point is poetically formulated by Nietzsche himself: "There are those who, whether from lack of experience or from dullness of spirit, turn away in scorn or pity from such phenomena, regarding them as 'popular diseases' while believing in their own good health; of course, these poor creatures have not the slightest inkling of how spectral and deathly pale their 'health' seems when the glowing life of Dionysiac enthusiasts storms past them" (*BT*, § 1, pp. 17–18).

12. The reader might wonder what is the nature of ancient Greek suffering? It is, for Nietzsche, connected to Silenus's, (or the Silens's) response, referenced in Aristotle's dialogue *Eudemos*, to the question of whether life is worth living: ". . . The very best thing is utterly beyond your reach: not to have been born, not to *be*, to be *nothing*. However, the second best thing for you [human beings] is: to die soon" (*BT*, § 3, p. 23). The Greeks, in other words, were dealing head-on with the problem of *living*. (Cf. also Raymond Geuss's introduction, pp. xvii–xviii, which explores the theodicean Platonic view of the power of good and Christian view of a good, all-resolving God, conceptions against which this view is posed.)

13. By "black creolized people," I mean the many African communities and varieties of non-African communities that have led to the formation of New World black cultures, although this does not preclude Old World mixtures as well. These mixtures are normative practices exemplifying the lived realities of such people. That is, they are not superficial. For a discussion of this conception of creolization and its relation to black peoples, see Paget Henry, *Caliban's Reason: Introducing Afro-Caribbean Philosophy* (New York: Routledge, 2000).

14. That this is a chapter exploring the contemporary relevance of Nietzsche's ideas, excrement is a fitting metaphor here, since for him the nihilism of leveling, of making all of the same, stinks.

15. Ralph Ellison, "What Would America Be Like without Blacks?," *Going to the Territory* (New York: Vintage, 1987), 108–109.

16. I am not here denying the realities of black mortality rates and other statistically and demographically significant information available by the U.S. Centers for Disease Control and other institutions offering quantitative epidemiological assessments. The Nietzschean argument does not lay claim to the absence of disease and physical illness.

17. See the introduction to Frantz Fanon's *Black Skin, White Masks*, trans. Charles Lamm Markman (New York: Grove Press, 1967). See also Lewis R. Gordon, *Existentia Africana: Understanding Africana Existential Thought* (New York: Routledge, 2000), chapter 1, "Africana Existential Philosophy." The question of rationality is affected by the reality of "racist rationality." For discussion, Lewis R. Gordon, see *Bad Faith and Antiblack Racism* (Amherst, NY: Humanity Books, 1995), part II, and also see Fanon's essay, "Racism and Culture," in *Toward the African Revolution: Political Essays*, trans. Haakon Chevalier (New York: Grove Press, 1967), 29–44. See as well David Theo Goldberg's very influential *Racist Culture* (Oxford: Blackwell, 1990) and, also by Goldberg, *The Racial State* (Oxford: Blackwell, 2001).

18. This aspect of American "mass" culture has received critical treatment from philosophers and social theorists ranging from Antonio Gramsci to Ortega Y Gasset to Herbert Marcuse and C. L. R. James.

19. This is a familiar feature of the American racial landscape. Their ongoing documentation can be found in the very vigilant *Journal of Blacks in Higher Education*. Consider Eldrick "Tiger" Woods: "Despite his success and celebrity, there still are [golf] courses in the United States on which he cannot play because of his race. Woods routinely receives death threats and hate mail. (At Stanford [University], he taped the most threatening and offensive letters to his dormitory wall, and to this day Tiger Woods insists that he be shown every piece of hate mail that he receives.) He channels this hate into repressed rage with which he is able to focus his energies on becoming the greatest golfer who has ever played the game" (*Journal of Blacks in Higher Education* 31 (Winter 2000–2001): 78.

20. Joe R. Feagin, *Racist America: Roots, Current Realities, and Future Reparations* (New York: Routledge, 2000). See, for example, pp. 31–32: "From at least the 1830s and the first decades of the 1900s new European immigrant groups, especially those not initially considered to be white—for example, the Irish and the Italians—by native-born whites, clamored to be defined as white in the U.S. Whiteness has long been the goal for all those who can squeeze into the category. . . . Historically [with regard to class and gender], most white workers and most white women have been uninterested in building unity of identity and protest with, respectively, black workers or black women across the color line." For a similar discussion, see Jane Anna Gordon, *Why They Couldn't Wait: A Critique of the Black-Jewish Conflict over Community Control*

in Ocean Hill-Brownsville (1967–1971) (New York: Routledge, 2001), especially chapters 3 and 4. And for a discussion of the complexity of Afro-Asian dynamics, see Vijay Prashad, *Everybody Was Kung Fu Fighting* (Boston: Beacon Press, 2001).

21. Premodern whiteness was primarily theological and infused with an aesthetics premised upon metaphysical realism. In other words, white skin was an indication of divine selection and distinction. For discussion, see William R. Jones, *Is God a White Racist?: Prolegomena to Black Theology*, 2nd ed. (Boston: Beacon Press, 1996). See also Gordon, *Bad Faith and Antiblack Racism*, part IV.

22. "It is not the victory of science that distinguishes our nineteenth century, but the victory of scientific method over science." Friedrich Nietzsche, *The Will to Power*, trans. Walter Kaufmann and R. J. Hollingdale (New York: Vintage, 1968), 261 (Book II, Part I, section 1, par. 466).

23. This calling is a consequence of the presumption of white leadership in the world. For discussion of why such conceptions of leadership require killers, see Elias Canetti, *Crowds and Power*, 219, 231–34.

24. There are many classic studies of this aspect of white identity. Fanon observed this in *Black Skin, White Masks*, chapter 6. See also Eric Erickson's *Childhood and Society*, 2nd ed. (New York: W.W. Norton, 1963). An immediate contrast emerges in psychological studies of black children, where the objective is not to raise a conqueror but to raise someone who can first survive and then (hopefully) excel in spite of anti-black racism. See, for instance, James Comer's and Alvin Poussaint's *Raising Black Children: Two Leading Psychiatrists Confront the Educational, Social, and Emotional Problems Facing Black Children* (New York: Plume, 1992).

25. This is not to say that there are not moments of upsurge. The swing, rock 'n' roll, and disco eras are recent examples. But all three were instances of colonizing *black* and *brown* creative upsurges.

26. Ralph Ellison, *Invisible Man* (New York: Vintage International, 1990), 264–65.

27. Many works are dedicated to the blues, but among the most poignant and insightful are Leroi Jones (Amiri Baraka), *Blues People: The Negro Experience in White America and the Music That Developed from It* (New York: William Morrow and Company, 1963) and Ralph Ellison's several wonderful essays on the subject in *Shadow and Act*, which includes an essay on Jones's work. See also Josiah Ulysses Young III, *A Pan-African Theology,* and Albert Murray, *The Blues Devils of Dada: A Contemporary American Approach to Aesthetic Statement* (New York: Vintage Books, 1997).

28. "Thus the blues—'the black slave lament'—was offered up for the admiration of the oppressors. This modicum of stylized oppression is the exploiter's and the racist's rightful due. Without oppression and without racism you have

no blues. The end of racism would sound the knell of great Negro music."
Frantz Fanon, "Racism and Culture," in *Toward the African Revolution*, 37.
Although not explicitly formulated as the blues, that quality of Fanon's writing
emerges in Nelson Maldonado-Torres's powerful analysis, "The Cry of the Self
as a Call from the Other: The Paradoxical Loving Subjectivity of Frantz Fanon,"
Listening: A Journal of Religion and Culture 36:1 (Winter 2001): 46–60.

29. See my discussion of this dimension of Fanon's work in my *Existentia
Africana*, chapter 2.

30. Fanon, *Black Skin, White Masks*, 11.

31. This interpretation of the path of black music, particularly hip-hop,
is based on some of the ideas I propounded in *Her Majesty's Other Children:
Sketches of Racism from a Neocolonial Age* (Lanham, MD: Rowman & Littlefield, 1997), part III, where my discussion of decadence in recent black music
is based on an understanding of black music as what Clevis Headley has right-
fully characterized as a metaphor for freedom. See Clevis Headley, "Race,
African American Philosophy, and Africana Philosophy: A Critical Reading of
Lewis Gordon's *Her Majesty's Other Children*," *Philosophia Africana* 4:1 (March
2001): 56–57. Commentaries on the movement from joy to social critique to
hypersexual play usually emerge in lamentations among hip-hop critics.
Among such critics most deserving of such attention in this regard is Ewuare
Osayande. See, for instance, his *So the Spoken Word Won't Be Broken: The Poli-
tics of the New Black Poetry* (Philadelphia: Talking Drums Communications,
1999), and *Caught at the Crossroads without a Map* (Philadelphia: Talking
Drum Communications, 2001).

32. The discussion of nihilism that follows the discussion of decadence
here is premised on Nietzsche's view, in *The Will to Power*, that nihilism is a
symptom of decadence, and decadence is a normal process of the life span of
living things. See, for example, Book I, chapter 1, par. 23. For a detailed discussion of Nietzsche's theory of decadence, see Jacqueline Renee Scott,
"Nietzsche and Decadence: The Revaluation of Morality," *Continental philosophy Review* 31 (January 1998): 59–78. See also Jaspers's *Nietzsche*, especially 391–92.

33. This is well known. For example, the emergence of Paul Whiteman
as "the King of Jazz," with his pale, saccharine versions of the music, is a story
that takes the chilling form of eternal recurrence in the history of black-white
relations in both popular and classical music. Think of the absurdity of this
early assessment of that dynamic by an influential white critic: "Nowhere have
I gone into detail about negro jazz bands. There are so many good ones, it
would be hard to pick out a few for special mention. None of them, however,
are as good as the best white bands, and very rarely are their best players as
good as the best white virtuosos." H. O. Osgood, *So This Is Jazz* (Boston: Little, Brown, and Company, 1926), 103. For a discussion of Paul Whiteman, see
Leroy Ostransky, *Understanding Jazz* (Englewood Cliffs, NJ: Prentice Hall,

1977), chapters 1 and 2, and Marshall W. Stearns, *The Story of Jazz* (London: Oxford University Press, 1958), chapters 14 and 15.

34. This is not to say that living under the weight and expectations of presumed "superiority" does not lead to a form of group "suffering" of its own— the suffering of untested existence. This was suggested earlier in our discussion of individual whites not really knowing whether they can live a day in the shoes of blacks. Bad faith can, however, allow such whites to transform the meaning of failure in such circumstances to *cultural superiority*, as Nietzsche himself does by making a comparison between blacks and whites on the question of the pain thresholds of each group: "[In prehistoric times]. . . pain did not hurt as much as it does now; at least that is the conclusion a doctor may arrive at who has treated Negroes (taken as representatives of prehistoric man) for severe internal inflammations that would drive even the best constituted European to distraction—in the case of Negroes they do *not* do so. (The curve of human susceptibility to pain seems in fact to take an extraordinary and almost sudden drop as soon as one has passed the upper ten thousand or ten million of the top stratum of culture" [*GM*, pp. 67–68].)

35. Paget Henry advances this interpretation of African struggles with existence in his book, *Caliban's Reason*, and his article, "Self-Formation and the Call: An Africana Perspective," *Listening: A Journal of Religion and Culture* 36:1 (Winter 2001): 27–45.

36. See Ellison, *Invisible Man*, 8.

37. I explore this observation in the chapter "Exoticism," in *Bad Faith and Antiblack Racism*, part III.

38. The distinction between mass and class emerges in a peculiar way with the achievement of the white middle "class." Although the working class wants a better life, it lacks the hubris of entitlement that characterizes the white middle class in the world, although the white members of the American working class often dream of it. Although obviously not the sentiment of every individual within the group, Ortega Y Gasset's depiction of mass consciousness provides a fairly accurate description of such an ethos: "*The characteristic of the hour is that the commonplace mind, knowing itself to be commonplace, has the assurance to proclaim the rights of the commonplace and to impose them wherever it will.* As they say in the United States: 'to be different is to be indecent.' The mass crushes beneath it everything that is different, everything that is excellent, individual, qualified and select. Anybody who is not like everybody, who does not think like everybody, runs the risk of being eliminated. And it is clear, of course, that this 'everybody' is not 'everybody.' 'Everybody' was normally the complex unity of the mass and the divergent, specialized minorities. Nowadays, 'everybody' is the mass alone. Here we have the formidable fact of our times, described without any concealment of the brutality of its features," *The Revolt of the Masses* (New York: W.W. Norton, 1932), 18. Need we mention malls and suburbs and gentrified white oases in dark cities?

39. Cf. Book I, chapter I, par. 22 of *The Will to Power*:

nihilism. It is *ambiguous*:
A. Nihilism as a sign of increased power of the spirit: as *active* nihilism.
B. Nihilism as decline and recession of the power of the spirit: as *passive* nihilism.

40. The Greek myths are more well known because of European identification with Greece. For the version offered here, consult Hesiod's *Theognis*. The much older Egyptian or East African ones are increasingly less familiar. For a wonderful outline and discussion of the influence of these myths, even on the early Mycenaean, Canaanite, and Sumerian myths, see Charles Finch III, *Echoes from the Old Darkland: Themes from the African Eden* (Decatur, GA: Khenti, 1996).

41. The popularity of John McWhorter's *Losing the Race* attests to this fact.

Part II

—

Prescriptions

5

Ecce Negro:
How to Become a Race Theorist

PAUL C. TAYLOR

"You had not yet sought yourselves when you found me. . . .
Now, I bid you lose me and find yourselves; and only *when
you have all denied me* will I return to you"

—Nietzsche, *Ecce Homo*

I.

I lost Nietzsche early on, though not in the willful way that
Zarathustra prescribes. I had read him almost continuously during my
junior year at Morehouse College, starting with *Beyond Good and Evil*
in a class and ending with a leisurely summertime perusal of *Zarathustra*. In a way this experience brought me to philosophy, in part by
demonstrating the possibility of doing whatever philosophers do in a
recognizable voice, or in what is recognizable as a voice, in part by giving
me words for my inchoate but unmistakable inclinations toward anti-
foundationalism and historicism.

I would soon learn to articulate my early inclinations in language
provided by philosophical pragmatists, mainly by John Dewey and
William James. But I was inclined in other directions as well, mainly
toward work that spoke to the conditions of black life in the United
States. In an effort to reconcile the impulse toward race work with my
philosopher's love for abstraction and theory, I embraced a variety of
Afrocentrism. But while that early accommodation fed my hunger for
historicism in ways that I will soon discuss further, it coexisted uneasily

101

with my instinctive anti-foundationalism. As I settled into my pragmatist convictions, my commitment to an Afrocentric model of intellectual race work became a commitment to the branch of Africana philosophy that concerns itself with race theory.

Both the move to pragmatism and the move to, then away from, Afrocentrism took me away from Nietzsche. He seemed at best indifferent and at worst positively hostile to my interest in race work—there was, after all, all that talk of masters and slaves, of blonde beasts, both of which I freely admit to misunderstanding, and of European culture(s). The resources I got from him I could get from pragmatism without the added burdens of rampant misogyny, explicit elitism, and the demand that literary forms bear philosophical weight. And his genealogical perspectivism seemed best suited to serve me simply as a preparation for the debunkings and reorientations of Afrocentric classicism, to which I will also return.

As it happens, though, some students became aware of my longstanding but long-dormant interest in Nietzsche and approached me about a directed studies course in some of the later works. I warned them that other people at the university who then employed me were better positioned to accompany them on this journey, but they persisted. I do not know how much they got out of our meetings, but I got an opportunity to notice and to rethink what I had never really thought of before as my denial of Nietzsche. And that opportunity led to this chapter.

I have never thought of pragmatism's displacement of Nietzsche in my intellectual life as a net gain, never forgotten that the costs of reading the likes of *Ecce Homo* come with their own hidden benefits. But I have also never explained to myself just why I should not think that way, and what the benefits are. So I would like to chart an alternate path from Afrocentrism to race theory, this time using Nietzschean resources.[1] Think of it as a first step toward seeing how the distinction between Deweyan pragmatism and Nietzschean perfectionism makes a difference. (A second step would involve comparing the two paths, but first things first.)

Afrocentrism: Uses and Abuses

Whoever does not merely comprehend the word "Dionysian" but comprehends *himself* in the word needs no refutation of Plato or Christianity or Schopenhauer—he *smells the decay*.

—Nietzsche, Ecce Homo

IIA.

In his writings, his editorship of the *Journal of Black Studies*, and his long stewardship of Temple University's Department of African American Studies, Molefi Asante has done more than anyone else to popularize and refine the notion of Afrocentrism. (Mostly for this reason, I will use Asante's name and "Afrocentrism" almost interchangeably.) In perhaps his best book, *Kemet, Afrocentricity, and Knowledge*,[2] he presents the view as a natural outgrowth of the postmodern decentering of Europe and the deflation of Western pretensions to objectivity, to neutrality, to the capacity to judge with context-independent universal validity. These Enlightenment ideals, Asante says, served as masks for the promulgation of local European values and interests, and recognizing this leaves us with two duties: to uncover the workings of interest in purportedly objective inquiry and neutral behavior, and to find a new model for conducting inquiry and guiding behavior. On Asante's view, Afrocentricity is the key to discharging both duties.

Asante's alternative to universality involves the excavation and embrace of *centrism*, which he describes as "the groundedness of observation and behavior in one's own experiences."[3] On his view, once we recognize that behavior and inquiry necessarily depend on context, in particular on epistemic and experiential contexts, we ought to excavate the relevant contexts and recognize the roles they play. Cultures provide the contexts that Asante takes most seriously, and the cultures he is concerned with are the ones that correspond, to the extent that they do, to what we think of as races. So his is a cultural, and a "racialist," centrism—where "racialist" appears in scare quotes because he explicitly rejects the idea of biological races. On this view there is an African culture, of course manifested in different ways in the local cultures of different African peoples, both on the Continent and in the Diaspora. There is also a European culture, similarly manifested in various ways. And while there are other broad cultures, these two play the crucial role in Asante's project, which is after all a blueprint for *African* centrism and for a greater understanding of the condition of "Africanity."

Here is what focusing on the European epistemic context reveals: Europe wrote itself into history as an autonomous unit, growing more or less steadily and alone from its Greek roots. It obscured both the relationships between its cornerstone, Greece, and other Mediterranean cultures, like Egypt, and the role that other cultures, like that of medieval Islam, played in its subsequent development. And along the way it denied that African cultures were civilized and, worse, that Africans had any culture worth the name. When the creativity, productivity, and sophistication of some African culture could not be denied, its African character had to be. So Egypt became part of the Orient or the Near or Middle East, and the ancient ruins of great Zimbabwe became the work of a shadowy non-African civilization with roots in Persia, India, or elsewhere.

Just as the move to embrace centrism and reject universality allows us to diagnose the obscurantist and self-serving nature of Europe's self-image, it also helps us replace that image with something better. Centrism requires that anyone seeking to understand a culture try as much as possible to do so from the standpoint of its participants. African centrism in particular encourages "the student . . . investigating African phenomena to view the world from the standpoint of the African."[4] Approached in this way, African cultural practices will not appear as failed attempts to do something that Europe does better, or as proof of an insensitivity even to the demands of culture, but rather as elements in a comprehensive way of life, with their own meanings. And African history would be a narrative not of Africa as passive Object, acted upon by others, but of Africa as active Subject, making its distinctive contributions to the world. Here we reach what Asante identifies as the central idea of Afrocentrism: "the absolute projecting of African agency"—as opposed to passivity and quiescence—"in every discourse and situation."[5]

Any student of culture can benefit from the Afrocentric perspective. But the injunction to understand "African phenomena from the standpoint of the African" also extends to such African phenomena as the lives of African-descended individuals. Since I am an African American, my attempt to fashion a satisfactory life for myself is an African phenomenon, and as such is inexplicable without reference to African culture. If I use European norms as guides, I will misunderstand my future and my forthcoming self. I will, in Asante's terms, have *lost my center* and risked my sanity. He has recently put it this way:

> Despite the persistent travails of the centuries, the twists and turns in the road to agency, Africans in the Americas are clearly headed in the right direction *for sanity*. And though we never had . . . *a collective therapy session to straighten out our heads* . . . we have been fortunate to inherit a trust in our instincts . . . and the ability to keep an eagle's eye on *the African compass*, not in the sense of some romantic vision of Africa or some exotic biological determinism but in the deliberate historical appreciation of the role of our ancestors in maintaining in their souls the knowledge of our continent of origin.[6]

The historical inability of African Americans to navigate by the African compass—evidenced, Asante explains elsewhere, by such traditions as giving our children names like Paul Christopher Taylor rather than, say, Nnamdi Azikiwe or Adib KMT – is the sort of problem that might benefit from "collective therapy."[7] But we are getting better at orienting ourselves around the African center, and are therefore "headed in the right direction for sanity." The opposite of sanity in this context is *dislocation*, as we see in this passage:

> Meaning in the contemporary context must be derived from the most centered aspects of the African's being. When this is not the case, psychological dislocation creates automatons who are unable to fully capture the historical moment because they are living on someone else's terms. . . . Where will the African person find emotional and cultural satisfaction if not in her own terms?[8]

IIB.

An obvious question to put to Asante is the question of essentialism: one might wonder about the sincerity with which Afrocentrism rejects "exotic biological determinism." This would produce a more nuanced conversation than many have thought, since Asante can get much of what he wants without biological races. But I find myself thinking instead that the first step along a Nietzschean path from Afrocentrism to race theory should involve the view that is usually identified, even on Nietzsche's behalf, as the pragmatic theory of truth. This label is fairly misleading, not least because Nietzsche, like William James, remained mostly unmoved by the questions that call forth what we now consider theories of truth. They were more interested in studying how we come to accept things as true, and in how that process enhances or inhibits life, than in explaining what it is for sentences to successfully represent the world.

In view of Afrocentrism's historicist sensibility, I am especially interested in exploring Nietzsche's discussion of truth and power in his early reflections on historical inquiry. In the essay "On the Uses and Abuses of History for Life,"[9] Nietzsche distinguishes three different ways of doing historical work, each with its characteristic dangers, practitioners, and areas of applicability. The monumental historian spins myths to embolden and inspire; he overlooks the unique confluence of circumstances that produced the past and produces a narrative that conforms to the needs of the present, all in order to find models for his own heroic activity. The antiquarian historian records and commemorates; he venerates the old and denigrates the new, all for the sake of maintaining for others the conditions that have proven favorable to the emergence of (his—and for Nietzsche it was always *his*) life. The critical historian, finally, questions and condemns the past in order to be free of it, to make room for the creative activity of fashioning the future. On Nietzsche's view we need all three approaches, judiciously recruited at the appropriate moments.

The point of all this, or one point, is that human life involves narration, telling stories, discursive emplotment: we need to establish a sense of ourselves, of who we are and what we are about, in order to get on in the world. Stories, like life, unfold over time, and humans are unique among animals in their awareness of their historicity. If storytelling is always selective, a matter of deciding what matters and what does not, then for storytelling animals like ourselves, *life* is always selective. We tell the stories, write the histories, that make sense to us, but sense making is shaped by extra-rational factors: by unconscious drives, by a preconscious sense of the context in which the act of inquiry takes place. One aim of "Uses and Abuses" is to make this aspect of the human condition explicit, to put us in a position to get better at the selective self-narrating that we will inevitably engage in anyway. Nietzsche aims here to make us aware of the different ways in which selectivity can operate, of the different kinds of partial stories we can tell about the past, so that we can recognize the importance of each approach.

It is tempting to say that Afrocentric classicism involves a kind of monumental history. Asante's Afrocentric reorientation of history typically, and most vividly in hands other than his,[10] does more than restore Egypt's place on the African continent and its relationship to Greek culture and philosophy. It establishes Egypt as the *classical* African civilization, as important to African peoples as Greece is to Europeans.

Still, I am not confident of the link between Afrocentric classicism and monumental history. Monumentalism, Nietzsche says, "pertains to the active and powerful human being, to the person who is involved in a great struggle and who needs exemplars, teachers, and comforters, but is unable to find them among his contemporaries" (*HL* 2). The use of this kind of history "lies in the great stimuli that a powerful person derives from it" (*HL* 2). This is one of the early appearances of the doctrine that Stanley Cavell prizes under the heading of Perfectionism, the idea that one's present self is something to be overcome, that an unattained but attainable self awaits recognition and approximation.[11]

Afrocentrism, it seems to me, is not attentive in this way to the goal of providing resources for individual self-creation. The aim of empowering the individual is always at the forefront of Afrocentric theory, but it is constrained by the individual's embedment in Asante's overarching cultural nationalist project. The project might be construed as a model for self-overcoming, but it posits a specific self—the Eurocentric, alienated, dislocated self—to be overcome, and a specific self—the centered Afrocentric self—that we are to become. Where Nietzsche undermines most of his specific recommendations regarding what the unattained self looks like – "I want no believers," he says, and "I erect no new idols" (*EH* "Destiny" 1, *EH* P 2)—Asante tells us directly that moving in the direction of greater health, as he can agree with Nietzsche to call it, means becoming a member of the African Cultural System.

Afrocentric history does not seem driven by the monumentalist aim of self-overcoming, but this may not yet provide grounds for criticism. Nietzsche urges us to blend the three historical modes, and maybe the dampening of the monumentalist's fervor comes from Asante's willingness to heed this injunction. There is, for example, a fair degree of antiquarianism in the Afrocentric effort to recover the suppressed history of African culture. Nietzsche seems almost to have been writing about the Afrocentrist when he describes the antiquarian as someone who

> looks beyond his own transient, curious, individual existence and senses himself to be the spirit of his house, his lineage, and his city. At times he even greets across the distance of darkening and confusing centuries the soul of his people as his own soul; the ability to . . . detect traces that are almost extinguished, to instinctively read correctly a past frequently overwritten . . . these are his gifts and his virtues. (*HL* 3)

The danger of antiquarianism is that "anything ancient and past . . . is simply regarded as venerable, and everything that fails to welcome the ancient with reverence—in other words, whatever is new and in the process of becoming—is met with hostility and rejected" (*HL* 3). Again, this seems not to apply to the Afrocentrist, since Asante, at least, works quite hard to link new practices and "African phenomena" to their ancient roots, or to the cultural predispositions that generated the ancient as surely as they do the contemporary. And again, perhaps the avoidance of this pitfall shows the Afrocentrist's successful blending of the different historical modes.

There is, however, a sense in which Afrocentrism does close itself to the future, a sense in which it fails to fuse its approach with the third

Nietzschean mode of *critical* history. As I have noted, the Afrocentric picture is locked into a kind of cultural racialism. Asante usually prefers not to call them races, but his cultural groups are coextensive with the races of the dominant strains of nineteenth-century Western race "science." In addition, he picks out the dislocated members of his culture groups by determining, in effect, what race they belong to—who counts as African descended and who does not, say—and evaluating their relationship to the culture of their "continent of origin." One wonders, what does this picture enjoin us to say about the growing recognition that a metaphysics of racial purity is untenable? In one place Asante concedes the "impurity" of all racial groups, especially African Americans. Nevertheless, he goes on simply to insist that "the core of our collective being is African," and that "we are by virtue of commitments, history, and convictions an African people."[12] But even if we can defend this effort to gloss over the "impurity" of the people we still categorize with intuitive ease, what are we to say about the growing numbers of people who resist stable categorization and identify themselves as biracial or multiracial—that is, who link themselves to more than one "continent of origin"?

We are back in the neighborhood of worries about essentialism, but the point here has more to do with how Asante handles the novelty that these essentialism-busting experiences and people represent. He might say that even if people embrace their heterogeneity and declare themselves mixed, the racialized distribution of social goods in places such as the United States will still proceed as if these people belong wholly to one group or another. But to say this is to make identity contingent upon the operations of white supremacy, and thereby to violate his basic principle: "the absolute projecting of African agency," the depiction of Africans as self-defining subjects rather than externally defined objects. As an alternative, he might say that it is politically important for black people to abide by the one-drop rule, to recruit anyone with any discernible black 'blood' into the race. But the claim so far has not been that people who misidentify are politically naïve; the claim is that they are *sick*. Finally, he might say that mixed-race people just have more options, that they can permissibly identify with any part of their ancestry. But it is hard to see how to reconcile this with the hypodescent-inspired *ipse dixit* offered in response to the general problem of purity, or with the apparent assumption that one culture or another clearly counts as mine.[13]

Whatever Asante might say, I have been unable to find any published accounts of what he *does* say, which seems to me to suggest a kind of imperviousness to an emerging future. Instead of following the path of the critical historian—and of the great historian, who artistically, poetically, blends the various modes in furtherance of life—instead of freeing himself from problematic aspects of our racial past in order to creatively imagine a novel future, the Afrocentrist venerates. In a way, in this way, Afrocentrism aligns itself with Nietzsche's great targets, Christianity, Socratism, liberal democracy, and so on: by privileging Being—in this case, racial and cultural purity—over the Becoming of fluid and ever-changing forms of life, Afrocentrism becomes unable to say yes when the world presents itself in ways that undermine the standing conditions of possibility for the likes of Asante.

A final example may make the point more completely. While arguing that African peoples should have African names, Asante asks, "Can you imagine a white European with a name like *Kofi Adegbola*? Or a Japanese in the United States . . . with a name like *Gerhard Casmir*?"[14] As it happens, I do not have to imagine the latter case, or one like it: I once had a student of Japanese descent who had been adopted as an infant, and, of course, named, by an Irish American couple. This student, whom I will call Siobhan O'Reilly—not her real name, but close to it—was interested in her Japanese heritage, and was in fact exploring it in her studies; but she was comfortable with and loved her adoptive family. I guess I am supposed to think of her as dislocated, as having gotten out of touch with her culture. This is an intuitively plausible way to think; it may even have motivated her study of Japan. There *is* a sense in which the home of her biological parents belongs to her, given the way the world is, the way we think about identity; and she should be free to explore it and create connections. There is even a sense in which denying any connection whatsoever, denying that her body and heritage make her subject in certain places to certain modes of treatment, to being approached as an Asian woman, with all that that means, might reveal her to be self-deceived. But should we have to say that she is dislocated, that she needs therapy, if she recognizes her interpellation as an Asian-American in a racialized society but does no more—if she refuses to *claim* her right not just to explore but to embrace Japanese culture?

The case of Siobhan O'Reilly encapsulates much of the complexity that attends contemporary social identities, the complexity that the Afrocentric approach denies in its constricted perspective on life. The transmissibility of culture and mobility of peoples, which makes possible an Irish American woman with, as it were, a Japanese body; the asymmetries of racialized desire, by which I mean, among other things, the disparity in the U.S. adoption "market" between the robust demand for infants from Asia and the stagnant demand for African American infants; the accumulating effects of a few decades of extremely relaxed—relative to its historical heights—state enforcement of racial identification in the U.S., on account of which interracial marriages are on the rise and even the census has abandoned the illusion of purity; the increasing awareness of the extremely parochial nature of United States racial practices and of the less than seamless fit between culture, nationality, and race—all of these conditions of contemporary social life have to drop out of the Afrocentric account, or appear as *maladies*, signs of the sickness of the age.

What if we were to embrace the conditions that make Siobhan's case so complicated? What if those of us concerned with intellectual race work took the complexity of race not as an incentive for disavowal and negation but as a challenge to our ability to creatively and productively engage with, which is to say to re-create, the world? What if we moved from antiquarian Afrocentrism to a critical, or critically historicist, race theory?

III. Race Theory: Cosmopolitan Prejudices

"The eye that had been spoiled by the tremendous need for seeing *far* . . . is here forced to focus on what lies nearest, the age, the around-us"

—Nietzsche, *Ecce Homo*

I use the expression "critical race theory" to denote alternatives to what I call "classical race theory." Classical race theory is the view of human variation that gained currency in the nineteenth century and that has shaped so much of U.S. history and society since; it is the view that the human population naturally comprises a small number of subpopulations, called "races," each of which is distinct from the others on account of its members' possession of distinct and inherited clusters of traits. For the classical racialist the race-defining traits are both physiognomic—skin color and hair texture, say—and nonphysiognomic—moral worth, intelligence, and culture; they cluster in ways that support scientific generalizations; and they motivate hierarchical rankings of the distinguished human types—some types are more beautiful, are smarter, and are more civilized than others.

Critical race theory, in contrast, begins with the recognition that the scientific "bases" for its classical predecessor are hopeless, that the world, the world of human physiology, just does not work the way classical racialism needs it to—that the nineteenth century needs in some sense to be shattered, condemned, dissolved (*HL* 3). One approach to critical race theory insists that the concept 'race' is useful despite the bankruptcy of classical racialism. Of the people who argue in this way, some hold that races are real, that the concept refers to real human populations, just not in the way or for the reasons that nineteenth-century theorists accepted. Others claim that even though there are in fact no races, the concept is important as a heuristic device, as a way of keeping us attuned to social dynamics of some importance. In contrast, practitioners of an alternative mode of critical race theory insist that race thinking does more harm than good, that there are no races and we would be better off if we quit acting as if there were. Some people refer to this approach as "eliminativism," because its adherents seek to eliminate races from our social ontologies.

An encounter with one of these eliminativists affirmed my choice of philosophical race theory over Afrocentrism: in graduate school I had the privilege of meeting K. Anthony Appiah. He was lecturing from the manuscript in African philosophy that would become his prize-winning book, *In My Father's House*, and his subtle and sophisticated analyses of what Asante calls 'African phenomena' bolstered my flagging hope that philosophy could be enlisted in the service of intellectual race work. But when I pored over the book some time later, I found myself vehemently disagreeing with the eliminativism I found there, as I would with its elaboration in his later book, *Color Conscious*. My worries about Appiah's approach have shaped my interest in race theory, as well as my effort to refine the pragmatic sensibilities that underwrote my complaints. Having disagreed with him as a pragmatist, I will take this opportunity to articulate my dissent in terms that I might have found if I had remained a Nietzschean.[15]

IIIA.

Appiah's influential strain of eliminativism allies itself with what is usually called a "cosmopolitan ideal." I am thinking here of writers like Ross Posnock, Paul Gilroy, and to some extent Naomi Zack; I am thinking of the view that Posnock describes as a species of universalism, distinguished by its aestheticist rejection of the demands of authenticity and embrace of the prospects for multiple cultural and affective attachments.[16] Appiah, for his part, explains that "the only human race . . .is *the* human race," and that racial identities are dangerously susceptible to, as he puts it, "going imperial." This is what happens when we subordinate individual personality and style to the requirements of racial "scripts," when we delimit the possibilities for human association so that relations like love and solidarity are locked within narrow racial bounds, and when we sacrifice individual autonomy to the demands of racial solidarity. As an alternative, he suggests that we "live with fractured identities; engage in identity play; find solidarity, yes, but recognize contingency, and, above all, practice irony."[17]

This cosmopolitanism sounds quite Nietzschean, especially in the Rortian, perfectionist form that Appiah endorses. Its advocates champion the virtues of individual self-creation and of independence from coercive cultural programs. And in their opposition to race thinking, they appear to exhibit the strength that Nietzsche demands of his free spirits and genuine philosophers, or at least of the philosophic "laborers" who prepare the way for these higher types: they are ready to make enemies of today's ideals, to appear to be "disagreeable fools and dangerous question marks," to take a "knife . . . to the chest of the very virtues of their time," if the still-influential faith in identity politics can count as a virtue (*BGE* 211–12).[18]

Unlike the mature Nietzsche, though, who eagerly and explicitly endorses an aristocratic radicalism, the cosmopolitans commit themselves to liberal democracy as the guarantor of their independence. Nietzsche claims that aristocratic society, with its "long ladder of differences in value between man and man," is a precondition for the enhancement of humanity. The "ingrained difference between strata" enables "the ruling class" to look down upon weaker, less healthy, less whole souls, thereby cultivating the "craving for an ever new widening of distances within the soul itself" and receiving a kind of training for perfectionist self-overcoming (*BGE* 257). He goes on to suggest that the next human enhancement might involve the creation of a new ruling class for Europe by, perversely, the processes of democratization. The same forces that "lead to the leveling and mediocritization of man— to a useful, industrious, handy, multi-purpose herd animal," would also, he says, "give birth to exceptional human beings of the most dangerous and attractive quality"—though only in "single, exceptional cases" (*BGE* 242). How would this work? Nietzsche explains:

> The Europeans are becoming . . . more and more detached from the conditions under which races originate [,] that are tied to some climate or class; they become increasingly independent of any *determinate* milieu that would like to inscribe itself for centuries in body and soul with the same demands.

Thus an essentially supra-national and nomadic type of man
is gradually coming up, a type that possesses . . . a maximum
of the art and power of adaptation. (*BGE* 242)

Nietzsche uses "race" here, as he often does, in one of the less
ambitious ways, to describe the historically, geographically, and linguis-
tically defined communities that were clamoring for political expression
in nation-states during his lifetime. We might distinguish here between
the four or five "color-coded" races of classical racialism—brown, black,
red, white, and yellow—and the myriad races of, for example, Anglo-
Saxonism, which imagined a variety of distinct European races constituting the broader white race. Nietzsche has in mind here the smaller
white races and suggests that they are becoming less important in the
face of the unifying forces of democratization—and, presumably, of
liberalism, industrial capitalism, and white supremacist colonialism
(he is, after all, writing just after the Berlin Conference of 1884–85
formalizes the scramble for Africa). A representative of the higher type
will emerge from humankind as, and as rarely as, before, but now as
an adaptive and a supra-national nomad, who will "turn out stronger
and richer than perhaps ever before – thanks to the absence of prejudice from his training, thanks to the manifoldness of practice, art, and
mask" (*BGE* 242). If these nomads turn out to become "exceptional and
dangerous" human beings, they can be cultivated into a ruling class,
on Nietzsche's view, only if there is a pathos of distance: if the multi-
purpose herd remains available to serve as a spur to self-overcoming.

All of this puts me in mind of Appiah's playful ironists—and of
Posnock's cosmopolitans, and Gilroy's transcultural humanists—for a
couple of reasons. First, their favored models are, as Nietzsche puts
it, nomads, people who, like Richard Wright, W. E. B. DuBois, and
themselves, are independent of any single, determinate, cultural
milieu. Second, and more important, these nomads are necessarily a
small minority of the human population. Most of us are not able to
explore traditions other than our own, whether by reading or by
travel. Most of us are not able to live and work in places far removed,
geographically and culturally, from the places of our birth, or, more
precisely, to do so in ways that we, unlike migrant laborers, find mostly
congenial. Since most of us simply lack the material resources to live
in this way, very few of us have the opportunity to have our cultural
prejudices excavated and undermined, or to visit places where others
have fewer, or different, settled expectations of us. Appiah raises the
problem himself, in a way, when he anticipates and responds to a
common complaint:

"It's all very well for you. You academics live a privileged life;
you have steady jobs . . . status from your place in maintaining
cultural capital. Trifle with your identities if you like; but leave
mine alone."

To which I answer only: my job as an intellectual is to call
it as I see it. I owe my fellow citizens respect, certainly, but not
a feigned acquiescence.[19]

I say that Appiah raises the problem *in a way* because he presents
the worry as a volitional one, as a matter of preference: the complainant
prefers not to be tampered with. The worry I have in mind, in contrast,
is a structural one: for example, the critic is, as a matter of political
economy, not likely to find herself in a position to raise the complaint.
Her identity, the identity that is *assigned* to her by society, is too closely
aligned with her life chances and store of social goods for her to be in
a position to play too fast and loose with it, to be too ironic about it.
That is, she can say *I prefer not to be thought of as a poor black mother*,
but if other people see her that way, she is likely to have to deal, at least
in some circumstances, with the world as it presents itself to poor black
mothers. Additionally, she may *choose* a black identity as an oppositional resource, as a tool for resisting the depredations of oppression
and injustice, or as a way of capturing her location on a racialized
social terrain in a compact and perspicuous formula (and, in this case,
in a partial formula, since I have stopped indicating, for reasons of space,
my interest in the convergence of race with such things as gender,
class, and citizenship).[20] Appiah may not have a duty to feign acquiescence,
but he probably does have a duty to remain sensitive to the conditions
under which identities are not just chosen or played with but used in
struggles for dignity and survival.

Appiah is quite sensitive to the uses of identity in everyday life,
so I do not mean to suggest that cosmopolitan nomads necessarily *require*
the pathos of distance in quite the way Nietzsche suggests, as a psychological condition for self-overcoming. My point is rather that the cosmopolitan is possible, as things now stand, anyway, thanks to political
economic conditions—call these late capitalism, or market liberalism,
or transformational globalization—that make pathos-generating distance inevitable. The cosmopolitan floats above, or slips in and out of,
the concrete practices that sustain and often constrain life in particular
places; and this freedom may gain some savor in contrast with the poor
souls who remain mired in the contingencies of the situations into
which they were thrown at, or by, birth. But I am less interested just

now in the psychological point than in this: Nietzsche has thought through and embraced the elitist consequences of his aristocratic radicalism; the cosmopolitans may not want to embrace their consequences, but they owe them a better thinking through than Appiah's gesture at "calling it like he sees it."

IIIB.

As I say, Appiah does remain sensitive to the conditions under which identities get used. In *Color Conscious* he goes so far as to moderate his eliminativism and grant the existence both of racial identities and of certain "sociocultural objects," created by human sorting practices, that correspond, more or less, to the groups we call races. Still, he insists that there *are no* races, and that racial identities are just *labels* rather than perspectives on the world or nodes in social networks of privilege and power. This is a peculiar ambivalence, and it flows, I think, from fundamental prejudices that philosophers have always cultivated in themselves. Before I discuss these prejudices, though, I have to say more about why Appiah insists on eliminativism, and about the view that his insistence closes off from him.

To say that historical and ongoing social practices sort people into populations and that we refer to these populations as races is nearly to say that races are socially constructed by assigning meaning to human bodies and bloodlines—much as states construct legal tender by assigning meaning to paper and metal, and *not* as Salem constructed witches by fantasizing about the devil's influence on woman. To say furthermore that membership in these populations can be an index of social location—of access to social goods and of likely modes of treatment under specified conditions—is to say that thinking in terms of these populations may be useful, that the idea of sorting people in this way is not simply a vehicle for injustice but perhaps a way of tracking and responding to it. Appiah concedes most of this but still refuses to speak of these populations as races, ostensibly because he thinks "race" necessarily refers to the impossible populations posited by nineteenth-century classical racialism. He supports this claim by examining the way "we" ordinarily use the concept of race in discourse and then concluding that what we say about race, what I'll call our race-talk, commits us to states of affairs that do not in fact obtain.

Appiah proposes to find out what we mean when we talk about race by means of historical inquiry because, as he puts it, "current ways of talking about race are the residue, the detritus, so to speak, of earlier ways of thinking . . . the pale reflection of a more full-blooded race discourse that flourished in the last century."[21] In that more "full-blooded" discourse, certain people—as it happens, "the intellectual and political elites of the United States and the United Kingdom"[22]—were accorded what Hilary Putnam calls "semantic deference." Putnam points out that we do not expect an adequate definition of, say, "proton" from the average layperson, even though we do not necessarily want to say that laypeople do not know how to use the word. So, he suggests, we allow most people to talk about protons, as it were, on credit: on the assumption that there are some experts somewhere who *do* know what "proton" means, and who can, if necessary, cash out or correct our attempts to use it. Appiah extends this offer to consumers of racial discourse and argues that the multitudes of ordinary people who have participated in and used race talk have been able to do so thanks to the "experts" who precisely established the meanings of the relevant terms.

Appiah takes Thomas Jefferson and Matthew Arnold as his representative experts, and he gets predictable results. The expert view turns out to be, more or less, what I have called classical racialism, the theory, Appiah reminds us, that our sciences of human variation are advanced enough now for us to reject with confidence. So if races just are the populations comprehended under the anthropology of Arnold and Jefferson, if that is just what "race" *means*, then of course there are no races.

An obvious objection to Appiah's position as I have presented it so far might point out that many people, like W. E. B. DuBois and Alain Locke, rejected classical racialism while striving to "conserve" races.[23] Appiah excludes such figures from his authoritative history of race talk on the grounds that their attempts to reconfigure the meaning of "race" end up relying on biological essentialism. His argument for this point focuses on DuBois, and I have discussed its limitations elsewhere in the pragmatic mood that I have been trying here to keep at bay. In the Nietzschean mood I am trying to cultivate, I prefer to discuss the prejudices that seem to me to motivate Appiah's approach.

Appiah begins his argument in *Color Conscious* with this thought experiment: imagine yourself, he says, at Angel Island in the 1920s, helping "an inquisitive immigrant from Canton . . . fill in an immigration form." Together you start to fill in the blanks: you ask the questions on the form, and the Cantonese woman gives you the answers. You proceed without incident through *name* and *date of birth*. Then you come to *race*. "This," Appiah says, "you do not have to ask. You write 'Oriental.'" When the woman asks what you have written, since you did not ask her anything first, according to Appiah you ("disingenuously") say, "I am writing down where you are from." That, of course, is not right, because, as we have said, the woman is from Canton. She persists in asking what you have written. Appiah wonders: "How do you answer this question? Seventy years ago, how would you have explained to someone from outside the modern West what our English word 'race' meant?" He adds a little later: "Would you give the same explanation today?"

Thought experiments are a standard device in analytic philosophy for imaginatively exposing and testing familiar intuitions. And like this Angel Island parable, they tend to be quite abstract about who the experimenter is supposed to be in the imagined case. Such details are not supposed to matter. But when the subject is as contextual and socially specific as race, this abstractness may itself be a bit disingenuous. Or it may express a casually dismissive approach to the personal, the perspectival, and the social dimensions of the subject matter, an approach that we should not be surprised to find affecting the development of the argument. Am I *me* helping the woman fill out the form? If I am, I do not think I *would* tell her that I had written down where she was from. Does my divergence from Appiah's intuitions about what I would do mean anything? Does it call into question his authority to speak for me on the subject of what we say? Are his intuitions even about me? If not, is he talking about any "we" of which I am a member? What is the significance of the fact obviously anticipated by Appiah's last question, if it is a fact: that I would explain "race" differently now than I would have in 1920? Is it any more significant than such facts as that the 1920s' version of me would have liked different music, or explained the rules of football differently?

I am not supposed to ask any of these questions. Appiah's questions, like his thought experiment, are supposed to make me take a God's-eye view of race, which will enable me to ask instead such questions as these: "What can race be if it is not objective and transhistorical?" And: "Can race really exist if it is as historically and geographically specific, and arbitrary, as it appears?" Of course, lots of things are neither objective nor transhistorical, both localized and in some sense arbitrary, like the rules of football and what counts as an acceptable before-dinner drink. Does that mean that touchdowns and aperitifs do not exist? Or just that the God's-eye view is an inappropriate way of approaching some states of affairs? Is it not the case, at least in normal life, that an appeal to some "we" just is an effort to be historically and socioculturally specific? And what would be the point of asking a nonspecific we, maybe Kant's community of rational beings, about race (or, for that matter, about football, or drinking)?

I ask these questions to register an as yet inarticulate dissatisfaction with Appiah's importation of analytic methods into a context of inquiry that calls for their interrogation. I am worried by his cavalier approach to the question, which seems not to be a question for him, of who we are. I might complain that Appiah's artificially circumscribed "we" leaves out the we that I, and many others, belong to, the home of at least one of the language games in which "race" makes sense. But I will just note that Appiah's silence about how his "we" gets chosen reflects a failure to consider certain personal factors that make him think of, or fail to think of, social reality in the way he does—a failure to avoid the first of the philosophical prejudices that Nietzsche teaches me to consider.
Nietzsche says that philosophers are

> not honest enough in their work. . . . They all pose as if they had discovered and reached their real opinions through the self-development of a cold, pure, divinely unconcerned dialectic . . . while at bottom it is an assumption, a hunch . . . a desire of the heart that has been filtered and made abstract. They are all advocates who resent that name. (*BGE* 5)

Analytic philosophy in particular exhibits this prejudice, in its continuing willingness to ask what we mean without taking seriously the questions of who we are, and of who is asking.
Nietzsche seems to be of two minds about philosophical isolation. He speaks eloquently about the philosopher's need for solitude (*EH* "Clever" 8), of the need to feel separated from the crowd and to "look down" (*BGE* 213); but he also discusses the way shared experiences create community, facilitate communication—and cultivate the herd (*BGE* 268). There are tensions here, partially manifested in the difficulty that the philosopher and the "ordinary" people have in making themselves intelligible to each other. But the true philosopher—the genuine philosopher, as opposed to the prejudiced "scholars" or philosophical laborers—will take this tension as an opportunity for self-overcoming; she will voluntarily take on "the burden and disgust" of "descending" into the mass, to engage in "the long and serious study of the average man" (*BGE* 26). I do not mean to endorse Nietzsche's lofty opinion of the philosopher and lowly opinion of the average person, not least because in these moments he certainly does *not* have in mind the distinction between professional scholars and nonacademics. But the tension between isolation and immersion is instructive when applied to analytic philosophy, which in one moment depicts itself as instructively idiosyncratic, as willing to think the thoughts that escape the mass of humankind,

and in the next moment, in the very method of conceptual analysis, tries to pass as representative, as speaking for "us."

If philosophers are, as Nietzsche says, advocates, not for "us" but, to borrow a metaphor that he applies to artists, for the cultural soil that they have fertilized and from which their work grows, then which we is Appiah representing (*GM* III:4)? If all philosophy is "involuntary and unconscious memoir," then what pre-theoretical commitments has his work excavated and made abstract? I am *not* working my way toward the too-easy suggestion that Appiah's cosmopolitanism proceeds from his Afro-European heritage, his upbringing on two continents, his current professional home in a third. He freely reports all this in various places, and his work deserves more than this slide from critical engagement into clinical diagnosis. I am instead working my way to a parallel but perhaps harder suggestion, perhaps working through Cambridge positivism, with its fidelity to the linguistic turn and its suspicion of the social, left in Appiah as large a deposit as any other affective attachment. Perhaps his intellectual approach to social phenomena was shaped by a philosophical education that encouraged him to write his first book in the philosophy of language.[24] I cannot help but think that someone with that training is much more likely to insist that the only real sciences are the natural sciences, or that the only real facts are the ones that can be described in the languages of the natural sciences.

This bias for the objects of "hard" science brings me to the second of the two prejudices that Nietzsche urges me to discuss: the mistrust of the "transitory, seductive, deceptive" world of appearance and the corresponding impulse to locate values in "the lap of Being, the intransitory, the . . . 'thing in itself'" (*BGE* 2). This mistrust translates into such corollary assumptions as that "the definite should be worth more than the indefinite, and mere appearance worth less than 'truth'" and that "a handful of 'certainty'" is preferable to 'a whole carload of beautiful possibilities" (*BGE* 81). I take this as one of Nietzsche's neo-Kantian deflations of Truth, of the (unattainable) property of those favored arrangements of symbols that accurately correspond to and represent the world as it exists prior to and independent of any perspective or representational scheme. But I will extend the point a step farther into a narrowing of the distinction between natural, or, as Ian Hacking says, *indifferent*, kinds, and *interactive* kinds.[25]

Kinds are sets of things about which we make generalizations, sets of things that behave in patterned ways; kind-concepts or kind-terms are the names for these sets. A common internal structure, explicable in the language of physics or chemistry or biology, causes the patterning that defines indifferent kinds. With interactive kinds the situation is somewhat different: these kinds are always human kinds—which is not to say that all human kinds are interactive—and human motivational sets *inspire* or motivate or encourage the patterning that defines them. To put it provocatively and a bit swiftly, indifferent kinds have causes, while interactive kinds have reasons. Natural kinds are reliable; unlike interactive kinds, their regularities do not depend on the acquiescence, participation, or agreement of fickle human agents. We can *create and abolish* interactive kinds, and do the same with tokens of the type that each kind represents—that is why they are interactive. To use one of Hacking's examples: having provided themselves at a certain point in their institutional (Foucault would say "disciplinary") history with the idea of child abuse social service workers, pediatricians, and school counselors then encourage certain people (clients, subjects) to see themselves not just as people who were in some fashion victimized as children but as a certain *type* of person, as an instance of or sufferer from a condition called child abuse. And seeing themselves in this way may cause the abused to behave in certain patterned ways.

None of this is to say, of course, that child abuse is not a real phenomenon, just that it owes its reality and persistence as *a* phenomenon to different conditions than, say, Jupiter does. Still, this different and less reliable reality can seem to philosophers like a debased reality, like a sham or counterfeit reality. And truths about these kinds of kinds can seem as if they are not really truths. Races, as I and I think many others understand them, may be interactive kinds: rather than proceeding from causes that reside in the austere realms of chemistry or physics, they proceed from reasons and motives, enunciable in the vocabularies of political economy, history, and psychology. True enough, the concept of race was originally presented as a natural kind term, a job we now know it cannot do. But to continue to focus on its inability to do this work is to privilege Truths about natural kinds over truths about the messy, transitory world of interactive kinds—where we most directly work out our prospects for life, death, joy, sorrow, deprivation, and flourishing. And in response to this focus and this bias toward Truth, I am encouraged to say with Nietzsche: "It is terrible to die of thirst in the ocean. Do you have to salt your truth so heavily that it does not even—quench thirst any more?" (*BGE* 81)

IV.

In a discarded draft for part of *Ecce Homo*, Nietzsche explains the difficulty that his work presents to would-be commentators.

To understand the most *abbreviated* language ever spoken by
a philosopher . . . one must follow the *opposite* procedure of
that generally required by philosophical literature. Usually
one must condense, or upset one's digestion; I have to be
diluted, liquefied, mixed with water. . . . I am *brief*; my readers
themselves must become long and comprehensive in order to
bring up and together all that I have thought, and thought
deep down. (*EH* appendix)

I have not been in a position to "dilute" Nietzsche's work. I have
sought instead to use it as I have been led to understand it by others
who have been long and comprehensive.[26] So I have been unable to say
much, when I have been able to say anything, about many issues in
Nietzsche scholarship that bear on what I have tried to do here. I have
said little about his distaste for nationalism, his undeserved reputa-
tion as the philosopher of Nazism, or his insistence on the future of
Europe; I have said even less about the relative levels of irony and
acquiescence I find in his (uneven) endorsements of traditional notions
of race and gender; I have only touched on the dispute between radical and traditional interpretations of his work, by revealing my own
view regarding the (Jamesian, neo-Kantian) status of truth in his
work; and I have said absolutely nothing about how to reconcile the
"great politics" of philosophic legislation and political power with the
radical democracy that I admire in Dewey. As I say, these are matters
to be dealt with at length and comprehensively.

My aim here has been to see how I might recover the Nietzsche
that brought me to philosophy, to see what he would have me say in
the presence of two figures who have profoundly shaped my intellectual life. My previous visits with these figures and their ideas were
almost always conducted in the company of Dewey, James, and DuBois
(among my canonical, which is to say my long-departed, teachers, and
setting aside, with the questions above, the matter of my other living
influences). I hope my engagement with Asante and Appiah has not
seemed malicious, but it is hard to judge this in proximity to Nietzsche's,
well, *vigorous* assaults on his targets. In deference to the possibility
that I have lapsed into emulating his sometimes-acrimonious approach
to criticism, I will close with one of his own self-exculpations: "I never
attack persons; I only avail myself of the person as of a strong magni-
fying glass that allows one to make visible a general but . . . elusive
[condition]" (*EH* "Wise" 7).

Notes

1. Assante and Appiah, my interlocutors here, are characters in my drama. I apologize for locking them into roles from the 1990 production.

2. Molefi K. Asante, *Kemet, Afrocentricity, and Knowledge* (Trenton: Africa World Press, 1990).

3. Asante, *Kemet*, 1.

4. Asante, *Kemet*, vi. Asante refers to inquiry so conducted as Africalogy, or "the afrocentric study of phenomena . . . related to Africa . . . based on the centrality of the African" (*Kemet*, 14).

5. Molefi Asante, Review of *Afrocentrism and World Politics*, by Errol Anthony Henderson, *African American Review* 31:3 (Fall 1997): 505–507.

6. Molefi Kete Asante, "The African American as African," *Diogenes* 45 (Winter 1998): 39–51, emphasis added.

7. See Molefi Kete Asante, *Afrocentricity* (Trenton: Africa World Press, 1988), 28–30. Nnamdi Azikiwe (1904–1996) was the first president of Nigeria (1963–1966).

8. Asante, *Kemet*, 35.

9. Friedrich Nietzsche, *Unfashionable Observations*, trans. Richard Gray (Stanford, CA: Stanford University Press, 1995), 83–167.

10. I am thinking here of, for example, the ASCAC—The Association for the Study of Classical African Civilizations). See Asa Hilliard, "Pedagogy in Ancient Kemet," in *Kemet and the African Worldview*, ed. Maulana Karenga and Jacob Carruthers (Los Angeles: University of Sankore Press, 1986), 131–150.

11. See Stanley Cavell, *A Pitch of Philosophy* (Cambridge, MA: Harvard University Press, 1994) 15, 50, 166; Stanley Cavell, *Conditions Handsome and Unhandsome: The Constitution of Emersonian Perfectionism* (Chicago: University of Chicago Press, 1988).

12. Asante, *Afrocentricity*, 27.

13. For another possible Afrocentric line on this problem, see Rhett S. Jones, "The End of Africanity? The Bi-Racial Assault on Blackness," *The Western Journal of Black Studies*, 18:4 (Winter 1994): 201–11.

14. Asante, *Afrocentricity*, 29.

15. K. Anthony Appiah, *In My Father's House* (New York: Oxford University Press, 1992). For an earlier discussion, see Appiah's "The Uncompleted Argument: DuBois and the Illusion of Race," in *"Race," Writing, and Difference*,

ed. Henry Louis Gates (Chicago: University of Chicago Press, 1986), 21–37. See also K. Anthony Appiah, "Race, Culture, Identity: Misunderstood Connections," in *Color Conscious*, ed. *K. Anthony Appiah and Amy Gutman* (Princeton, NJ: Princeton University Press, 1996), 30–105. For my dissent, see Paul C. Taylor, "Appiah's Uncompleted Argument: DuBois and the Reality of Race," *Social Theory and Practice* 26:1 (Spring 2000): 103–28. For the larger view that motivates the dissent and much of this chapter, see Paul C. Taylor, *Race: A Philosophical Introduction* (Cambridge, UK: Polity Press, 2003).

16. Ross Posnock, *Color and Culture* (Cambridge, MA: Harvard University Press, 2000); Paul Gilroy, *Against Race* (Cambridge, MA: Harvard University Press, 2000); Naomi Zack, *Race and Mixed Race* (Philadelphia: Temple University Press, 1993).

17. Appiah, "Race, Culture, Identity," 103–104.

18. Friedrich Nietzsche, *Beyond Good and Evil*, trans. Walter Kaufmann (New York: Random House, Vintage Books, 1966).

19. Appiah, "Race," 104.

20. For an explanation of this argument, though in the context of what she calls cultural rather than racial identity, see Paula Moya, "Postmodernism, 'Realism,' and the Politics of Identity," in *Reclaiming Identity*, Paula Moya and Michael Hames-Garcia (Berkeley: University of California Press, 2000), 67–101.

21. Appiah, "Race," 38.

22. Appiah, "Race," 41.

23. See W. E. B. DuBois, "The Conservation of Races," in *The Oxford W. E. B. DuBois Reader*, ed. Eric Sundquist (New York: Oxford University Press, 1996), 38–47.

24. K. Anthony Appiah, *Assertion and Conditionals* (New York: Cambridge University Press, 1985).

25. Ian Hacking, *The Social Construction of What?* (Cambridge, MA: Harvard University Press, 1999).

26. See Maudemarie Clark, *Nietzsche on Truth and Philosophy* (New York: Cambridge University Press, 1991); Keith Ansell-Pearson, *An Introduction to Nietzsche As Political Thinker* (New York: Cambridge University Press, 1994); Peter Berkowitz, *Nietzsche: The Ethics of an Immoralist* (Cambridge, MA: Harvard University Press, 1995), with reservations about his framework, but with gratitude for his close readings of individual texts; Arthur Danto, *Nietzsche As Philosopher* (New York: Columbia University Press, 1965); also see Walter Kaufmann's many notes in his translations of *BGE* and *EH*.

6

Nietzsche's Proto-Phenomenological Approach to the Theoretical Problem of Race

DANIEL W. CONWAY

Our Europe of today, being the arena of an absurdly sudden attempt at a radical mixture of classes, and *hence* races, is therefore skeptical in all its heights and depths.

—Nietzsche, *Beyond Good and Evil*, 208

Nietzsche was not the first philosopher to cultivate a nomadic existence. Nor was he the first to credit his itinerancy with the development of a powerful, new critical perspective. But he was certainly among the first of the philosophers-errant to allow his travels to fund his reflections on race. Although presented to his readers as a solitary wanderer, he usually sojourned in the company—if not always the companionship—of other travelers, some of whom regaled him with tales of their previous journeys.[1] He typically frequented destinations, moreover, that were popular with other travelers: Sils-Maria, Zürich, Nice, Venice, Genoa, Turin, and so on.[2] Like many of these fellow travelers, Nietzsche restlessly sought climates, locales, and meteorological conditions that would be ever more conducive to the restoration and/or amplification of health.[3]

While his journeys did not admit of an impressive degree of adventure,[4] they did afford him the opportunity to observe a wide range and diversity of human types, at a time when Europeans enjoyed an unprecedented mobility. Whether sitting quietly in a railroad car, dining in the common room of a *pension*, or strolling alongside other sunseekers, he witnessed firsthand the effects of the "racial mixing" that characterized Europe, or so he believed, in the late nineteenth century. (He did so, moreover, under the conditions he most preferred in an observational setting: relative anonymity and a safe, clinical distance from his unsuspecting research subjects.) As a direct result of these observations, in fact, he was able to supplement his deeply personal psychological conjectures with evidence of a more recognizably sociological nature.

It is safe to say, in fact, that Nietzsche's travels directly and indirectly influenced his reflections on race. He succeeded, for example, in discerning a broad range of differences between and among supposedly fixed racial designations.[5] The attunement he displayed in general toward subtle shadings, fine gradations, and unnoticed variations similarly informed his appreciation for the wide diversity of human types. He was thus able to infuse the nascent science of race with a welcome measure of scholarly objectivity. This is not to say, of course, that his reflections on race were innocent of ideology and idiosyncrasy, for they were not.[6] But he was more willing than most to accommodate the growing body of empirical evidence and, on that basis, to question the most popular (and rigid) racial theories of his day. He consequently accepted as a non-negotiable fact of his own descent the "racial mixing" that rival theorists feared as an imminent threat to racial purity (*GS* 377). He was no doubt encouraged in his acceptance of this putative fact by the testimony of his fellow travelers, whose persistent pursuit of "health" may have confirmed his suspicions of a pandemic degeneration of European culture.[7]

The influence of Nietzsche's travels on his reflections on race is especially striking in light of the skeptical, iconoclastic bent of his thinking. As we see in the epigraph to this chapter, he viewed the recent trend toward skepticism—including, presumably, his own—as a result of the "racial mixing" that had plunged European culture into disarray. Indeed, if any philosopher of the nineteenth century would have been inclined to conclude that race is simply an illusion, or that racial designations are reducible without remainder to ideological proclamations, Nietzsche should have been that philosopher. His current standing as the patron saint of postmodern philosophy is by no means undeserved. He was generally suspicious of the pet categories and dichotomies employed by philosophers, and he delighted in exposing the prejudices at work behind the scenes of most philosophical explanations. He also was an unabashed champion of science, at least as he imagined its ideal practice, and he regularly urged philosophers, historians, and psychologists to conform more strictly to the stringent methods and strict naturalism of the emerging scientific paradigm. He was deeply skeptical, therefore, of the most influential theories of race in circulation at the time, especially those that linked racial identity to the unbroken continuity of supposedly pure bloodlines of familial descent. He sought not only to expose these theories as motivated by nationalistic, xenophobic concerns but also to treat their currency as symptomatic of the spread of European decadence.

In light of his skepticism and iconoclasm, it would be plausible to assume that Nietzsche was at least tempted to conclude, like Herder,[8] that race is simply a fiction. If he was so tempted, however, his writings bear no trace of it. In fact, the diversity and variations he observed while traveling only fortified his belief in the underlying reality of race. As he suggests in the passage from which the epigraph to this chapter was extracted, in fact, Nietzsche traced his skepticism to the "absurdly sudden" miscegenation that largely defines "our Europe of today." He apparently regarded both the races undergoing mixture and the mixture itself as all-too-real. He consequently forwarded what might be called a "racial formalism," which attributes the cultivation of race to the operation of a coherent, self-perpetuating system of acculturation. In developing his racial formalism, he broke decisively with the blood-based accounts of race that were popular in his day. As a result, he may be considered one of the first theorists of race to resist the ideological allure of materialist explanations and classifications.

But Nietzsche is just as interesting for what he did not resist. While openly suspicious of appeals to blood purity, he was nevertheless convinced that race inheres in, and is transmitted by, the body. He hoped, in fact, that his formalism would position him to theorize the "material" component of race, which in turn would enable a more productive, scientific engagement with the racialized body. Rather than reject all appeals to the biological transmission of traits, he recommended that the science of race acquaint itself more honestly with the growing body of empirical evidence and avail itself of more creative methods of scientific inquiry. In particular, he urged a proto-phenomenological attention to the body, which, he believed, would reveal ever more basic expressions of racial embodiment. It is in this promotion of a contestatory union of philosophy and science, or so I maintain, that his most enduring contribution to contemporary race theory lies.

Race and the Priority of Form

The imposition of form onto matter is a familiar, even dominant, motif of Nietzsche's philosophy. Virtually every artifact or achievement that he praises, in areas of endeavor as diverse as philosophy, poetry, music, the plastic arts, religion, statecraft, and morality, is the product—or so he believes—of an imposition of form onto matter. So, too with his account of the dynamics of racial cultivation: Race is the product of the imposition of a single, overarching cultural form onto an otherwise undefined collection of families, clans, tribes, and peoples. Although its material component is by no means insignificant, a race derives its identity and sense of destiny from the cultural form it receives. The cultivation of race thus involves the incorporation of diverse human types (or materials) under a single system (or form) of acculturation. The greater the diversity of human types collected under the umbrella of a single system of acculturation, the richer the resulting culture and, as Nietzsche sees it, the *purer* the race it produces.

Nietzsche's racial formalism thus accounts for his uniquely prescriptive use of the term *race*. He often treated race as an achievement, as a mark of distinction that elevated certain peoples and nations above others. The races that he most admired all played an active, decisive role in constituting themselves as such. They assumed responsibility for the cultural form imposed on them and thereby arrogated to themselves a measure of control over the direction of their future development. Upon acceding to racehood, he believed, a people or nation thus acquires privileges and responsibilities previously unknown to it. As an example of the possibilities that are uniquely available to genuine races, Nietzsche draws an instructive contrast between the Hebrew Bible and the Christian New Testament:

> The Bible in general suffers no comparison [with the Gospels]. One is among Jews: *first* consideration to keep from losing the thread completely. The simulation of "holiness," which has really become genius here, never even approximated elsewhere in books or among men, this counterfeit of words and gestures as an *art*, is not the accident of some individual talent or other or of some exceptional character. This requires *race*. (A 44)

The clear implication of this passage is that we should not expect the New Testament to measure up to the Hebrew Bible. The latter is a work of unparalleled "genius," a work of "art" so inspired that it cannot be traced to the accident of individual achievement. Art of this magnitude can be produced only by a genuine race, of whose nobility it is a natural—and indeed necessary—expression. Genius and art are possible, he thus implies, only for a race. Lesser peoples and nations may be graced by an "individual talent" or "some exceptional character," but only by accident. True genius and art are never accidental but are cultivated through generations of self-imposed discipline and order. He thus maintains that the success of the Jews in constituting themselves as a race has very little to do with their success in safeguarding the purity of their blood. Rather, he explains, the Jews have equipped themselves with a durable apparatus of acculturation, which enables them to withstand the fads and fashions that have seduced the lesser peoples and nations of modern Europe:

> The Jews . . . know how to prevail even under the worst conditions (even better than under favorable conditions), by means of virtues that today one would like to mark as vices—thanks above all to a resolute faith that they need not be ashamed before "modern ideas"; they change, *when* they change, always only . . . according to the principle, "as slowly as possible." (*BGE* 251)

As these extracts confirm, however, Nietzsche's admiration for the Jews was by no means unadulterated. The Jews are a race, to be sure, and in fact the purest race known to European modernity. But they *became* a race by implementing questionable formative measures (e.g., "simulation," "counterfeiting," "prevailing under the worst conditions"), which he suspects have prevented other races—especially the Aryan-European race—from simultaneously flourishing.[9]

It is by virtue of his racial formalism that Nietzsche departs most dramatically from the anti-Semites and Aryan enthusiasts to whom he expressly opposes himself. As we have seen, his formalism authorizes him to reject the common wisdom of his day and to derange conventional evaluations of racial superiority. He lauds the Jews as being "beyond any doubt the strongest, toughest, and *purest* race now living in Europe" (*BGE* 251),[10] while he describes the Germans, the self-styled claimants to pure Aryan descent, as "a people of the most monstrous mixture and medley of races" (*BGE* 244).[11] Those anti-Semites who vowed to protect the purity of their Aryan blood—including Bernhard Förster, the inept colonial governor and cowardly suicide who became Nietzsche's brother-in-law in 1885[12]—were roused to action only well after the degeneration of Europe's Aryan-influenced culture had commenced. It is no coincidence, in fact, that the Aryan myth gained a wider currency at a time when, according to Nietzsche, the undoing of the Aryan conquest of Europe was already well under way.

Nietzsche's formalist challenge thus announces his intention to place into question the very notion of race itself. Rival theories of race are burdened not only by the ideological ends they are obliged to serve but also by a naïve, unimaginative understanding of what race is and comprises. By appealing to blood purity, rival theorists can at best explain the transmission of only the most superficial physical resemblances among (some) members of a race. A blood-based theory of race may therefore succeed in partially certifying the identity of a family, tribe, or clan, but it cannot account for what any family, tribe, or clan shares in common with the other subgroups that compose a single race. Blood-based theories are therefore unable to account for the most interesting and enduring aspects of race. What makes a race distinctive, Nietzsche maintained, is not purity of blood but the purity of a single cultural form distributed across an aggregate of otherwise unrelated families, tribes, and clans.

Nietzsche thus believed that his formalism uniquely accounts for the *dynamic* character of racial cultivation. According to his theory, races are made, not born. (They are also—and just as surely—unmade, as their regnant systems of acculturation naturally decay.) Races typically strengthen and purify themselves through the continued absorption of diverse "materials," usually through the conquest and assimilation of neighboring tribes and families.

Nietzsche's controversial appropriation of the mythic Aryan conquest of Europe serves his philosophy as both the example *par excellence* of racial cultivation and the blueprint for his own political designs.[13] On his rendition of this myth, Europe received its familiar form and identity as a consequence of raids conducted by a marauding "blond" barbarian race against "dark-haired" aboriginal peoples (*GM* I:5).[14] The Aryan conquest of aboriginal Europe subjected a vast population of disparate tribes and peoples to a single system of acculturation. From this massive imposition of form onto matter emerged the uniquely European (or Aryan-European) race that Nietzsche admired and wished to conserve.[15]

He was therefore concerned that European decadence threatens to undo the formative, unifying effects of the Aryan conquest. Immediately after identifying the Aryans as "the conqueror and *master race*," he conspicuously wonders if they are not in fact "succumbing physiologically" (*GM* I:5). The disintegration of European culture can be traced, he further speculates, to a belated *"counterattack"* on the part of the "suppressed" aboriginal peoples of Europe (*GM* I:5). It is with this disintegration in mind that he submits his judgment that the contemporary "descendants . . . of the pre-Aryan populace" of Europe in fact "represent the *regression* of humankind" (*GM* I:11). This "regression" appears most noticeably in the formerly noble Germans, for "between the old Germanic tribes and us Germans there exists hardly a conceptual relationship, let alone one of blood" (*GM* I:11). In what is perhaps his most direct affront to the anti-Semites of his day, he proposes—albeit "cheerfully"—to restore the Germans to their former glory by authorizing their selective intermarriage with Jews (*BGE* 251).[16]

Regardless of what one may think of Nietzsche's story of the rise and fall of Europe, the priority he assigns to cultural form is indisputable. In light of this priority, in fact, the oft-remarked racial diversity of late nineteenth-century Europe can be placed in its proper context. What these various nations and peoples all share in common is the more basic inheritance of a single, unifying culture. They stand out as "separate" peoples and nations only against the unifying backdrop of European culture, even (or especially) as this backdrop noticeably decays. That the nation-states of modern Europe neglect and even renounce their common inheritance is evidence not of their independence and autarky but of their devolution into petty, squabbling splinter states (*GS* 377).

Nietzsche regularly acknowledges the importance of the "material" component of race,[17] but he rarely treats its contribution as decisive, especially in comparison to that of cultural form. While it is true that he admires those races whose cultural forms encompass a wide diversity of human types, he values none of these constituent types in its own right. He values each people, tribe, clan or family only for its unique contribution to the overall diversity of the material component of race. Once absorbed and assimilated into the newly formed race, moreover, these constituent types exhaust the (purely instrumental) value of their contributions to its material component. Indeed, he tends to treat the material component of race as little more than an anonymous, undefined substratum, onto which the ennobling form of race is amorally imprinted. This is why he typically neglects to name the constituent peoples who contribute to the formation of any particular race. Whether discussing the fashioning of his beloved "Greeks," or of the original state, or of the mythic, Europe-defining Aryans, or of the envisioned pan-European race of the future, he focuses almost exclusively on cultural form.[18]

The Dangers and Deficiencies of Nietzsche's Racial Formalism

Nietzsche presents his racial formalism as motivated in part by the unique historical conditions of late modernity, in particular, the widespread decay of European races and culture. He thus reduces what he calls the "problem of race" to the problem of *decadence* (*BGE* 264), which he understands as an inherited organic affliction that burdens successor generations with a degenerate set of bodily traits.[19] As the formerly unifying culture of Europe decays, he thus maintains:

> The Europeans are becoming more similar to each other; they become more and more detached from the conditions under which races originate that are tied to some climate or class; they become increasingly independent of any *determinate* milieu that would like to inscribe itself for centuries in body and soul with the same demands. Thus an essentially supra-national and nomadic type of man is gradually coming up, a type that possesses, physiologically speaking, a maximum of the art and power of adaptation as its typical distinction. (*BGE* 242)

This (self-serving) account of his transitional historical epoch in turn licenses his allegiance to the political ideals that have earned him such widespread disdain. Estranged by rampant miscegenation from the "determinate" settings in which they acquired and expressed their racial identities, these "supra-national" and "nomadic" Europeans now lead an indeterminate, aimless existence. As a result, they now require cruel leadership, the assignment of menial tasks, and the form-giving imprint of culture:

> [T]he overall impression of such future Europeans will prob-ably be that of manifold garrulous workers who will be poor in will, extremely employable, and as much in need of a master and commander as of their daily bread. But while the democra-tization of Europe leads to the production of a type that is prepared for *slavery* in the subtlest sense, in single, exceptional cases the *strong* human being will have to turn out stronger and richer than perhaps ever before—thanks to the absence of prejudice from his training, thanks to the tremendous mani-foldness of practice, art, and mask. (*BGE* 242)

Fortunately for European posterity, however, the very conditions that have allowed for "the democratization of Europe" are also likely to pro-duce the "tyrants" who will provide this new breed of Europeans with the cultural determination they lack (*BGE* 242).

Nietzsche's formalism thus conveys a disturbingly cavalier indif-ference toward the peoples and tribes—not to mention the individuals—

who constitute the material component of race. This indifference finds its most notorious expression in his occasional references to racial culti-vation as exercises in *breeding* [*Züchtung*]. In one particularly troubling passage, he explains that

> the philosopher as *we* understand him, we free spirits—as the man of the most comprehensive responsibility who has the conscience for the over-all development of man—this philoso-pher will make use of religions for his project of breeding and education, just as he will make use of whatever political and economic states are at hand. (*BGE* 61)

As I have argued elsewhere, Nietzsche's references to breeding cannot simply be dismissed as either careless or rhetorically amplified.[20] By modeling the cultivation of races on the domestication of animals, he implies that the recipients of cultural form are *mere* animals, ante-cedently lacking in meaningful culture and education. (I will simply note in passing that even animals do not deserve to be regarded as raw materials for human design and experimentation.)

That these constituent human types already possess form and order of their own, as evidenced by the wealth of their investments in tradition, culture, ritual, education, and history, is of no lasting concern to Nietzsche and the amoral lawgivers whom he hopes will preside over the "cultivation of a new caste that will rule Europe" (*BGE* 251). Indeed, the overall effect of his references to "breeding" is to render anonymous the constituent peoples and tribes who furnish the material component of race. If form is everything, then matter is significant only insofar as it aptly receives the imprint of form. The anonymity of these constituent peoples and tribes in turn obscures—and perhaps erases—the violence involved in collecting them under a novel appa-ratus of acculturation.

Nietzsche's experiment with racial formalism thus essays a cautionary tale for contemporary theorists who are inclined, even with good intentions, to circumvent or minimize the material com-ponent of race. Perhaps because he endeavored to provide a credible alternative to blood-based accounts of race, his formalism betrays some of the very defects that fault these rival accounts. Although he decries the petty nationalism and xenophobia that motivate these rival accounts (*GS* 377), he produces an alternative theory of racial cultivation that is similarly objectionable on moral grounds. In par-ticular, we might say, his formalism threatens, in the words of Anthony Appiah, to "go imperial," dominating not only people of other identities, but the other identities, whose shape is exactly what makes each of us what we individually and distinctively are.[21]

In Nietzsche's case, of course, the threat of imperialism is not idle, even if it is fantastic. He sincerely hoped to contribute to the cultivation of a ruling elite that would preside over the renewal of a pan-European empire (*BGE* 251).[22]

Bodily Cultivation and the Reality of Race

It is certainly fair at this point to wonder if Nietzsche's formalism delivers an account of race at all. If race is understood to involve the biological transmission of physical traits, then his formalism sponsors, at best, a minimal conception of race. On the one hand, perhaps, he should be commended for developing an account of race that neither exaggerates nor ignores the role of biologically transmitted characteristics. On the other hand, the priority he assigns to cultural form suggests that by *race* he actually means something more like *ethnicity*.[23] Has he rescued the science of race from its ideological nonage, or has he in fact supplanted it with a science of culture?

According to Nietzsche, a race is distinguishable from other (i.e., lesser) peoples and nations by the apparatus of acculturation that empowers it to project its will into the future. It is the unique work of acculturation, he further believes, to equip individual bodies with a trusty set of instincts, on which members of a particular race may pre-reflectively rely for their most basic dispositions of embodiment. He thus avers that

> one cannot erase from the soul of a human being what his ancestors liked most to do and did most constantly. . . . It is simply not possible that a human being should *not* have in his body the qualities and preferences of his parents and ancestors, whatever appearances may suggest to the contrary. This is the problem of race. (*BGE* 264)

Nietzsche consequently treats the making (and unmaking) of race as largely a matter of educating (or not) the body. While recounting the cultural exploits of his beloved Greeks, for example, he draws from their success the following generalization:

> [A] breeding of feelings and thoughts alone is almost nothing (this is the great misunderstanding underlying German education [Bildung], which is wholly illusory); one must first persuade the body [Leib]. Strict perseverance in significant and exquisite gestures [Gebärden] together with the obligation to live only with people who do not "let themselves go"—that is quite enough for one to become significant and exquisite, and in two or three generations all this becomes inward. (TI 9:47)

As this passage confirms, Nietzsche expressly identifies the body as the primary focus of the kind of education that will facilitate the development of a people or nation into a genuine race. The education of the body takes hold, he explains, only when the gestures in question "become inward," which can be accomplished, he believes, over only "two or three generations." The accession of a people or nation to racehood thus requires that the desired patterns of corporeality acquire the status and function of a new "second" nature. He consequently recommends a program of education that will equip individual bodies with a coherent, uniform set of pre-reflective habits and dispositions, which in turn will facilitate the transmission of acquired traits to successor generations. It is the uniformity of these traits across an entire population that allows for the consolidation and purification of a race.

Nietzsche's attention to the body's "significant and exquisite gestures," especially in contradistinction to its "thoughts and feelings," furthermore conveys his intention to address this program of education to an expression of corporeality that is generally regarded as too primitive to be receptive to education. He thus goes on to explain that

> it is decisive for the lot of a people and of humanity that culture should begin in the *right* place—*not* in the "soul" (as was the fateful superstition of the priests and half-priests): the right place is the body, gesture, diet, physiology; *the rest* follows from that. (TI 9:47)

That is, educators typically place the cart before the horse: they begin with the "soul" and fail accordingly. They unwittingly concern themselves with a body that is already equipped with the instincts that will enable it to flourish (or not) within a particular culture.[24] In contrast, he implies, an education that begins with the body will naturally encompass the "soul" in due course. (Although he does not say so here, he may mean to imply that an education that begins with the body will actually summon an educable soul into existence.) As this passage also confirms, a proper education of the body should begin with the most basic of bodily needs.

But what are these needs? Nietzsche's unusual attention to "gesture, diet, physiology" and the like may strike some readers as simply too idiosyncratic to merit serious consideration. His enthusiasm for the cultivation of "significant and exquisite gestures" may furthermore call to mind a finishing school for European dandies. Indeed, how can matters of such trivial concern figure into his grandiose plans for the renewal of a distinctly European race and culture?

Here we should note that the gestures in question are only indirectly indicative of the body whose education Nietzsche advocates. He is ultimately concerned, in fact, *not* with the visible body known to anatomists and laymen alike but with what might be called the "invisible" body—namely, the instinctual microstructure that informs and supports the living, animal organism.[25] With respect to this most basic expression of corporeal vitality, he explains,

> Every animal—therefore *la bête philosophe*, too—instinctively strives for an optimum of favorable conditions under which it can expend all its strength [*Kraft*] and achieve its maximal feeling of power [*Machtgefühl*]; every animal abhors, just as instinctively and with a subtlety of discernment that is "higher than all reason," every kind of intrusion or hindrance that obstructs or could obstruct this path to the optimum. (*GM* III:7)

His program of education—already novel in its primary focus on the body—is in fact dedicated to the training of the human animal organism, so that fully acculturated individuals might attain the "maximal feeling of power" that is consistent with their expenditures of strength. It is here, at this primal, instinctual level of corporeal expression, that races are made and unmade.[26]

It is not clear whether Nietzsche means for his attention to the "invisible" microstructure of animal instincts to contribute to a disclosure of the body in a "natural," preracialized expression of its corporeality. If this is what he means—and his relationship to nature is notoriously vexed—then his program for educating the body is probably vulnerable to the very objections that he lodges against other philosophers who find their way back to nature. His reflections on racial embodiment are welcome nonetheless, for they encourage us to consider the presence of race at ever more primitive (and ever subtler) expressions of corporeal existence. He may not position us to isolate the precise point at which bodies contract their defining racial characteristics (if this even makes sense), but he does help us to detect previously invisible indices of racial embodiment. Indeed, his speculations on the racial specificity of gesture find both confirmation and reprise in the influential research of Omi and Winant, whose observations of "racial etiquette" disclose the imprint of race on even the most rudimentary expressions of corporeal existence.[27]

Thus we see that the successful education of the body—and, so, the successful cultivation of race—is largely a matter of equipping individual bodies with the instincts they will need to participate prereflectively in the defining *ethos* of the race. So long as an apparatus of acculturation remains intact and operational, individuals naturally inherit the habits, customs, instincts, and other prereflective patterns of corporeality that were acquired by their ancestors. Acculturated to enact prereflective patterns of activity and response, individuals educated in accordance with this model may confidently minimize their reliance on conscious deliberations concerning their most basic bodily needs. They may do so, moreover, in full confidence that others will do so as well. It is with this model of acculturation in mind that Nietzsche identifies "attain[ing] the perfect automatism of instinct" as the "presupposition of all mastery, of every kind of perfection in the art of life" (*A* 57). If properly installed and faithfully maintained, that is, a governing system of instincts can transform a motley collection of families, clans, and tribes into a genuine race.

Nietzsche thus asserts that *culture* performs the work of racial transmission that rival theorists prefer to assign to blood. In what is perhaps his most novel contribution to our understanding of the dynamics of racial cultivation, he insists that race is a characteristic of individual bodies, but only insofar as these bodies have been educated within particular systems of acculturation. Bodies propagate the defining characteristics of race, but not by means of the blood that circulates within them.

On the one hand, then, we should fully expect racialized bodies to resemble one another in discernible ways. Notwithstanding the priority he assigned to cultural form, Nietzsche was by no means inattentive to outward, physical expressions of race.[28] On the other hand, these resemblances inhere *not* in the outward, physical markers—such as skin, eye, and hair color, and cranial and facial morphology—that typically inform racial classifications but in more primitive expressions of corporeality, such as gesture, habit, bearing, and custom. He apparently means to imply, moreover, that these subtler indices of corporeality, on which his program of education trains its focus, furnish the unifying backdrop against which the more familiar physical markers of racial identity are discernible as such.[29] If bodies contract their racial identity in their most primitive expressions of corporeal existence, then perhaps it is this background source of uniformity that encourages in some observers the illusion of a more uniform distribution of outward, physical markers. Although he does not say so, his attention to the "invisible" body may help explain the persistence of racial classifications ostensibly based on stereotypical physical markers.

To be sure, Nietzsche's reflections on racial embodiment are at best suggestive. His insights, albeit promising, provide only a sketchy account of how and when individual bodies contract their racial characteristics. His Lamarckian sympathies further complicate his reception by a scientific establishment that favors a more recognizably Darwinian account of racial cultivation. Still, his attention to the microstructure of the "invisible" body provides the science of race with a promising agenda for its future research.

While it would be anachronistic to situate Nietzsche in the tradition of existential phenomenology, he certainly belongs at or near its historical wellspring. His influence on the formation and development of this tradition is undeniable, especially with respect to leading figures, most notably Heidegger. As we have seen, moreover, his attention to the "invisible" body contributes significantly to the articulation of a phenomenology of racial embodiment.[30] This influence should not surprise us. Nietzsche's brief to philosophers and scientists bears a strong family resemblance to the challenge presented by existential phenomenology—namely, to understand the body in its full complexity and contextuality. With particular respect to the dynamics of racial cultivation, he avers that philosophers and scientists have not yet engaged—much less explained—the phenomenon of embodiment in its most primitive expressions of animal existence. It is here, he believes, that the body receives its initial dose of education, including its acquisition of a distinctly racial identity.

Rejecting the crude biologism favored by rival theorists of race, Nietzsche instead advocates what might be called a proto-phenomenological account of embodiment. It is not biology per se that he rejects but the narrow, ideological biology practiced and endorsed by his unscientific contemporaries. As we shall see in the next section, his interest in the cultural transmission of acquired corporeal habits may encourage theorists of race to pursue their research outside the conventional bounds of the biological sciences.

A Nietzschean Perspective on the Science of Race

Nietzsche's greatest contribution to contemporary race theory may lie in his promotion of a mutually contestatory and mutually elevating relationship between philosophy and science. He both recommends a more scientific treatment of race *and* warns against the prejudices embedded in even the best of scientific practices. The spirit of mutually productive contestation is most visibly embodied in what he advertises as his contribution to the articulation of the "gay science" [*die fröhliche Wissenschaft*].

In order to appreciate Nietzsche's advocacy of the "gay science," let us consider his reflections on race in light of Anthony Appiah's controversial dismissal of race as an unscientific fiction. In the context of his attempt to "complete" W. E. B. DuBois's argument about race, Appiah famously concludes that

> the truth is that there are no races: there is nothing in the world that can do all we ask "race" to do for us. The evil that is done is done by the concept and by easy—yet impossible—assumptions as to its application. What we miss through our obsession with the structure of relations of concepts is, simply, reality.[31]

In arriving at this conclusion, Appiah appeals to the decisive status of contemporary scientific explanation, which, he believes, does not provide adequate evidentiary support for the supposed reality of race. In particular, he relies on the findings of the biological sciences, which, he suggests, either command a unique access to what is real or uniquely prevent us from mistaking language and/or textuality for reality.[32]

Appiah's proffered completion of DuBois's uncompleted argument has drawn a great deal of comment and criticism. From Nietzsche's point of view, however, there need be nothing objectionable about Appiah's appeal to the decisive status of scientific explanation, as long as the practice of science itself is treated as contestable. Although Nietzsche regularly demands that philosophy follow the methodological lead of the physical sciences, he also enjoins philosophers to subject the enabling prejudices of science to ongoing exposure.[33] So although Appiah's initial conclusions about race were perhaps too boldly stated, and too narrowly focused on current biological evidence,[34] his appeal to scientific explanation was not itself problematic. If our best scientific evidence fails to support what we believe we mean by "race," then certainly we must subject the concept of race—as well as its overlapping contexts of discourse—

to further scrutiny. At the same time, however, we would do well to investigate the nature and limitations of our best scientific evidence. Especially if construed fairly narrowly, biology may very well support the conclusion that race is an unscientific illusion. As Appiah's critics have variously pointed out, however, race is not simply a matter of biology—or at any rate should not simply be assumed to be. From a Nietzschean perspective, it would be welcome at this point in the discussion to conduct a genealogical inquiry into the historical conditions that have facilitated the installation of biology as the master discourse of scientific explanation. We might then be in a position to expose any unscientific prejudices that have contributed to the historically specific ascendency of the biological sciences as superior domains of scientific explanation.

In Essay III of *On the Genealogy of Morals*, Nietzsche exposes the "will to truth" [*der Wille zur Wahrheit*] that, according to him, animates every scholarly venture. Although the will to truth authorizes the scope and method of scientific investigation, it can do so only because it rests on a hidden *faith* in truth—namely, the "belief that truth is inestimable and cannot be criticized" (*GM* III:24). Owing to its untruthful reliance on an enabling faith in truth, the operation of the will to truth informs the scientific enterprise with a conservative, contractionary economy. Prompted by the will to truth, scholars not only seek the truth but also endeavor to do so within boundaries that are drawn as cleanly and narrowly as possible. This means that scholars do not typically pursue the truth wherever their research might lead them, for they always seek the truth in tandem with their (equally zealous) efforts to circumscribe the relevant domain of inquiry. Although conventional scholars may appear to be, and even describe themselves as, daring and intrepid, they rarely pursue their quarry beyond familiar disciplinary boundaries. Their will to truth recoils from uncertainty and ambiguity just as surely (and naturally) as it advances upon truth.

As an antidote to the contractionary impulse of the will to truth, Nietzsche recommends the practice of what he calls the "gay science," an example of which he supposedly displays in *On the Genealogy of Morals* (*GM* P7). The desired effect of the gay science is to exert a countervailing, expansionary force on the pursuit of truth, such that "new" truths might be discovered via experimental methods in nontraditional fields of inquiry.[35] Nietzsche associates this countervailing force with the airy lightness of his "cheerfulness" [*Heiterkeit*], which he contrasts with the leaden weight of his scholarly "seriousness" [*Ernst*] (*GM* P7). As the union of *Heiterkeit* and *Ernst* suggests, moreover, the aim of the gay science is not in fact revolutionary.[36] Rather than disrupt or subvert conventional scientific practice, the gay science endeavors instead to nudge scholars toward and across the boundaries of the comfort zones in which they instinctively enclose themselves and their research.

While Nietzsche's readers tend to emphasize the *gaiety* of the gay science (i.e., its "cheerfulness"), its *scientific* pedigree (i.e., its "seriousness") is equally integral to its practice. (He acknowledges as much when he volunteers that he too has faith in truth, even as he attempts to steer the will to truth into collision with itself (*GM* III: 24).) Whatever else it may be or involve, the gay science is and must remain a serious truth-seeking and truth-telling enterprise.[37] Rather than dispense with all established standards of logic, rigor, and methodicity, the practice of the gay science extends the application of these standards into domains of inquiry that are not widely recognized as "scientific" in the strictest, purest sense of the term. It does so by opposing the disambiguating, self-enclosing impulses at work in any scientific venture. Practitioners of the gay science thus seek the truth outside the disciplines to which its pursuit is usually confined.

There may be no better example of this expansionary impulse than the operation of genealogy itself, which Nietzsche appropriates as a novel method for ascertaining the *"origin* of our moral prejudices" (*GM* P:2). Noting the failures of predecessor genealogists of morality (*GM* I:1), he collects evidence and borrows resources from unlikely precincts of scholarly inquiry, including etymology, psychology, sociology, and ethnography. In doing so, he neither abandons nor neutralizes the will to truth that motivates his inquiry. If anything, *his* will to truth is emboldened by the "cheerfulness" that allows him to pursue his quarry where more conventional scholars fear to tread.

If Nietzsche is right about the contractionary economy of the will to truth, then we should certainly expect Appiah to appeal to biology, narrowly construed, and conclude that race is a fiction. Doing so not only places Appiah squarely within the mainstream practice of established science but also implicates him in the self-certifying prejudices to which scientists are naturally prey. What the science of race needs at such a contractionary moment, just as it needed at the time of Nietzsche's initial intervention, is an expansionary infusion of gay science. The will to truth must be faced with its own untruthfulness. Theorists of race must be convinced to suffer the ambiguity that invariably attends the expansion of scientific exploration into less familiar fields of inquiry.

Rather than simply accept Appiah's initial conclusion, that is, we might treat it as an occasion to call into question the articulation of scientific explanation that supports it. If anything, Appiah's provocative challenge illustrates just how unsatisfying it is to conceive of race in narrow biological terms. Perhaps unwittingly, in fact, he has exposed the perils involved in reducing the project of scientific explanation to a narrow construal of the biological sciences. If scientific inquiry is to remain true to its self-avowed naturalism, then it will eventually need to transgress the familiar (and very recently circumscribed) confines of biology and pursue the questions of race and embodiment in other, less strictly defined fields of investigation. As the trajectory of Appiah's own research confirms,[38] a commitment to scientific naturalism will lead us to pursue the question of race in fields as diverse as sociology, geography, demography, anthropology, and history.[39]

As Nietzsche's novel appropriation of genealogy is meant to convey, an expansion of the focus of this investigation need not oblige us to renounce our allegiance to scientific naturalism. When entering the domains of these social sciences, one need not surrender oneself to the dark forces of irrationalism or folk science. These fields too admit of rigorous empirical investigation, even if the models of inquiry native to them may be less clearly defined than those of the biological sciences. The proto-phenomenological turn that he recommends is thus designed to call science itself to order. His novel attention to the "invisible" microstructure of the body is intended not as a departure from scientific explanation but as a liberation of science from the artificial, self-observed limits of conventional treatments of the body (and so of race).

In the end, Nietzsche's approach to the problem of race will be most appealing to those scholars who are both mindful of the lack of scientific warrant for racial classifications and reluctant to dismiss race as a simple fiction or ideological construct. His attention to the "invisible" body encourages us to treat race as real, as inhering in observable traits of the body, which we are in turn encouraged to investigate in its phenomenological complexity. It is to his lasting credit, in fact, that he urged us to consider the body as it is educated—and racialized—in its most primitive expressions of corporeal vitality. Even if we do not accept his account of racial embodiment, we may certainly welcome the urgency of his call to revisit the body and reconsider its fluid capacities for agency and patiency.[40]

Notes

1. On one such occasion, related by Krell and Bates (1997), "Nietzsche clearly learned about Oaxaca from a group of Swiss colonists on vacation in Sils" (149). He later referred longingly to "the highlands of Mexico, near the

Pacific" in his letter to Köselitz of 14 August 1881 (*KSB* 6, #136, p. 113), and he extolled the climate of Oaxaca in his letter to Elisabeth of August 1883 (*KSB* 6, #453, p. 431).

2. I am indebted here to Gary Shapiro's (1989) apt depiction of Nietzsche as "the philosopher of the postal age, that is, of the era in which the universality of communication and transportation are taken for granted" (1).

3. Moore (2004, 71–73).

4. Especially in light of Nietzsche's penchant for travel, it is fascinating to take note of the cities and countries that he did *not* visit. As Krell and Bates (1997) observe, "[Nietzsche] never left the continent of Europe. Nor did he ever see many of the places a good European would find 'essential' to his or her culture. He never made it to Paris or Barcelona, St. Petersburg or Copenhagen, London or Brussels or Prague" (1). The failure to visit Paris is almost incomprehensible for this unabashed Francophile. Despite noting that "much new seriousness, much new *passion* of the spirit, have migrated to Paris" (*TI* 8:4), he never saw fit to participate in this migration.

5. Nietzsche's reflections on race may be instructively contrasted with the views of his famously place-bound predecessor, Immanuel Kant. Whereas the former's travels exposed him to a wide range of human types, the latter's attachment to Königsberg limited his firsthand access to a wider database, thus ensuring his dependence on the empirical claims advanced in travelogues (see Bernasconi [2001, 14–15]). It is perhaps not too great a stretch, moreover, to conjecture that Kant's aversion to travel contributed to his articulation of a relatively rigid theory of race. Indeed, he believed that races, once exspeciated, are permanent and unchanging (Kant [2001, 41–43]; see also Bernasconi [2001, 23–24]). For his own part, Nietzsche regarded all races as works in progress, as responding subtly to shifts and stimuli in their surrounding environment.

6. For a survey of Nietzsche's cosmopolitan, Eurocentric, and Germanocentric prejudices, see Conway (2002b), 187–90).

7. Moore (2004, 71–73).

8. Herder (2000, 23–26).

9. I develop this argument in Conway (2002a, 185–90).

10. Emphasis added.

11. See Schank (2000, 51–60, 73–88).

12. See MacIntyre (1992, 119–48); Lampert (2001, 255–57).

13. Cancik (1997) persuasively maintains that Nietzsche's plan for a new European order is modeled on his earlier account of the origin of the Greeks as an identifiable race or nation. As Cancik explains, this account denies the popular myth of a progenitor race of "pure" Greeks, claiming instead that the various peoples and tribes who eventually acquired a Greek identity did so

only when they came to Greece and developed under the discipline of Greek culture and custom (55–58). Cancik thus traces the racism inherent in Nietzsche's plan for a unified Europe to this earlier account of the "origin" of the racial identity of the Greeks (59–60).

14. Nietzsche's etymological discussion in Essay I of *GM* is intended in large part to demonstrate that specific terms denoting "nobility" in Greek, Latin, and Gaelic corroborate this theory of a "blond" (or an Aryan) conquest of "darker" aboriginal races, tribes, and peoples (*GM* I:5). His notorious admiration for the "blond beast" is directly attributable to its alleged role in producing a distinctly European race, which successfully blended the most desirable traits of the conqueror race with those of the tribes and peoples it conquered. He honors the "blond beast," that is, as the unwitting architect of the European race and culture, as inadvertently wringing order from chaos. That is why some of the races in whom Nietzsche celebrates the form-giving predation of the "blond beast"— most notably the "Roman, Arabic, and Japanese nobility"—do not express the outward characteristics typically associated with a blond race (*GM* 1:11).

15. My discussion of Nietzsche's references to an Aryan conquest of Europe is generally indebted to Schank (2000, 51–60).

16. See Lampert (2001, 255–57).

17. He goes so far as to use the word *Material*, as in the following passage: "To say it briefly (for a long time people will still keep silent about it): What will not be built any more henceforth, and cannot be built any more, is— a society [*Gesellschaft*] in the old sense of that word; to build that structure [*um diesen Bau zu bauen*], everything is lacking, above all the material [*Material*]. All of us are no longer material for a society" (*GS* 356).

18. His blueprint for European cultural renewal, for example, identifies by name only the Germans, French, and English. He also identifies the Jews, whom he does not consider a genuinely European race (*BGE* 250–56).

19. As this passage confirms, Nietzsche links the "problem of race" not to the threat of miscegenation but to the unalterable fact that all races are eventually subject to decline. Even the most robust apparatus of acculturation eventually must decay, thereby precipitating the demise of the culture and race it previously supported.

20. See Conway (2002b, 180–82).

21. Appiah and Gutmann (1996, 103).

22. For a discussion of "Nietzsche's empire," see Conway (2002a, 175–81.

23. For an instructive taxonomy, see Schank (2000, 147–49). Outlaw helpfully distinguishes between "race" and "ethnie" (136–37), where the former concept comprises "biologically transmitted physical factors," while in the latter "the constitutive factors that are shared (more or less) by members of the

group are for the most part cultural" (136). Outlaw thus understands "a 'race' to be wider, more encompassing than an 'ethnie' such that a particular 'race' can have a number of 'ethnies'" (136). See also Lott (1999, 56–57).

24. He consequently insists that this kind of education can aspire at best to a grand deception: "If one knows something about the parents, an inference about the child is permissible: any disgusting incontinence, any nook envy, a clumsy insistence that one is always right. [T]hat sort of thing must as surely be transferred to the child as corrupted blood; and with the aid of the best education one will at best deceive with regard to such a heredity" (*BGE* 264).

25. For a discussion of Nietzsche's investigation of the "invisible" body, see Conway (1997, 23–34).

26. For a careful account of Nietzsche's treatment of the body as a "sociocultural artifact," as "inscribed" by political forces and historical events, see Grosz (1994, 115–34).

27. See Omi and Winant (1986, 60–69). See also Alcoff (2001, 270–72).

28. In support of his assertion of an Aryan conquest of aboriginal Europe, for example, he remarks, "The same is true of virtually all Europe: the suppressed race has gradually recovered the upper hand again, in coloring, shortness of skull, perhaps even in the intellectual and social instincts" (*GM* I:5). While the resurgence of the "suppressed race" is observable in the accession of its defining physical traits, its most telling effect is the disintegration of the unifying cultural form that the original Aryan conquest provided. As these outward, physical traits accede, Nietzsche believes, the more subtle indices of European racehood recede from view.

29. On this point, Nietzsche's position is similar to that of DuBois: "[S]till, my tie to Africa is strong. On this vast continent were born and lived a large portion of my direct ancestors going back a thousand years or more. The mark of their heritage is upon me in color and hair. These are obvious things, but of little meaning in themselves; *only important as they stand for more real and more subtle differences from other men*" (116–117, emphasis added).

30. Nietzsche's attention to the prereflective racialization of the body anticipates, and instructively complements, Merleau-Ponty's attention to the "habitual body," especially as the latter's contribution is taken up and fortified by scholars such as Alcoff. I am particularly indebted to Alcoff for her extension of Merleau-Ponty's analysis to "postural attitudes and modes of perception taken in interactions with others whose identities are marked by gender, race, age, and so on" (2001, 271).

31. Appiah (2000, 134).

32. Appiah frames his essay on DuBois with an introductory—and approbatory—discussion of what "contemporary biologists" think about race (2000, 118), and a concluding—and dismissive—account of what "those of us in the

humanities," laboring "under Saussurian hegemony," make of race (134). Clearly preferring the findings of biology to those of the humanities circa 1985, Appiah completes DuBois's "uncompleted argument" and exposes race as an "illusion." In his later book, he makes a similar point about the biological basis for race: "I have no problem with people who want to use the word 'race' in population genetics . . . [T]here are biological races in some creatures, but not in us" (Appiah and Gutmann 1996, 73).

33. Nietzsche's charge to science—namely, that it continue to perfect its avowed commitment to naturalism—is echoed in his reproach of Spencer for proposing "adaptation" as the fundamental feature of life: "Thus the essence of life, its *will to power*, is ignored: one overlooks the essential priority of the spontaneous, aggressive, expansive, form-giving forces that give new interpretations and directions, although 'adaptation' follows only after this" (*GM* II:12).

34. In fairness to Appiah, it should be noted that his strongest, most controversial claims about race appear in a section of his essay called "Concluding Unscientific Postscript." The homage to Kierkegaard and the explicit avowal of his "unscientific" aims perhaps attest to a measure of self-reflection (or even irony) that Appiah's critics are not generally willing to grant him.

35. In his review of *On the Genealogy of Morals*, Nietzsche reveals that toward the end of each of the three essays, "in the midst of perfectly gruesome detonations, a *new* truth becomes visible every time among thick clouds" (*EH* "Books" *GM*).

36. See Schacht (1995, 190–92).

37. Ibid., 195–201.

38. Although he continues to maintain that "there are no races" in the sense—dependent upon the belief in "racial essences"—intended by thinkers "from Jefferson to Arnold" (Appiah and Gutmann 1996, 71), Appiah outlines an account of "racial identity" that draws heavily on evidence provided by research conducted not only in the social sciences but in phenomenology as well (76–80).

39. See Bernasconi (2001, 1–3).

40. I am grateful to the editors of this volume for their generous, instructive comments on earlier drafts of this chapter.

Works Cited

Alcoff, Linda Martín. 2001. "Toward a Phenomenology of Racial Embodiment." In *Race*, ed. Robert Bernasconi. Oxford: Blackwell, 267–83.

Appiah, Anthony. 2000. "The Uncompleted Argument: DuBois and the Illusion of Race." Reprinted in *The Idea of Race*, ed. Robert Bernasconi and Tommy L. Lott. Indianapolis, IN: Hackett, 118–35.

Appiah, K. Anthony, and Amy Gutmann. 1996. *Color Conscious: The Political Morality of Race*. Princeton, NJ: Princeton University Press.

Bernasconi, Robert. 2001. "Who Invented the Concept of Race? Kant's Role in the Enlightenment Construction of Race." In *Race*, ed. Robert Bernasconi. Oxford: Blackwell, 11–36.

Cancik, Hubert. 1997. "'Mongols, Semites, and the Pure-Bred Greeks': Nietzsche's Handling of the Racial Doctrines of his Time." In *Nietzsche and Jewish Culture*, ed. J. Golomb. London: Routledge, 55–75.

Conway, Daniel W. 1997. *Nietzsche's Dangerous Game: Philosophy in the Twilight of the Idols*. New York: Cambridge University Press.

Conway, Daniel W. 2002a. *"Ecce Caesar*: Nietzsche's Imperial Aspirations." In *Nietzsche, Godfather of Fascism?*, ed. Jacob Golomb and Robert S. Wistrich. Princeton, NJ: Princeton University Press, 173–95.

Conway, Daniel W. 2002b. "'The Great Play and Fight of Forces': Nietzsche on Race." In *Philosophers on Race: Critical Essays*, ed. Julie K. Ward and Tommy L. Lott. Oxford: Blackwell, 167–94.

DuBois, W. E. B. 1975. *Dusk of Dawn: An Essay Toward an Autobiography of a Race Concept*. New Brunswick, NJ: Transaction Publishers, 1984.

Grosz, Elizabeth. 1994. *Volatile Bodies: Toward a Corporeal Feminism*. St. Leonards, New South Wales, Australia: Allen & Unwin.

Herder, Johann Gottfried. 2000. *Ideas on the Philosophy of the History of Humankind*, excerpted and reprinted in *The Idea of Race*, ed. Robert Bernasconi and Tommy L. Lott. Indianapolis, IN: Hackett, 23–26.

Kant, Immanuel. 2001. "On the Use of Teleological Principles of Philosophy." In *Race*, ed. Robert Bernasconi. Oxford: Blackwell, 37–56.

Krell, David F., and Donald L. Bates. 1997. *The Good European: Nietzsche's Work Sites in Word and Image*. Chicago: University of Chicago Press.

Lampert, Laurence. 2001. *Nietzsche's Task: An Interpretation of Beyond Good and Evil*. New Haven, CT: Yale University Press.

MacIntyre, Ben. 1992. *Forgotten Fatherland: The Search for Elisabeth Nietzsche*. New York: Farrar, Straus, Giroux.

Moore, Gregory. 2004. "Nietzsche, Medicine, and Meteorology." In *Nietzsche and Science*, ed. Gregory Moore and Thomas H. Brobjer. Hampshire, England: Ashgate, 71–90.

Nietzsche, Friedrich. 1974. *The Gay Science*. Translated by Walter Kaufmann. New York: Random House/Vintage Books.

Nietzsche, Friedrich. 1980. *Sämtliche Werke: Kritische Studienausgabe in 15 Bänden*. Edited by G. Colli and M. Montinari. Berlin: dtv/de Gruyter.

Nietzsche, Friedrich. 1982a. *The Antichrist*. In *The Portable Nietzsche*. Edited and translated by Walter Kaufmann. New York: Viking Penguin.

Nietzsche, Friedrich. 1982b. *Twilight of the Idols*. In *The Portable Nietzsche*. Edited and translated by Walter Kaufmann. New York: Viking Penguin.

Nietzsche, Friedrich. 1986. *Sämtliche Briefe: Kritische Studienausgabe in 8 Bänden*. Edited by G. Colli and M. Montinari. Berlin: dtv/de Gruyter.

Nietzsche, Friedrich. 1989a. *Beyond Good and Evil: Prelude to a Philosophy of the Future*. Translated by Walter Kaufmann. New York: Random House/Vintage Books.

Nietzsche, Friedrich. 1989b. *On the Genealogy of Morals*. Translated by Walter Kaufmann and R. J. Hollingdale; *Ecce Homo*. Translated by Walter Kaufmann. New York: Random House/Vintage Books.

Omi, Michael, and Howard Winant. 1986. *Racial Formation in the United States: From the 1960s to the 1980s*. London: Routledge.

Outlaw, Lucius T. 1996. *On Race and Philosophy*. New York and London: Routledge.

Schacht, Richard. 1995. "How to Naturalize Cheerfully: Nietzsche's *Fröhliche Wissenschaft*." In *Making Sense of Nietzsche*, ed. Urbana: University of Illinois Press, 187–205.

Schank, Gerd. 2000. *"Rasse" und "Züchtung" bei Nietzsche*. Berlin: Walter de Gruyter.

Shapiro, Gary. 1989. *Nietzschean Narratives*. Bloomington: Indiana University Press.

7

The Price of the Ticket: A Genealogy and Revaluation of Race

JACQUELINE SCOTT

Friedrich Nietzsche was an outsider to, and critic of, traditional philosophy and proposed his own revaluation of it, while at the same time he proposed a positive philosophy whose motivating factor was the flourishing of the culture. In both the critical and positive aspects of philosophy, he wrote about race and how a revalued form of the concept might play a role in making the culture healthier. It is Nietzsche's revaluation of race that I will discuss in this chapter, in particular, what a revaluation of race might mean in the twenty-first century and what the ramifications for it might be.[1] First I will discuss the ways in which race has been conceived of as a problem by critical race theorists. Then I will argue that Nietzsche contended with a similar problem in his time and will highlight his method for addressing this problem: by doing a genealogy and revaluation of the concept of race. His genealogy and revaluation of race is inextricably bound to his larger genealogy and revaluation of moral values.

I will contend that both treatments of race and values are part of his attempt to act as a physician and treat his culture for the disease of decadence that was causing its decay. In the last section, I will evaluate the use of Nietzsche's treatments for decadence for the problems of race that plague our own culture. In particular, I will argue that Nietzsche's treatments serve as both helpful examples and cautionary tales for those of us who are concerned about the problem that race poses for African American cultures (and, by extension, other cultures). Specifically, I will maintain that Nietzsche's genealogy and revaluation of race is instructive for us (in both positive and negative senses) regarding issues of identity formation. I will focus on the price that I think we will have to pay for this revalued, healthier concept of race. It is the price of the ticket for a concept of race that allows for a fuller blossoming of both individual and communal identities and for an increased freedom from the internal and external constraints imposed by a static, stagnant notion of racial identity.

The Problem of Race

Everything now, we must assume, is in our hands; we have no right to assume otherwise. If we—and now I mean the relatively conscious whites and the relatively conscious blacks, who must, like lovers, insist on, or create, the consciousness of the others—do not falter in our duty now, we may be able, handful that we are, to end the racial nightmare, and achieve our country, and change the history of the world. If we do not now dare everything, the fulfillment of that prophecy, recreated from the Bible in song by a slave, is upon us: "God gave Noah the rainbow sign, No more water, the fire next time!"[2]

Those of us who care about the health of our society and in particular about the threat posed by "the racial nightmare" must take seriously Baldwin's challenge. Though he wrote it in 1962, his diagnosis of the historical challenge still applies to us now (though I would add that it is the responsibility of conscious people of *all* races). We find ourselves at a crucial time in the history of race: the definition of and values assigned to race are in flux. The biological foundations upon which our contemporary notions were founded in the eighteenth and nineteenth centuries have been called into question and found to be empirically false. Those scientific findings, along with the opportunities afforded by political and social challenges to racism, present us with the opportunity to end the racial nightmare by doing something with our racial theories.

W. E. B. DuBois proclaimed that the problem of the twentieth century would be "the problem of the color line."[3] In terms of the contemporary debates within the field of race theory, I hypothesize that the problem of the twenty-first century will be the problem of the reconception of racial identity. This reconceived identity will necessarily involve a rejection of the strict biological foundations of race (race as color, as morphology). There are some, such as Naomi Zack, who contend that because the eighteenth- and nineteenth-century biological foundations for our contemporary notions of race have been found to be empirically false, we should do away with race altogether and move forward to a time without race.[4] I have serious doubts that doing away with races is now possible, and I would argue that it is not advisable. The problem of race is not a problem with racialized identities per se but rather with the type of racialized identities that have emerged from the traditional concept of race as well as the values that have been placed on them. Nietzsche might seem to be a counter intuitive source for contemporary race theorists, but he undertook the task of healing his culture by revaluing the prevailing concept of race.

As we find ourselves at this turning point in history, we are presented with an amazing opportunity. The question is how best to take advantage of it, and it seems that there are few easy answers. How do we imagine moving beyond the stolid racial categories that bind and separate us when so much of our identity and history is tied to these racial categories? How do we find the language for moving beyond fixed, confining racial categories? I am concerned that eliminating race might be tantamount to throwing the baby out with the bath water. Might it not be prudent first to assess its value in our society? Is race completely unhealthy, or has it contributed, or can it potentially contribute, to individual and cultural health?

Many academics also have contended with this opportunity in the history of race, and I will resist the urge to summarize all of their views. I want to examine briefly the views of Lucius Outlaw and Charles Mills in order to highlight two other paradigmatic and important contributions to the literature. Outlaw and Mills have argued that race has had, and might potentially have, a more positive role to play in our culture. They want to resist doing away with race and instead want to reconceptualize the concept of race (as well as the resultant racial identities based on it).

Outlaw, following DuBois, argues that race and ethnicity have played, and could continue to play, important roles in both our individual and cultural lives, and they should therefore be "conserved." For Outlaw, cultures provide "the means of constructing necessarily meaningfully ordered life-worlds," and these "cultural resources constitute "the defining practices and fabrics of meanings vital for the formation and maintenance of anthropologically crucial personal and social identities and histories (i.e., biographies and traditions) that socialize individuals and tie them together into the making and re-making of social wholes."[5] For him, race is intimately tied to culture in the sense that an individual's "embodied identity" and the ways in which a given culture defines itself as physically and culturally distinct from foreigners "are important to how native individual and social life is ordered". In particular, Outlaw cites the "somatic aesthetics that help to regulate the preferences and practices in terms of which partners are chosen for the intimacies that frequently (must) result in the birth of new members and in terms of the offspring are bonded with, nurtured, and socialized into the collectivity."[6] In other words, contrary to the prevailing understanding, Outlaw is contending that races are not constituted by an essentialized nature, and instead the biological component of race is due to gene pools created by the ways in which people have chosen their reproductive partners. In this sense, Outlaw is arguing that races are "real" and not merely social constructs—they are historically contingent, yet anthropologically necessary.[7]

Outlaw's alternative to doing away with race altogether is intriguing and brings out some important points: namely, that races play a part in helping us as individuals and communities create meaning in life (Nietzsche held a similar view, as will be discussed in the next section), and as such they cannot blithely be dismissed solely because they have historically been intimately tied to the pernicious effects of racism. Outlaw also has offered a fruitful approach to a way of reconceptualizing race that replaces biological essentialism (and determinism) with an anthropological description of a human need to create meaning in life. In these ways, I see many similarities in his views and those of Nietzsche, but as I will argue in the last section of this chapter, Outlaw also seems to be making the same mistake as Nietzsche in the sense of being too much a child of his time—in failing to move far enough away from the problematic racial views of his time and thus in part replicating the very problem he wants to solve. In short, the emphasis on race conservation (and in particular the maintenance of the biological components of race) might actually *prevent* people from creating meaning in their lives.

Charles Mills shares Outlaw's desire to understand race as something that is real and potentially plays an important role in our lives. As he eloquently wrote in his book *Blackness Visible*, "Room has to be made for race as both real and unreal: that race can be ontological without being biological, metaphysical without being physical, existential without being essential, shaping one's being without being in one's shape."[8] On my reading, Mills's emphasis is on the ways in which races have been socially constructed and the ontological, metaphysical, and existential roles (both positive and negative) that they have played. In this way, Mills is more successful in avoiding the biological pitfalls than Nietzsche and Outlaw. However, after doing the incredibly important work of tracing the historical, sociological and philosophical paths of the concept of race, he does not take the next step of exploring the concept of race that might emerge once race as a created ontology has been taken seriously.

Returning to Zack's views, she argues that race is a fiction and the best way to get to a state of "racelessness" is by the concept of mixed race.

> Because race means pure race, the opposite of race is not race-lessness but racial impurity, or what I have here called micro-diversity. The next step after microdiversity is racelessness. Racelessness is the next freeing stage after microdiversity and my continuing work on racial theory will address the subject.[9]

According to her, the very notion of "mixed race" (I will use that term instead of microdiversity), disrupts the assumption of race purity. If purity is assumed, then one can only be one race and not two or three. If some individuals refuse to ascribe to this strict categorization, and instead insist on the simultaneity of being multiple races, then this insistence necessarily calls into question the exclusionary nature of those categories. Zack's argument is that when this notion of mixed race is seriously accepted (as is happening in our society), our racial categories will be proved irrational, and then we can move on to the state of racelessness.

Zack is not alone in recognizing the radical potential of the con-cept of mixed race. Linda Alcoff and David Theo Goldberg also have written about it, and each has argued that while it calls into question the "racializing project," it also in some sense reifies it.[10] As Goldberg points out, race mixing still involves race talk. It is precisely because of this dual role (questioning and reifying) that Zack contends that mixed race must be the intermediary step to racelessness. In her view, as we emphasize and insist upon the mixed race identity we critical race (or maybe it should be racelessness) theorists should prepare our-selves for racelessness by "turn[ing] back in chronological time to the last period in Western history before the ordinary modern idea of race had been formulated," and this period is the seventeenth century because it is just prior to the time when "the ideas of race, gender, and even the self . . . were first developed."[11]

I would like to interrogate this role assigned to mixed race in order to see if there might be alternative outcomes to that of racelessness. I will use Nietzsche as a way of exploring these alternatives. As opposed to going back to the seventeenth century, I propose studying the nineteenth century in order to carry out a genealogy of our racial terms and to see if there is a healthy possibility for "saving" race. Like Outlaw, Mills, Alcoff, and Goldberg, I want at least initially to resist doing away with race, and because Nietzsche proposed a culturally healthier way of conceiving of race that in many ways is in keeping with the views of Mills and Outlaw, I think that we might learn from him in our search for alternatives.[12]

Nietzsche's Genealogy of Race

For Nietzsche, genealogy was a tool of investigation. He used it to examine the origins, but more importantly the evolution, of concepts. In particular, he was concerned with the concepts that were being used by his contemporaries in the creation of cultural and individual identities.[13] While the primary purpose of his genealogies was to understand how contemporary moral concepts came about, the knowledge of their origins and evolution was then meant to serve in an evaluation of those concepts (*GM* P 6).[14] This understanding comes about through a close reading and interpretation of "texts" that have provided the context in which these concepts have been historically deployed and in which they developed (*GM* P 8).[15] Nietzsche's most famous genealogy is the one in *On the Genealogy of Morals* in which he examines the "slave" origins of the prevailing Christian morality, and he used this examination to evaluate the problematic nature of this morality. He evaluated these moral concepts based on their ability to promote the health of the culture and the species as opposed to conveying transcendental truths.

> . . . under what conditions did man devise these value judgments good and evil? *and what value do they themselves possess?* Have they hitherto hindered or furthered human prosperity? Are they a sign of distress, of impoverishment, of the degeneration of life? or is there revealed in them, on the contrary the plenitude, force, and will of life, its courage, certainty, future? (*GM* P 3)

In this way, Nietzsche teamed up the investigative aspect of genealogy with the evaluative aspect of his symptomatological critical philosophy. With the latter, Nietzsche's goal was to act as a physician of the culture and to diagnose diseased cultures by closely examining the symptoms they displayed.[16] In the end, the disease from which all cultures suffer is decadence, but the symptoms they display and the ways in which they contend with it differ.

The organizing principle of Nietzsche's positive philosophy in the late works (those after *Thus Spoke Zarathustra*) is the problem of decadence. Nietzsche took up the "problem of decadence" with renewed vigor in the late works, especially in relation to the political aspects of his positive philosophy (*CW* P).[17] He viewed decadence as a decay of the instincts that becomes manifest in the performance of our most human task: that of creating what I have called rationales for existence, meaning the values we create that lend meaning to our initially meaningless lives.[18] We create moralities (systems of values) to avoid the suicide-inspiring state of nihilism (*GM* III 28). It is here that decadence becomes a problem: we have to create meaning in life, but any meaning we create will eventually prove ineffective and decay. The meaning we create acts as an organizing principle and a catalyst for action. It gives us a reason to get out of bed in the morning, confront the myriad of life's daily challenges, and strive for a "better" life (as determined by the values derived from the meaning attributed to life). This meaning is created by or for a particular person in a specific time and place. As times and places change and as the person changes, the meaning will be less effective (will decay), and the individual will have to modify it or face nihilism.

Because we cannot live in a state in which there are no values, the question posed by decadence is, how are we to come to terms with the initial meaninglessness of life and the fact that any values we create will decline? Traditionally, philosophers have responded by denying the meaninglessness of life, claiming to have "discovered" the Truth of it as well as the objective, universal values based on this Truth. They therefore denied the fact that their values would decay.[19]

As self-designated cultural physicians, Socrates, Wagner, Nietzsche, and the ascetic priest all assumed the task of treating the decadence of their respective cultures. The differences in their remedies are telling in that they reveal each cultural physician's view of decadence *as well as* the extent to which he suffered from the disease. In general, there are two categories of remedies: antidotes and cures. The problem with the second category for Nietzsche is that there can be no cure for decadence—either for an individual or a culture.[20] Decadence (the inevitable decay of values) is an inextricable part of the human condition, and to attempt to remove or avoid it is to deny a key fact of life and to fail to fulfill the human task of continually creating rationales for existence.

This is why Nietzsche always associated nihilism—the lack of rationales for existence—with suicide. It is a state of being that human beings are unable to maintain. Nietzsche's self-appointed task was to find a healthier way of contending with the disease of decadence. He accepted the fact that there is no cure for it.

In the late works he attempted to distinguish himself from traditional approaches to the problem of decadence by making an implicit distinction between strong and weak decadents.[21] Nietzsche did not explicitly make such a distinction, but he implicitly used it as a criterion in his evaluation of both himself and others who grappled with decadence.[22] Strong decadents are able to contend with decadence by changing the value they place on it (*GS* 382).[23] As opposed to denying the fact that all values are subjectively created, and will eventually decay, the strong decadent celebrates these facts. Nietzsche's contention was that we must move away from attempting to discover Truth and instead try to create values that do not deny their subjectivity. These values would celebrate and affirm the life of the individual and others like him or her, their purpose being the enhancement of the creator (a celebration of the flourishing of him or her) and, by extension, the enhancement of the species. In turn, cultures are evaluated based on the strong types they are able to produce (*A* 3).[24]

The type who creates such values is a strong decadent because she or he is creating values in the face of the meaninglessness of life and is therefore a decadent, but this individual is considered "strong" in that she or he acknowledges this decadence and affirms it as part of life. Strong decadents like their weak decadent counterparts, are afflicted with the disease of decadence, but unlike these counterparts, they are not debilitated by it. Therefore, strong decadents were prescribing an antidote to decadence instead of a cure.

One of the primary effects of weak decadent morality had been that this more valuable, strong type was not being bred, and had in fact been vilified. Nietzsche's response was that one should question the values that had led to the breeding and survival of a large group of mediocre types. The primary way that Nietzsche suggested instituting this treatment of revaluing values was to persuade his readers that the prevailing values were not ones that led to flourishing but instead to nihilism, and then to convince "all the sciences" (e.g., linguistics, physiology, medicine, and philosophy) to determine new values (and based on the connection he made between values and human types) and new types of people.[25]

Nietzsche did not present a fully comprehensive theory of race in his books, and the racial theory that is there is not necessary for understanding Nietzsche.[26] It does serve to highlight Nietzsche's theories about cultures: their evolution, their health, and the treatment for unhealthy cultures. For Nietzsche, cultures are evaluated based on the people they produce, and they also evolve as the people that characterize them evolve. In short, cultures are organic and have a physiological component. The physiological constitution of human beings affects the character of a culture, and once established, the culture will in turn affect the groups of people or races that characterize it (*BGE* 242).[27]

European culture was undergoing a "physiological process" that caused Europeans to become similar because of the cultural conditions that caused people to differentiate (to form races) had been removed by a weak decadent approach to valuation. R. J. Hollingdale defined Nietzsche's notion of race as "a group of people who had to live together a long time and as a result had certain needs and certain characteristics in common."[28] Using this definition and the way in which race operates in Nietzsche's texts, groups of people (nations) constitute races and the characteristics that emerge from these races, when combined with the characteristics of other races, coalesce into cultures.[29] While the aim of cultures is stability, cultures evolve as the various races that constitute them vie for dominance. Races then can be understood as catalysts for cultural change. Democracies resisted that change by assigning a high value to similarities between their people and thus undercutting the growth of races. In Nietzsche's time a "national feeling" was trying to eliminate all races that were not Aryan in order to "purify" Germany (and Europe) of "tainted blood," and it resulted in the stagnation of the culture. It was this stagnation that Nietzsche claimed was a primary symptom of the "sickness" (e.g., weak decadence) of his culture (*BGE* 201-3, 242).

Nietzschean races then are a combination of physiological and psychological traits that are primarily inherited but also can be affected by the individual's desire to alter these traits and/or by external forces. The prime catalyst for racial evolution though is race mixing, which is generally brought about by blood mixing. This blood mixing can occur in two ways: discriminant and indiscriminant race mixing. Nietzsche referred to the first type as breeding or cultivation (*Züchtung*). As is the case with "blood," *Züchtung* is another word that was used by the nationalists in their attempts to render Germany an Aryan nation.[30] For Nietzsche, breeding is an aspect of morality, and it had been used badly by weak decadents.[31]

Züchtung plays an important role in defining who has the right to create values. That right is determined at least in part by "one's origins, one's ancestors, one's blood," and several generations are required to ensure that the correct virtues have been "acquired, nurtured, inherited, and digested singly" (*BGE* 213). One can then see that cultivation (in both a biological and sociological sense) is intimately tied to morality and the philosopher. This cultivation involves not only a biological inheritance but also the instilling of virtues by education, religion, politics, and economics (*BGE* 61).[32] This cultivation is not always conscious or voluntary. The creation of meaning in life (the creation of values or moralities) is undertaken for the sake of survival (at the worst) or flourishing (at the best), and in this way, this creation of values is part of the process of cultivating—of breeding (*Züchtung*)—particular human beings who will be able to hold off the suicidal nihilism by embodying this meaning (*GM* III 28).

Nietzsche claimed that the decline in the isolation of European nations and the resulting mixing of races were inevitable. Germany was so dominated by the morality of mediocre, weak decadent types that its goal was the artificial preservation of the Aryan type as opposed to an active breeding of new strong types. It was this desire for preservation that, according to Nietzsche, explained the rise in national hostilities whose goal was to encourage Germans to bond together and keep themselves from being "contaminated" by other races—particularly Jews.

Revaluation of Race

In his attempts to heal this sickness, Nietzsche called for a revaluation of weak decadent values—and by extension a revaluation of the nationalist notion of race. This is the reason that Nietzsche prescribed a fresh infusion of healthy races (e.g., contemporary Jews) as a treatment. Nietzsche then was agreeing with his nationalist contemporaries that their culture was physiologically ailing, and that the introduction of healthier "blood" was required. The difference between them was the type of "blood" each prescribed.[33] The nineteenth century German nationalists called for a "pure" Aryan blood to heal their culture, and Nietzsche prescribed "blood mixing."

He called for the reader to "work for the amalgamation of nations" (*HH* I 475).[34] In particular, he called for the mixing of positive Jewish characteristics ("their energy and higher intelligence, their capital in will and spirit") with those of Europeans so as to breed a new mixed race—the Good European.[35]

As soon as it is no longer a question of the conserving of nations but of the production of the strongest possible European mixed race, the Jew will be just as usable and desirable as an ingredient of it as any other national residue. . . . Christianity has done everything to orientalize the occident, Judaism has always played an essential part in occidentalizing it again: which in a certain sense means making of Europe's mission and history a *continuation of the Greek.* (*HH* I 475)

Nietzsche admitted that, like all races, Jews also had negative characteristics (those of the "youthful stock-exchange Jew [who] is the most repulsive invention of the entire human race"), but that it was worth the risk of involving those qualities in the process of breeding, because Jews held the key to a continuation of the "enlightenment of Graeco-Roman antiquity" (*HH* I 475). In other words, if a creation of a modern strong European type to rival those of the ancient Greeks and Romans were possible, then a new type must be created by mixing races. The German nationalists who claimed to be breeding a strong, pure Aryan race by excluding Jews were actually merely preserving a mediocre type, calling for the elimination of a strong race, and they were thus endangering the culture.[36]

One of the tasks of cultures or nations then is the cultivation of types of human beings who will create meaning in life that will in turn, ensure its continuation, and hopefully, its flourishing. Nations, then, for Nietzsche are not static entities, they are "*res facta,*" something made: "something evolving, young, and easily changed." Eventually, a nation might take on "race" status if it can prove its strength through long endurance. This endurance is not attained by attempting to survive but by a combination of hostile external forces and the attempt to flourish despite them. For Nietzsche, "There are probably no pure races but only races that have become pure," and even these *res facta* races are "extremely rare" (*D* 272). A race becomes pure by mixing with other races, taking the energy produced by the resulting contradictory qualities, and channeling them so that they "will stand at the command of the total organism." Nietzsche then suggested revaluing the concept of race in claiming that it is only healthy for the culture if one assumes that "pure races" are mixed races.

Race, then, is a component of Nietzsche's call for cultural revitalization. Nietzsche tried to carry out a revaluation of the definition and function of race in this revitalization. I propose that we learn from this attempted revaluation in our efforts to revitalize our own culture. As opposed to doing away with race altogether (which would lead to nihilism), Nietzsche suggested that we call healthy those races that admit to and enhance their strength through "race mixing." By calling into question the value of pure races, Nietzsche not only undercuts the value system of his nationalist opponents but also highlights the illogicality of trying to preserve so-called pure races.

Nietzsche's revalued definition of race also might be of interest to us today because it not only denies that "pure races" are culturally optimal but questions the possibility and advisability of attaining the Aryan standard of purity. Instead, Nietzsche's race is fluid in the sense that strong, healthy races are created through the continual mixing of races. In other words, races are subjective, fluid, and, by definition, mixed. At the same time, Nietzsche also might serve as a cautionary note for us.[37] His views of race were progressive for his time and countered some of the most heinous assumptions of his Aryan counterparts, but they also conserved the biological assumptions of his time. In terms of his talk of "breeding" and race mixing as "blood mixing," Nietzsche remained a child of his time, and at least to our eyes and ears, he resembled the very group from whom he wanted to distance himself. While Nietzsche was still stuck in race talk (meaning that he was reifying it), he was simultaneously expanding the way in which race could be used in the push for cultural health.

In other words, my argument here is that Nietzsche could be understood as a first essay in responding to the call of those (e.g., Zack, Alcoff, and Goldberg) who want to emphasize the concept of mixed race as a way of subverting the still accepted "purity"-based conception of race. In the end, we might end up with an understanding of race that following Charles Mills is both "real and unreal."[38] We might then come to understand race as having been constructed in part by humans (and thus having no metaphysical basis) but as real in the sense that it can provide healthy identities and a sense of history for groups of people without restricting them, as might Outlaw's "conserved" racial concept, to the confining racial identities of the purity-based model. Following Nietzsche, I am proposing that we might be able to find a way to bring about cultural health in terms of race, without doing away with race altogether or merely conserving those aspects that have contributed to cultural ill health.

The Price of the Ticket

We need to carry out a Nietzschean revaluation of our concept of race. First we need to carry out a genealogy of the concept: to look at its origins, the ways in which it has evolved and been used to serve the aspirations of particular groups. In many ways, this type of genealogy has been undertaken by scholars in various fields, and I want to encourage the continuation of it. Especially, we should examine the multiple ways in which race has been used to empower and disempower groups and individuals. Philosophy has been slower in carrying out this genealogy, but in the last few years several books have emerged that cull texts from the history of philosophy that reflect the changing concept of race.[39]

As Outlaw has pointed out, on the positive side races have provided an important sense of culture, and, by extension, individual identity. It is around the concept of race that groups have organized politically and socially, and it is based on an often-evolving definition of race, that individuals of those groups have chosen reproductive partners. As Mills has argued, in the United States, this identity creation has been secondary to the primary role of race, the creation of "a system of advantage and disadvantage," and in fact at times, these two roles have been connected.[40] Where one stands in this system of advantages and disadvantages will then have a profound impact on how one sees oneself and the world, how one is treated and treats others, and how one perceives of the interests of one's racial group. In other words, this system creates a "racial self" that is "biologically fictitious" and "socially real."[41] For black Americans, then, our identities emerged from a debased (to the point of invisibility) value in this system, and as such they were in large part a reaction against this proffered debased identity and entailed, as Mills put it, "an affirmation simultaneously of individual and group existence."[42]

A genealogy of race in the United States would then reveal the origins and evolution of both this system and racialized identities. I anticipate that what emerges from this genealogy is view of race as monolithically thick. It is "thick" in the sense of its profound effects on individuals, groups, and the country in virtually every realm of existence. It is "monolithic" in that within individual races, the concept does not allow for diversity or variation. In other words, a race is a discrete, undifferentiated whole into which one is born, and because of one's "blood" one is in general consigned to that racial designation for life. In some sense, one is born into a racialized culture and its attendant values, and one is therefore provided with the values that might help one organize a meaningfully ordered life-world, to borrow Outlaw's terminology. At the same time, due to internal and external pressures, one is expected to accept, and punished for failing to accept, these "life-world" values based on one's perceived racial identity.[43]

This is the "purity" model of race. On this model, races are valued based on their ability to remain untainted by the "blood" of other (particularly "lower" races). Races try to maintain "purity" through a combination of fear of contamination (and possible extinction) and group pride. There is a defined "tipping point" (which has changed throughout history) in which an individual is determined to have been too "contaminated" by the blood of another race and is thus labeled to be of that other race. The "one-drop" rule in the United States is a clear example of how this purity-based model of race has operated.[44] Because race is also "thick," a change in the race of family members from one generation to the next (where, say, the child is determined to be of a different race than his or her grandparents) will reverberate in every aspect of this child's life.

Races were created to fulfill certain needs and desires—both in a positive sense (identities) and in a negative sense (creating hierarchy of groups). A genealogy forces us to ask whether we still have those needs and whether race still meets them. A genealogy would then reveal the conditions (or, using Nietzschean terminology, the "health") under which the concept of race was created and the ways it was valued. Because of these healthy roles race has played, Outlaw calls for its reconception (as based more on anthropology than biology) and conservation. I wonder, though, if this conserved conception of race will attain the goal of creating flourishing and meaningful cultures and individuals. I question whether because this conceived concept of race still operates in part on the purity model it can provide a meaningful life-world for all or even most members of a given race. In short, I think Outlaw might be conserving too much of the emphasis on the biological than on the traditional concept of race.

Therefore, we need to carry out the second part of the project: questioning the value of the concept. Because race has been based on this purity-based model, which I liken to the view of moral values based on objective and universal truths, it also has been "unhealthy." Following Nietzsche's argument, creating rationales for existence based on universal and objective truths has not led to human flourishing but instead to the decline of cultures and, by extension, the decline of the species. Nietzsche then extends this argument to concepts of races and cultures that claim to be uncontaminated and thus pure. Just as the "discovery" of universal and objective truths cannot solve the problem of decadence, the maintenance of "purity" will not lead to the flourishing of the race. In fact, the focus on "purity" freezes individuals in a monolithically narrow group identity (a racial nook), and will not allow the healthiest of the individuals to create new, innovative rationales for existence.

As Alcoff, Goldberg, and Zack have argued, the purity-based model of race does not reflect the "life-worlds" of those who claim to be racially mixed. Their voices are often silenced due to a fear of exile from one or all of the racial groups.

> [T]he problem may be deeper, in that foundational concepts of self and identity are founded on purity, wholeness, and coherence. A self that is internally heterogeneous beyond repair or resolution becomes a candidate for pathology in a society where integration of self is taken to be necessary for mental health. We need to reflect upon this premium put on internal coherence and racial purity and how this has been manifested in Western concepts and practices of identity as a public persona as well as subjectivity as a foundational understanding of the self. We need to consider what role this preference for purity and racial separateness has had on dominant formulations of identity and subjectivity, and what the effects might be if this preference was no longer operative.[45]

As Alcoff indicates in the preceding quote, the purity-based model often has led to the decline (in terms of mental fitness) as opposed to the flourishing of individuals within particular races. Relating this to Nietzsche's revaluation of decadence, one might then ask if there needs to be a concomitant revaluation of race where "health" and flourishing are defined based on the acceptance of "contamination." As opposed to assuming that there is a "pure" uncontaminated concept of race that is attainable, we recognize the fact that we are all contaminated, we are all of mixed race.[46] This is Nietzsche's strong decadent approach to the disease of decadence, and I am proposing that we take a strong racialist approach to the problems brought about by race. As opposed to thinking that we can cure ourselves of the disease of race, we search for an antidote that will allow us to flourish with the help of racial identities.

In critical race theory, we have already begun to borrow from the Nietzschean approach to the revaluation of morality and races in terms of a rejection of the purity-based model of race. Not only has it finally been put to rest that there are racial "genes" that definitively make a person a particular race, and that a person must be a single race, but it is generally accepted in critical race theory that races are not scientifically real and are instead, to varying degrees, socially constructed. A new, revalued concept of race is emerging: race is less about one's biological history and more about one's chosen identity. This revalued concept of race recognizes that racial identities are constructed by individuals and communities and can provide a sense of history and healthy identities.

In this way, race is not only being reconceived but it is also being revalued. In general, this revaluation is not emerging out of a weak racialist desire to escape racial designation but rather from a desire to be a part of a given race or races on one's own terms. It is based on an active attempt at self-definition as opposed to a passive acceptance of one's identity. If we were to surrender the race purity talk, then we would lose its attendant pathologies and gain a more fluid notion of racial identity. Races would then be ticks on a continuum as opposed to discrete, mutually exclusive entities. Race would still be embodied, but no longer would biology (in terms of one's somatic aesthetic) be the *sole* legitimate determinant of one's race. Race, because it lacked biological determinacy, would be devalued in terms of its ability to express who one is, in its ability to act as an organizing principle.

This revalued concept of race would replace the traditionally monolithically thick one with one that is multifariously thin, "multifarious" in the sense that individual races would allow for more diversity within themselves as well as between themselves and other races. It would be "thin" in that one's racial identity would not determine virtually every aspect of one's life. This "impurity"-based model of race would more readily reflect the multicultural and intercultural nature of our world, where race is less construed solely based on similarity of appearance and more on the multiple communities and cultures in which individuals live and create life-worlds. In this world, the purity-based model of race fails to play the legitimating role it played in the past. One would not *have* to primarily identify oneself according to race— it would be one identity among many. Race would be less a noun than an adjective, less essentially constitutive than existentially reflective.

Before we carry out this revaluation, we need to try to anticipate the ramifications of this revaluation and seriously consider whether or not we are comfortable with them. In closing, I want to anticipate some of these ramifications and argue that the price of this ticket out of our racial nightmare is a good value. In other words, in order to win freedom from the misleading, stifling, race purity concept, we will have to surrender the security that accompanied it. We will have to learn how to construct consciously our own racial identity without depending on the false security of biological inheritance. One would then claim to be of a particular race less because of one's parentage but more based on the communities from and in which one creates a meaningful life, based on the way in which one practices one's art of living.

In theory, this price might seem negligible, but in practice for many, it is a price not worth paying. It involves changing our expectations and assumptions—it challenges that which we have always claimed to know. Racial identities would tell us relatively little about a given person. Many people refuse to accept that there are no racial genes, because they do not want to surrender the security of predetermined racial identities—even while recognizing the history of the deleterious effects of such assumptions. As Nietzsche put it, they have

> a metaphysician's ambition to hold a hopeless position [and] may participate and ultimately prefer even a handful of "certainty" to a whole carload of beautiful possibilities; there may actually be puritanical fanatics of conscience who prefer even a certain nothing to an uncertain something to lie down on— and die. But this is nihilism and the sign of a despairing, mortally weary soul—however courageous the gestures of such a virtue may look. (*BGE* 10)

Conserving the last vestiges of the purity-based model of race is the hopeless position that, at the expense of an illusory certain survival, one is willing to risk the flourishing of communities of people.

Conclusion

A genealogy of race reveals the attention, thought, and planning that went into the creation and maintenance of race (on the purity-based model) and argues that we should not hesitate to devote equal attention, thought, and planning to the revaluation of this concept. This revaluation would involve a paradigm shift, a shifting of the foundation, a moving of the tectonic plates, and when this happens, that which is known to be immovable moves like liquid. The revaluation of race could cause a similar shift in our worldviews. We need to consider seriously whether or not we are willing to pay the price of relinquishing the security of monolithically thick racial identities. I have argued that perhaps with such a racial revaluation we just might be able to heed Baldwin's call for seizing the opportunity for ending the racial nightmare. It is up to us, those racial transgressors (in Nietzschean language, "homeless ones") who can see beyond our current illogical conceptions of race and the values assigned to them to new horizons (*GS* 377). While it is a hard task to undo the hundreds of years of racializing that have resulted in the calcification of political and social power, as well as group and individual identities, to fail to undertake the task might be equally as hazardous.

> For the sake of one's children, in order to minimize the bill that *they* must pay, one must be careful not to take refuge in any delusion—and the value placed on the color of the skin is always and everywhere and forever a delusion. I know that what I am asking is impossible. But in our time, as in every time, the impossible is the least that one can demand—and one is, after all, emboldened by the spectacle of human history in general, and American Negro history in particular, for it testifies to nothing less than the perpetual achievement of the impossible.[47]

Notes

1. In this chapter, the discussion of the concept of race will focus on the American concept of race.

2. James Baldwin, "The Fire Next Time," in *The Price of the Ticket: Collected Non-Fiction 1948–1985*, ed. (New York: St. Martin's Press, 1985), 379.

3. W. E. B. DuBois, *The Souls of Black Folk* (Boston: Bedford Books, 1997), 45.

4. Naomi Zack, "Life After Race," in *American Mixed Race*, ed. Naomi Zack (Boston: Rowman & Littlefield, 1995), 307.

5. Lucius Outlaw, *On Race and Philosophy*, (New York: Routledge, 1996), 16.

6. Outlaw, *On Race and Philosophy*, p. 16–17: "This is the historically contingent, yet anthropologically necessary, sociocultural matrix that must be appreciated in endeavoring to understand how physical and cultural factors are taken up and given social meanings so as to become mutually reinforcing in the processes through which social collectivities are "constructed": that is, the processes in and through which geographically determinant populations and subgroups of sexually reproducing individuals become adaptively differentiated biologically and culturally, groupings we have come to call "races" and "ethnies" (though there have been other designations for such groupings, in various languages, throughout human history)."

7. Outlaw, *On Race and Philosophy*, 8, 17.

8. Charles Mills, *Blackness Visible* (Ithaca, NY: Cornell University Press, 1998), xiv.

9. Zack, "Life After Race," 301.

10. David Theo Goldberg, "Made in the USA: Racial Mixing 'n Matching," in *American Mixed Race*, 238; and Linda Alcoff, "Mestizo Identity," in *American Mixed Race*, 257.

11. Zack, "Life After Race," 307.

12. Alcoff, "Mestizo Identity," 272, 275–78; Goldberg, "Made in the USA," 253–54.

13. Much has been written about Nietzschean genealogies. For examples, see the essays in *Nietzsche, Genealogy, Morality: Essays on Nietzsche's On the Genealogy of Morals*, ed. Richard Schacht (Berkeley: University of California Press, 1994).

14. Friedrich Nietzsche, *On the Genealogy of Morals*, trans. Walter Kaufmann (New York: Random House, 1967).

15. David Couzens Hoy, "Nietzsche, Hume, and the Genealogical Method," in *Nietzsche, Genealogy, Morality*, 258–59; and Alexander Nehamas, "The Genealogy of Genealogy: Interpretation in Nietzsche's Second *Untimely Meditation* and in *On the Genealogy of Morals*," in *Nietzsche, Genealogy, Morality*, 275.

16. Eric Blondel, "The Question of Genealogy," in *Nietzsche, Genealogy, Morality*, 314; Daniel Conway, "Genealogy and Critical Method," in *Nietzsche, Genealogy, Morality*, 321–22.

17. Friedrich Nietzsche, *The Case of Wagner* [*CW*], trans. Walter Kaufmann and R. J. Hollingdale (New York: Random House, 1967).

18. See Jacqueline Scott, "Nietzsche and Decadence: The Revaluation of Morality," *Continental Philosophy Review* (formerly *Man and World*) 31 (January 1998): 60–61.

19. See also Daniel Conway, *Nietzsche's Dangerous Game* (Cambridge: Cambridge University Press, 1997), 107–16.

20. I am using the terms *cure* and *antidote* in very specific senses. A cure permanently heals a disease, and an antidote treats the symptoms without directly affecting the disease itself.

21. In *Nietzsche's Dangerous Game*, Conway makes a distinction between passive and active nihilists that is analogous to my strong versus weak decadence dichotomy (114–16). Conway has argued that Nietzsche portrayed himself as "our best example of an active nihilist" (114). While I agree with Conway that Nietzsche did make a distinction between active and passive nihilism, they are only *symptoms* of decadence. As I will argue later, it is the *disease* itself with which Nietzsche attempted to contend, and that is why in the late

works he emphasized decadence and the fact of his own decadent status. Nihilism is only one of the many symptoms of decadence (e.g., timeliness, bad conscience, dogmatism, etc.), and while it is arguably one of the most problematic for Nietzsche, his attempt at a revaluation of values was meant to be an antidote for the most rabid symptoms of decadence, and not for nihilism alone. Nietzsche's primary task involved a revaluation of decadence (weak to strong decadence) and not nihilism.

22. Scott, "Nietzsche and Decadence," 63–68.

23. Friedrich Nietzsche, *The Gay Science*, trans. Walter Kaufmann (New York: Vintage Books, 1974).

24. Friedrich Nietzsche, *The Antichrist*, trans. R. J. Hollingdale (London: Penguin Books, 1968). There is a school of thought that Nietzsche abandoned his cultural physician status in the late works. See Alexander Nehamas, *Nietzsche: Life as Literature* (Cambridge, MA: Harvard University Press, 1985) as an example.

25. "The question: what is the *value* of this or that table of values and "morals?" should be viewed from the most divers perspectives; for the problem *"value for what?"* cannot be examined too subtly. Something, for example, that possessed obvious value in relation to the longest possible survival of a race (or to the enhancement of its power of adaptation to a particular climate or to the preservation of the greatest number) would by no means possess the same value if it were a question, for instance, of producing a stronger type. The well-being of the majority and the well-being of the few are opposite viewpoints of value: to consider the former *a priori* of higher value may be left to the naiveté of English biologists.—*All* the sciences have from now on to prepare the way for the future task of the philosophers: this task understood as the solution to the *problem of value*, the determination of the *order of rank among values"* (*GM*: I 17).

26. For a more extensive analysis of Nietzsche's concept of race and its connection to decadence, see Scott, "On the Use and Abuse of Race in Philosophy: Nietzsche, Jews and Race," in *Race and Racism in Continental Philosophy*, ed. Robert Bernasconi, (forthcoming); Daniel Conway, "The Great Play and Fight of Forces," in *Philosophers on Race*, ed., Julie Ward and Tommy Lott (London: Blackwell, 2002), 167–94.

27. Friedrich Nietzsche, *Beyond Good and Evil*, trans. Walter Kaufmann (New York: Vintage Books, 1955).

28. R. J. Hollingdale, *Nietzsche: The Man and His Philosophy* (Baton Rouge: Louisiana State University Press, 1965), 224.

29. It would seem, then, that nations are mere political units that, due to time and circumstance, might progress to become races and cultures (see *BGE* 251 and the discussion of breeding that follows).

30. Walter Kaufmann claimed that the terms *Zucht* and *Züchtung* appear occasionally in the *Will to Power*, and that there are even fewer references to either word in the published works. He further claimed that "[i]f one looks for a philosophic precedent for Nietzsche's strange concern with breeding, one will have to seek it not in his German predecessors but in Plato" (Walter Kaufmann, *Nietzsche: Philosopher, Psychologist, Antichrist*, 4th ed., (Princeton, NJ: Princeton University Press, 1974), 304–305). Actually there are quite a few references to *Zucht* and *Züchtung* in the published works, and they are not "throwaway" lines. Contrary to Kaufmann, I think that Nietzsche, at least in part, was borrowing from "his German predecessors" in his use of the terms, but it was not a wholesale borrowing.

31. Unlike their true Aryan predecessors of "Indian morality," Christians were breeding "the poor and lowly." According to this account, the Indian Aryans' task was the breeding of four races, with the "virtuous . . . people of race" (the Aryans) at the top of the hierarchy (*TI* "Improvers" 3). These Aryans were of "pure blood," but the Christians inherited the "Chandala" (Untouchable) values, and as such, they are "the *anti-Aryan* religion *par excellence*" (*TI* "Improvers" 4). In short, breeding is a part of morality, but some breeding is preferable to others.

32. "Even the beauty of a race or a family, the charm and benevolence of their whole demeanor, is earned by labor: like genius, it is the final result of the accumulatory labor of generations. . . . Supreme rule of conduct: even when alone one must not 'let oneself go.'—Good things are costly beyond measure: and the law still holds that he who *has* them is different from who *obtains* them. Everything good is inheritance: what is not inherited is imperfect, is a beginning. . . . For one must not mistake the method involved here: a mere disciplining of thoughts and feelings is virtually nothing (—here lies the great mistake of German culture, which is totally illusory): one first has to convince the *body*. The strict maintenance of a significant and select demeanor, and obligation to live only among men who do not 'let themselves go', completely suffices for becoming significant and select: in two or three generations everything is already *internalized*. It is decisive for the fortune of nations and of mankind that one should inaugurate culture in the *right place—not* in the 'soul' (as has been the fateful superstition of priests and quasi-priests): the right place is the body, demeanor, diet, physiology: the *rest* follows. . . . This is why the Greeks remain the *supreme cultural event* of history—they knew, they *did* what needed to be done; Christianity, which despised the body, has up till now been mankind's greatest misfortune—" (*TI* "Skirmishes" 47).

33. My reading of Nietzsche is contentious, because there are some who claim that Nietzsche divorced his racial claims from any biological assumptions. In part, they do this to remove the stain of anti-Semitism from Nietzsche. Others admit that there might be some links to biology, but that he "rejects value difference linked to biology alone," and therefore he accepts race but rejects racism (see Yovel Yirmiyahu, *Dark Riddle* 135).

34. Friedrich Nietzsche, *Human, All-Too-Human* [*HH*], trans. R .J. Hollingdale (Cambridge: Cambridge University Press, 1986).

35. *GS* 377.

36. See also *GS* 377. In *Beyond Good and Evil* 251, Nietzsche claimed that the primary motivation for German anti-Semitism was the weakness of German culture. The "physiology" of the German culture could not digest any more Jews. For this reason, Nietzsche called for the mixing of German "blood" with that of Italians, French, and English, because they had "stronger digestive systems." Only then could Europe digest the blood of the Jews who were the "strongest, toughest, purest" race and who wanted to be "absorbed and assimilated by Europe."

> to that end it might be useful to and fair to expel the anti-Semitic screamers from the country. Accommodated with all caution, with selection; approximately as the English nobility does. It is obvious that the stronger and already more clearly defined types of the new Germanism can enter into relations with them . . . it would be interesting in many ways to see whether the hereditary art of commanding and obeying . . . could not be enriched with the genius of money and patience (and above all a little spirituality, which is utterly lacking among these officers). But here it is proper to break off my cheerful Germanomania and holiday oratory; for I am beginning to touch on what is serious for me, the "European problem" as I understand it, the cultivation of a new caste that will rule Europe. (*BGE* 251)

Earlier in *Dawn* 205, Nietzsche also has called for the absorption of Jewish values by Europe, and there he said after this assimilation had brought about the creation of "great men and great works," then the Jews would have "transformed its eternal vengeance into an eternal blessing for Europe." In other words, then they would have atoned for having produced Paul and, by extension, Christianity. Nietzsche also suggested that Europe could use Chinese blood to counteract the restlessness and fretfulness of Europeans (see Friedrich Nietzsche, *Dawn*, trans. R. J. Hollingdale [Cambridge: Cambridge University Press, 1982], 206).

37. See Conway, "The Great Play and Fight of Forces," in *Philosophers on Race* for a fuller account of the problematic nature, and the political implications, of Nietzsche's concept of race as well as his call for the breeding of a new caste of Good Europeans.

38. Mills, *Blackness Visible*, xiv, 47–49.

39. See Michael Banton, *Racial Theories* (Cambridge: Cambridge University Press, 1987); Robert Bernasconi and Tommy L. Lott, eds., *The Idea of Race* (Indianapolis, IN: Hackett, Inc., 2000); Robert Bernasconi, ed., *Race* (Oxford: Blackwell, 2000); Emmanuel Eze, ed., *Race and the Enlightenment* (Oxford: Blackwell, 1997); Charles Mills, *The Racial Contract* (Ithaca, NY: Cornell University

Press, 1997). In addition, Paul Taylor has undertaken a philosophical account of race in *Race: A Philosophical Introduction* (Cambridge: Polity Press, 2004).

40. Mills, *Blackness Visible*, p. 134.

41. Ibid.

42. Ibid., 11.

43. The criteria for a given racial identity have changed in the United States such that in one historical period one might have been "white" and in another "black." While such changes might seem to undercut my contention about the monolithic nature of race, it actually only emphasizes my point. While the criteria for a given category of race might evolve, the fact of the stringent, narrow, exclusive category of racial identity has not changed—except for in the last thirty years.

44. Banton, *Racial Theories*; Ariela Gross, *Double Character* (Princeton, NJ: Princeton Woodrow Wilson Center Press, 1996); Hanry López, *White By Law: The Legal Construction of Race* (New York: New York University Press, 1996).

45. Alcoff, "Mestizo Identity," 261.

46. "We who are homeless are too manifold and mixed racially and in our descent, being "modern men," and consequently do not feel tempted to participate in the mendacious racial self-admiration and racial indecency that parades in Germany today as a sign of a German way of thinking and that is doubly false and obscene among the people of the "historical sense." We are in a word—and let this be our word of honor—*good Europeans*, the heirs of Europe, the rich, oversupplied, but also overly obligated heirs of thousands of years of European spirit" (*GS* 377).

47. Baldwin, "The Fire Next Time," 379.

Part III

—

Regimens of Recovery

8

Unlikely Illuminations: Nietzsche and Frederick Douglass on Power, Struggle, and the *Aisthesis* of Freedom

CHRISTA DAVIS ACAMPORA

This chapter strives to illuminate affinities between Frederick Douglass's conception of freedom and the slavery he escaped and Nietzsche's view of struggle, which indicates a similar conception of the dynamic of perversions of power and its transfiguring possibilities. The two complement each other in unexpected ways. Douglass provides accounts of slave experience that illustrate how his resistance through struggle offered him a transformative aesthetic experience of *meaningful* freedom. This realization of power is specifically one not motivated by revenge and resentment of the sort Nietzsche describes as characteristic of slavish morality in the first essay of his *On the Genealogy of Morals*. Much of Nietzsche's writing aims at investigating how meanings or values are produced, and especially the ways in which their genealogies are marked by efforts to effect *sensations of power*. Nietzsche provides some relevant criteria for distinguishing creative from destructive struggles, the kinds of transformations they effect, and the forms of power they afford and cultivate. This Nietzschean framework supports Douglass's impression that he has a superior character when emerging out of struggles that enable him to gain a sense of his freedom.

To some, my objective here might seem perverse, perhaps even repulsive—why endeavor to bend Douglass to Nietzsche, or attempt to read Nietzsche as if he were a progressive egalitarian? After all, does not one powerfully articulate the moral reprehensibility of slavery while the other is a philosopher of mastery and domination who actually advocates a new kind of slavery[1] and is perhaps even "a cruel racist"[2] through and through? What is to be gained by performing the hermeneutic gymnastics required to illuminate any similarity between these two writers, and would not doing so constitute an injustice to the intent of each?[3] I am quite mindful of these concerns, although the confines of this chapter do not permit me to thoroughly address all of them. Ultimately, I argue that both Douglass and Nietzsche share a conception of human power and how it might seek or produce meaningful freedom. The purpose is not to show that they ultimately share the same ends in their projects but rather that they hold certain complementary positions that, when considered in tandem, deepen our appreciation of the respective projects in which they were involved. The goal of reading Nietzsche alongside Douglass is not to render Nietzsche more palatable or to offer his apology against the charges of racism, as if by mere association with Douglass Nietzsche appears more sympathetic to the concerns of oppressed blacks. Nor is it my objective to show that what Douglass can merely express as his personal experience in narrative form Nietzsche actually renders more truly philosophical. I am not trying to give Nietzsche the face of Douglass or see the specter of Nietzsche illuminating Douglass's experience. Instead, the real work of this chapter is to further explore the relevance of imagination for moral deliberation (broadly conceived to include consideration of the sort of person one aims to become). Reading Douglass and Nietzsche together on power as it relates to the felt quality or *aisthesis* of freedom provides entrée to further investigation of practices of resistance and the relation between aesthetic and moral freedom. Attentive to these *unlikely illuminations*, we can better appreciate ways in which the acquisition of meaningful freedom is an accomplishment achieved through a dynamic of social and individual cooperation and resistance that is not necessarily hostile to the pursuit of meaningful community. In fact, I draw an even stronger conclusion—far from destroying or minimizing the significance of our relations to others, the *aisthesis* of agency, realized in struggle, educes erotic and imaginative resources vital for shaping a collective identity of who we are and the future we want as ours.

I.

Douglass's oft-cited account of his fight with the slave-breaker Covey in his second autobiography, *My Bondage and My Freedom,*[4] clearly indicates that despite the tortures of slavery, Douglass longed not to simply reverse the terms of his subjugation in order to brutalize his captors. Douglass cites his resistance to Covey as the ignition of his struggle for freedom. A striking feature of Douglass's account is the way in which he perceives the use of power and the value of struggle. He is careful to distinguish his defensive from his aggressive acts, and these distinctions have less to do with an interest in being a good Christian than they do with his concern to not exert force abusively. Douglass's descriptions of his experience distinguish his passionate desire to develop as a mature human being from a ruthless, nearly desperate urge to secure recognition of one's superiority by any means necessary. Douglass, no doubt, seeks recognition, but he pursues his quest in a way that specifically avoids abuse and cruelty. Sheer dominance clearly does not constitute legitimacy in his eyes. In fact, Douglass suggests that those who are compelled to *destroy* others as a means of expressing their desire to assert themselves fail to create the communities within which their honor might genuinely have any worth.

One day, as Douglass is tending the horses in the stables, Covey sneaks, "in a peculiar snake-like way," into the barn and tackles him unawares. Covey attempts to tie Douglass's legs so that he can beat him with less resistance. Although weakened from a beating that had, only days before, injured him so severely that he nearly lost his life, Douglass still manages to successfully prevent being bound. Douglass notes that it seemed as though Covey thought he had him "very securely within his power," when he "resolved to fight": "The fighting madness had come upon me, and I found my strong fingers firmly attached to the throat of my cowardly tormentor; as heedless of consequences, at the moment, as though we stood as equals before the law" (*MB*, 242). Douglass at once broke loose of the belief, inculcated from his birth, that the "masters are superior, and invested with a sort of sacredness" that could not be challenged (*MB*, 251). Douglass describes how he met every blow Covey attempted to make, but that he did not strive to injure him in return. Surprised by the resistance of the slave he had so thoroughly abused just two days earlier, Covey began to tremble. Prior to this time, Douglass claims, the contest had been equal, but Covey could not stand to engage in such a fight. Covey "lustily" cried out for help, Douglass recalls, "not that I was obtaining any marked advantage over him, or was injuring him, but because he was gaining none over me, and was not able, single-handed, to conquer me" (*MB*, 243). Soon enough Covey secured the help he needed, and Douglass was forced to meet the disruption of the balance of power with greater force. He writes, "I was still *defensive* toward Covey, but *aggressive* toward [his cousin] Hughes," who had come to his aid (*MB*, 243).

Douglass quickly dispensed with Hughes by kicking him so hard that he swaggered away in pain. Still, his actions toward Covey remained the same. Even when it appeared as though Covey was about to bludgeon him with a piece of wood, Douglass tossed him into a pile of cow manure rather than taking the wood from him in order to use it to beat him. Readers are told that the fight continued for several hours. Covey repeatedly attempted to gain an advantage by enlisting the help of other slaves, but all refused. Finally, Covey gave up the fight, telling Douglass, "I would not have whipped you half so much as I have had you not resisted" (*MB*, 246). But Douglass claims Covey had not whipped him at all, and he never attempted to whip him again.

Earlier in the work Douglass reflects on the nature of the abuses slaveholders perpetrate. He notes that masters choose to beat slaves who do not resist, not necessarily because they are concerned for their own physical well-being, but because their sense of their own self-worth is inextricably linked to their ability to completely dominate others encountered in these matches. In a description of the brutal flogging of a slave named "Nellie," whose only offense was having the courage to look her master in the eye, Douglass notes how the master succeeded in bruising her flesh but left "her invincible spirit undaunted" (*MB*, 94). Consequently, she was almost never beaten again. Douglass writes, "They prefer to whip those who are most easily whipped. The old doctrine that submission is the best cure for outrage and wrong does not hold good on the slave plantation. He is whipped oftenest, who is whipped easiest; and that slave who has the courage to stand up for himself against the overseer, although he may have many hard stripes at first, becomes, in the end, a freeman, even though he sustain the formal relation of a slave" (*MB*, 95).

It is that sense of freedom that Douglass claims for himself following the fight with Covey. It reflects the "turning point" in his "*life as a slave*" and "rekindled . . . the smouldering embers of liberty" that had been beaten out of him since his youth. Douglass writes, "I was a changed being after that fight. I was *nothing* before; I WAS A MAN NOW" (*MB*, 246). To be a man[5]—and it would seem from his descriptions of Covey's "breeder," Caroline, to be human—is to have force: what Douglass calls "the essential dignity of humanity" (*MB*, 247). "Human nature," he writes, "is so constituted, that it cannot *honor* a helpless man, although it can *pity* him; and even this it cannot do long, if the signs of power do not arise" (*MB*, 247). But we should take special note of the kind force that Douglass exercised in the aforementioned description above and that with which it is contrasted.

Douglass tells us that "Covey was a tyrant, and a cowardly one, withal." As to why he did not report Douglass to the authorities for breaking the law that forbids resisting a master on the penalty of death, Douglass speculates that "Covey was, probably, ashamed to have it known and confessed that he had been mastered by a boy of sixteen. [. . .] The story that he had undertaken to whip a lad, and had been resisted, was, of itself, sufficient to damage him; for his bearing should, in the estimation of slaveholders, be of that imperial order that should make such an occurrence impossible" (*MB*, 248). Covey was in many respects like one of Douglass's earlier masters, Captain Auld. Douglass describes him as a man in whom there was "all the love of domination, the pride of mastery, and the swagger of authority, but his rule lacked the vital element of consistency." "He could be cruel," Douglass continues, "but his methods of showing it were cowardly, and evinced his meanness rather than his spirit. His commands were strong, his enforcement weak" (*MB*, 192).

Speaking of the force that distinguishes him, Douglass writes, "This spirit made me a freeman in *fact*, while I remained a slave in *form*" (*MB*, 247). Further, he claims, "When a slave cannot be flogged he is more than half free. He has a domain as broad as his own manly heart to defend, and his is really '*a power on earth*'" (*MB*, 247). For Douglass, it is the character of the power he exercises in action that distinguishes the free man from the slave, despite his formal conditions.[6]

What does the fight with Covey give Douglass? He describes it himself as acquiring recognition (*for* himself, not *by* Covey) that he is *not* helpless. But his physical bondage persists, and it is unclear that much changes in the social order following the incident, except that Covey is understandably wary of Douglass and chooses to pursue more pliant subjects for his violent outbursts. The struggle itself obviously did not earn Douglass manumission. It did not result in recognition by his torturer that he had a claim or *entitlement* to freedom. So what was it that gave Douglass the experience of being "a man now, of being" a power on earth"?

According to the prevailing conception of justice, he continued to be a slave; his condition was justified in terms of the institution that secured and enforced his slavery, in terms of the white, masculine model of the rational, autonomous, sovereign individual, coupled with views concerning who was and was not capable of such self-government. That institution simply refused to recognize Douglass as having even the possibility of attaining what was recognized as legitimate human agency. He was considered *essentially* deficient. Cast in those terms, it was impossible to *see* him *ever* as anything more than a slave, property. What enables Douglass to see himself as something *more*?

In the course of the struggle Douglass does more than seize the standards of measure of the master and apply them to himself. In fighting, in the activity of struggling—of transforming the situation and the outcome—Douglass derives a new sense of justice (and not merely a new route to it for himself). This new sense of justice enables him to see himself not as someone with (the right to) dominion but rather *as an agent full of possibilities*. It is *that* which produces the *feeling* of himself as free—this is what I call the *aisthesis* of agency. The *aisthesis* of agency is more than simply a sensation. It is an experience that carries cognitive import—something previously unknown is disclosed, and this opens new possibilities for action and the production of meanings.

It is significant that this experience stems from a physical, bodily encounter[7] rather than from the intellectual or spiritual labors characteristic of the nineteenth-century *Bildungsroman* tradition, among which Douglass's writings might be included but from which they should be distinguished. Meaningful freedom is not just a state of mind for Douglass: it is fully *embodied*; it gives the body new meaning. The occasion of his naissance into freedom was not a contest or game or rite of passage that was abstracted from the ordinary and everyday as in the heroic tradition of ancient Greek literature. What Douglass acquires is not a concept of himself as a person with a claim to *power over* others but rather the feeling of having forged a path to a new domain—one "as broad as his own manly heart," one characterized not by recognition of autonomy or self-control but rather by possibility and the power to imaginatively create a future.

Douglass's fight with Covey provides him entrée to what Drucilla Cornell describes as "the imaginary domain," "that psychic and moral space in which we [. . .] are allowed to evaluate and represent who we are."[8] She considers how such imaginative resources are crucial for the formation of identity and one's capacity for self-representation. The imaginary domain, she writes, is what "gives to the individual person, and her only, the right to claim who she is through her own representation of her [. . .] being."[9] This capacity, Cornell suggests, is what gives real import to our concerns for autonomy, which she conceives not simply as freedom from others but rather as the *power to* be the authors of our lives, to be the *sources* of the lives we live and the ways in which they differ from the lives of others.

A new kind of agency is possible in the imaginary domain, and this is particularly significant for those whose situation is utterly abysmal and lacks options for viable action for change. Cornell writes that "the imaginary domain is the space of the 'as if' in which we imagine who we might be if we made ourselves our own end and claimed ourselves as our own person."[10] In the imaginary domain, we are *free* to imaginatively experience not only possible *objects* of desire but the *kind of desire* (or the *shape of desire*) that will animate our actions and orient our larger goals and projects. When, in the fight with Covey, Douglass feels himself to be "a power on earth" rather than merely an agent who either lacks or possesses superior force, he acquires a different sense of human possibility. In this encounter, the intelligible end of the meaning of human being shifts from being cast only in terms of domination— the completion and perfection of which might be total subjection or even annihilation—to being considered in terms of agency that aims chiefly at becoming a creator of ends and the standards by which they might be judged. He moves, in short, from conceiving the good of human reality as power that is realized in terms of possession to defining that good in terms of possessing the possibility of *reshaping the good itself*. When one is free to be good not merely in terms of values constituted by others but free to participate in the determination of those values oneself, one engages a thoroughly different, and I would argue more powerful, sense of agency than before. As Douglass himself plays a role in defining the terms of his fight with Covey, as he determines for himself what will constitute superior moral character in his resistance, he experiences the felt quality of the imaginary domain in which his freedom positively acquires its significance and meaning. It is an experience that opens a whole new set of possibilities, and it enables him to surmount if not the physical subjection of his body the subjection of his desire that gives that body and all of its actions its meaning and future possibilities. Empowered by *the feeling of his freedom*, Douglass is enabled to imagine innumerable ways in which it might be further realized, which is not to be free of the demands of others.[11]

    The kind of freedom exercised in the imaginary domain is called "freedom of personality" by Cornell, which "is valuable because it is what lets us make a life we embrace as our own."[12] This, I take it, is what Douglass means when he claims "Now I AM A MAN," not that the fight has made him *manly* or summoned from him manly qualities, or that previously he was somehow deficient in human being, but rather that he had a palpable experience of the felt quality of himself as an agent full of possibility—to exercise restraint, to resist, to vie for determining the terms of his struggle and what its end should be—and that this was a life he could embrace as his own. It does not represent a discovery of a pre-fabricated autonomous, metaphysical self, and it is not just the building of himself as a "self-made man" who achieves his freedom by ruling himself.[13]

The struggle that marks Douglass's freedom represents a conquest over the anesthetized, mutilated aesthetic issuing from the lived, enslaved body. Why this would be vital emerging from the experience of slavery should be easily understood: the institution of slavery aims to exercise its control, force compliance, and justify itself on the basis of the idea that the slave is merely a *thing*, his or her body an object of commerce, property of another. The *aisthesis* of freedom deploys creative resources that enliven and enable the power of human agency. This is what Douglass achieves in his momentous struggle. He becomes, in the words of Simone de Beauvoir, "apprenticed in freedom" and hence enabled and empowered to revolt against the values that reduce his existence to useful property and exclude him from legitimizing human community.[14] Slavery cements its hold by effecting transmogrified desire and impairment of any sense of the erotic that would enable one to see oneself as a maker of pleasure and beauty, one who shares and introduces meaningful value in the world. What Douglass acquires in the fight with Covey is a kind of *visibility* (both a kind of seeing and being seen) activated by what has been called by others "loving perception," a way of seeing the world such that one seizes upon and finds one's ecstasies in the *possibilities* of what one perceives.[15]

So what can Nietzsche contribute to this vision, and how might we revise Nietzsche's own conception illuminated by that vision? Nietzsche looks to mythic origins of struggle to challenge modern conceptions of competition. Out of this account he develops criteria for ascertaining the use and abuse of power that will allow us to draw, redraw, and recognize limits of power—cooperatively and communally defined—without denying the benefits of resistance for human development or threatening its legitimacy in the course of political struggle. Tracing the elastic social space of the contest (*agon*), Nietzsche locates the emergence of values in an erotic economy of contest. It is this vision that I wish to briefly sketch and consider in light of his conception of moral development and the production of meaning.

Before moving to my discussion of Nietzsche, I wish to draw attention to one more way in which Douglass distinguishes productive expressions of power from those that are destructive. He describes the way in which the slaves' spirit of resistance is further sapped by forcing it into futile outlets. The fight with Covey stands in contrast to the pseudo contests permitted to slaves on holidays. Douglass notes that these events served as a means of "keeping the minds of the slaves occupied with prospective pleasure, within the limits of slavery" (*MB*,

253). They were encouraged to participate in "only those wild and low sports, peculiar to semi-civilized people" (*MB*, 255). On these holidays the masters would encourage a kind of saturnalia that would produce petty and destructive rivalry and drunkenness, suggesting that these characterized the true life of freedom. Once the aftereffects of these activities became apparent, Douglass claims, liberty looked significantly less desirable. Throughout his account, the abusive and corruptive physical force of the community that produced slavery is contrasted with the value of a strengthened spirit (*MB*, 272), one buttressed by the feeling of freedom that is theirs.

II.

What Nietzsche can add to Douglass's vision as I have described the kind of *seeing* made possible through the feeling of power that struggle brings forth is a typology of different kinds of struggles and how they cultivate different desires relating to the pursuit of freedom. Nietzsche interestingly holds a similar view regarding the potentially valuable experiences that are had in the course of struggles or contests, and he considers the opportunities and potential dangers found in both the forms of struggle and the ways of acting within them. Such a framework might provide us with further evaluative criteria for considering Douglass's fight with Covey, in ways perhaps most interesting for those concerned to reconcile Douglass's professed pacifism at the time with his willingness to commit violence in the fight.[16]

Nietzsche's model for struggle is drawn from his consideration of the ancient Greek contest, or *agon*. Although Nietzsche's most extended discussion of that particular form of struggle is found in his unpublished preface to an unwritten book, "Homer's Contest," he develops those ideas and expands them throughout his writings. Most significant for my purposes here is Nietzsche's interest in the different view of competition that he thinks the Greeks held and how that view is relevant to their ethics. Of particular interest to Nietzsche is how a dynamic of localization and circulation of power, specifically put to creative and constructive purposes, can be cultivated through contest and how that mechanism is vulnerable to degeneration and may become deformed if the contest is put to other purposes.[17]

Those discussing Nietzsche's agonism frequently make reference to his account of the text of Hesiod's *Works and Days* that Pausanias is supposed to have seen during his travels in Greece. Unlike the text that the scholars of Nietzsche's day considered legitimate, the copy that Pausanias cites describes two Eris goddesses. Eris is ordinarily associated with strife, conflict, and war. She was considered the source of envy and jealous rage. What is curious about Pausanias's reference to the twin goddesses is that one is considered good: that which brings about dissention bears a strong family resemblance to a fruitful desire, namely, the urge to excel. Nietzsche carefully maps the first goddess to what he describes as a desire to bring about complete destruction of what one opposes—a thirst for destruction—while he identifies the other as inciting a drive to bring out of oneself a performance that exceeds that of the opponent.[18]

Struggles can have either creative or destructive ends and corresponding means to reach them. In his *Human, All-Too-Human*,[19] Nietzsche further distinguishes different kinds of contests when he highlights the modes of action of *rising above* [*erheben*] and *pushing down* [*herabdrücken*] what one opposes: "The envious man is conscious of every respect in which the man he envies exceeds the common measure and desires to push him down [*herabdrücken*] to it—or to raise himself up [*erheben*] to the height of the other: out of which there arise two different modes of action, which Hesiod designated as the evil and the good Eris" (*HH* II (2):29). Just as individuals can manifest these actions, so too can cultures and institutions that regulate the available forms of contest. Nietzsche speculates in "Homer's Contest" that the proliferation of outlets organized on an agonistic model, the form of contest best suited to fostering and rewarding the activity of rising above, accounts for the monumental accomplishments in ancient Greek culture.

That Nietzsche goes beyond simply admiring "a little healthy competition" becomes clear when he subsequently turns his attention to investigating the struggles at the heart of tragic art (*The Birth of Tragedy*), the contest for truth and virtue in Socratic and Platonic philosophy (especially *The Gay Science* and *Beyond Good and Evil*), the adaptation of spiritualized struggle in Christian morality (especially *Daybreak, On the Genealogy of Morals*, and *The Antichrist*), and the scientific conceptions of life and health (especially in his lecture notes and *On the Genealogy of Morals*). Nietzsche is particularly interested in how what is distinguished as appropriate and acceptable struggle follows certain political ends and how the corresponding dispositions about competition, resistance, and struggle are reflected in ethical perspectives. Nietzsche considers striving and struggle to be a basic condition of existence, not merely for human beings but for everything that is.

Given that, he asks, what form of struggle might best advance human possibilities generally?

Several features of productive contest emerge, although Nietzsche never offers a full exposition of the relevant question.[20] Beyond potentially inspiring excellence, which would presumably be relative to some previously existing standard, agonistic contest is supposed to be radically open, at least this seems to be a feature that Nietzsche specifically designates as exceptional about the view he finds in ancient Greece.[21] The openness is achieved in two respects: first, the viability of challenge must be preserved; second, the contest must be flexible enough to generate decisions about excellence that are relative not only to past performances but also in accordance with new standards produced through the contest itself.[22] In other words, although rare and exceptional, every contest at least extends the possibility that the prevailing standards of measure themselves could be reformed.

The significance of this openness to the community as a whole is evident to Nietzsche in what Diogenes Laertius reports as the original purpose of ostracism: anyone who emerged as an undefeatable opponent had to be banished, as great as such a person might be. This was not because greatness itself was despised; rather, it was out of concern for cultivating the pursuit of excellence as a whole. The latter was to be effected not through reduction to the lowest common denominator but by ever extending the prospect of being able to earn a title to greatness, to participate in creating the standard for what would count as best. Moreover, those standards of judgment were being constantly formulated and renegotiated in every instance of rendering a decision. Nietzsche cites the most exemplary contestants as those who not only offered an exceptional performance in the contest but also revised the very standards by which they were judged. Nietzsche's admiration of these features of contest makes it clear that he is not simply nostalgic for a heroic ethic of nobility lost, and he is not pining for a return to the good old days of Homer. Moreover, it is worth considering the relations between victors, competitors, and the community that will provide the institutional framework for such agonistic enterprises to occur.

Although contests typically end when a particular individual distinguishes himself or herself in whatever way the contest sets up as decisive, there is a significant communal basis to this distinction. Victors can only become such by virtue of the institutions that make their activities meaningful in such a way; they require a certain kind of communal recognition for their actions to afford them any sort of status or special significance; victories are always contingent upon the community whose judgment provides the basis of legitimacy for any such claim to superiority. Thus victors are always indebted for their honor to those who would bestow it; it is not simply taken or even independently earned. Moreover, victors are significantly indebted to other competitors, those immediate and those who have preceded them. Their actions both supply a contest relative to which the victors' actions appear as excellent and draw out the particular performance that earned the victor his or her distinction.[23]

The fragility of these arrangements is underscored by Nietzsche as he charts examples of corruption of agonistic relations. These are interesting to consider, because they provide further insight into how Nietzsche refines his understanding of the distinction between creative and destructive expressions of power. Although the Greeks are Nietzsche's exemplars of agonism, they clearly failed to sustain this remarkable feature of their culture.[24] Exceptional victory has a tendency to induce *hybris*, a belief in invincibility that can lead to the commission of violence, and a lack of respect for one's opponents and the shared institutions that legitimate the triumph.[25] Nietzsche claims that this happened in Athens following the Persian Wars—when the Athenians showed themselves to be such decisive victors in the war against the Persians, they disrupted the rivalry among the Greek city-states that had previously prevailed and served to regulate the significance of what it meant to be "Greek".[26] Public contests that provided creative outlets for the desire to strive deteriorated into spectacle. Without the creation of a new outlet for struggle, Nietzsche imagines, the Greeks might have become so brutal as to engage in wanton destruction and annihilation of each other (*BT* 15). Instead, what emerged as a replacement for the kind of contests he admired was Socratic philosophy with its dialectic, which had the *appearance* of the old kind of struggle.[27] But dialectic was significantly different, according to Nietzsche, because it failed to provide the openness described earlier. First, dialectic was dominated by an unbeatable opponent, namely, the Socratic position of truth, and, secondly, the standards of judgment were absolutely uncontestable—reason rules tyrannically in Nietzsche's caricature. Moreover, with the Socratic game struggles that constituted the public sphere were replaced with spiritual ones waged by individuals. And with that, the cultural (social) possibilities withered.

Nietzsche's tale continues to unfold as he traces the genealogy of the spiritual contest of Socratic-Platonic philosophy to Christian morality and even in contemporary scientific theory of organic development and health. Throughout, Nietzsche remains attentive to *forms* of the struggles, the kinds of actions within them they encouraged, and their prospects for providing the benefits of earlier forms of contest. Nietzsche's account depicts the contest becoming increasingly closed and increasingly more violent, even when, and perhaps most especially when, aggressive actions of struggle, resistance, and challenge are deemed inappropriate in the name of advancing civilization or morality. On Nietzsche's account, as this process continues, human beings also become less free, not because their will to be brutal is restrained but because they have less access to creative struggle than before.

But what is the goal of creative struggle? Ultimately and at their best, creative struggles aim at the production of new values and meanings. Nietzsche thought the productive kind of contest was at the heart of tragic art. The *agon* of the Apollinian and Dionysian artistic forces created an arena in which the best was drawn out of each in a dynamic through which neither was allowed to dominate. Unlike Aristotle, Nietzsche thought the real fruit of tragedy was not *catharsis* but an *aisthesis* of human being through which what it means to be human is given a *felt sense*, which is inaccessible solely through the idealized image of the Apollinian or the rapturous Dionysian. Tragic art, for Nietzsche, effected a magical transformation in which the entire symbolism of the body was called into play (*BT* 2). Rather than purging the audience of pity and fear, tragedy provided its witnesses opportunities "to see oneself transformed before one's own eyes and to begin to act as if one had actually entered into another body." Tragic art dramatized the struggle between competing perspectives of the individualized and undifferentiated, the intelligible and the mysterious. It represented the creative appropriation of opposition and resistance.[28]

It is this emphasis on the transformative and liberating affects of the felt quality of the experience of struggle that I think Douglass and Nietzsche share, at least insofar as they are attentive to the sense of agency that potentially emerges in such engagements. Clearly Douglass did not figure his fight with Covey in terms of the ancient Greek *agon*, and certainly Nietzsche did not look to the struggles for freedom enacted by enslaved Africans as a model for the kind of struggles he admired as genuinely liberatory. But I think Douglass and Nietzsche do share a conception of agency requisite for realizing meaningful freedom. Both highlight how such a form of agency can emerge through specific experiences of struggle, mindful of how those struggles differ from the commission of violence. And both give consideration to how what is at stake in such interactions is not simply recognition as a member of a community of those entitled to rule but rather understanding oneself as a participant in the community of those who determine the qualities of legitimate power.

Thus far my account of how Nietzsche thinks about the use and abuse of power in relation to struggle and its transformative possibilities, leaves unaddressed several serious ways in which Nietzsche diverges from Douglass on these matters, and these concerns have a bearing on the charge of racism mentioned in the introduction. It should be clear that although I do not think Nietzsche is an advocate of cruelty and violence—the evidence for which is his condemnation of anti-agonistic views on the grounds that they actually constitute a celebration of cruelty and torture as they shut down opportunities for creative expressions of force as discussed above—Nietzsche is clearly no pacifist, and he acknowledges that there is no ultimate constraint against abusive expressions of power. Nonetheless, Nietzsche thinks we will be less interested, less in need of pursuing a sense of ourselves as agents through violent force if and when we have the opportunity to cultivate a sense of ourselves as powerful in ways that actually enhance the significance of our possibilities generally. Nietzsche's genealogies of slavish moralities highlight well this very concern and render more intelligible his discussion of suffering.[29]

III.

Nietzsche's *Genealogy*[30] provides multiple histories of births of moralities and the sets of values they found. More specifically, Nietzsche is interested in the origin and mechanics of value creation. The text traces several, mythic births and the struggles that form the basis of these inventions. Essay two considers the "breeding" of "the animal who is permitted to make promises" (*GM* II:1; translation my own).[31] The point is to trace the psychic evolution of morality, which Nietzsche sees as loosely analogous to physiological development. Like the physical body, the psyche has a process of nutrition. Nietzsche's account of morality in the second essay considers the cultivation of the capacities that enable us to be morally responsible and prone to guilt and bad conscience, for which memory is necessary, interrupting or blocking the process of "inpsychation." Inpsychation is Nietzsche's term of art for describing "the fact that what we experience and absorb enters our consciousness as little while we are digesting it [. . .] as does the thousandfold process, involved in physical nourishment—so-called 'incorporation'" (*GM* II:1). In psychic digestion, forgetting plays an *active* role; without it, "there could be no happiness, no cheerfulness, no hope, no pride, no *present*" (*GM* II:1). The introduction of memory, Nietzsche suggests, potentially clogs that process to the point of resulting in psychic dyspepsia. Morality in requiring practices of memory that incapacitate vital forgetting could be considered, on this account, a *disease*.[32]

The rest of the second essay of the *Genealogy* investigates the preconditions that make human being susceptible to psychic indigestion. He describes the emergence of the "sovereign individual" (*GM* II:2), an ideal type whose signature features are being conscious of his own power and freedom, a master of free will, and in possession of conscience. This figure appears in many discussions of Nietzsche's vision for what it might mean to advance "beyond good and evil," beyond the slavish morality that Nietzsche thinks we still embrace. An important consideration, though, is *whose* ideal the sovereign individual is supposed to be. I have argued at length elsewhere that it is definitely *not* Nietzsche's.[33] The relevant evidence for this, in the context of the present discussion, is Nietzsche's characterization of the practices of memory required to make it possible for our *present morality* (perhaps synonymous with Kantian morality with its emphasis on autonomy[34]) to hold up the ideal of sovereignty as its highest moral aim, how this has made it *diseased* (as discussed earlier) and how this has a basis in *destructive violence*. Conscience—as the right to stand security for oneself, as a prerequisite for having the right to affirm oneself—requires *memory*. Among the *mnemotechnics*, as Nietzsche describes the techniques for producing memory, about which "the oldest psychology" teaches us is enduring pain, which produces the most-lasting memories (*GM* II:3). Systems of cruelty, sacrifice, and mutilation—and all ascetic practices generally—serve the function of "fixing ideas," of burning memory into the flesh, of infusing the body with remembrance.

In this particular telling of the story of the development of morality, guilt and bad conscience emerge not out of a sense of responsibility but rather out of an economic system that required memory for the repayment of debts. Nietzsche discusses the logic of compensation that brings with it warrant and title to cruelty (*GM* II:5). He notes how evaluations become tied to the body, its parts and limbs construed in terms of equivalences. Recompense takes the form of pleasure in violation, whereby a creditor earns as his tribute the right to abuse, to vent his power freely over others (*GM* II:5). Moral debt, guilt, and responsibility are as soaked in blood and torture, as Nietzsche tells the story, and once these ideas took root in the moral realm, cruelty became even more refined and memory—through the intensification of suffering and pain—even more enduring.

One might ask, "[t]o what extent can suffering balance debts or guilt?" Nietzsche conjectures, "To the extent that to *make* suffer was in the highest degree pleasurable, to the extent that the injured party exchanged for the loss he had sustained, including the displeasure caused by the loss, an extraordinary counterbalancing pleasure: that of *making* suffer—a genuine *festival*" (*GM* II:6). Higher culture is built upon these practices of torture and cruelty. Nietzsche does not note this to celebrate the fact or invite even greater torture in order to advance culture further still. The prevailing question of the *Genealogy* is whether and how human beings might be able to get beyond these ascetic practices as their method of advancement.

Nietzsche's discussion of suffering in the seventh section of the second essay occurs in the context elaborated earlier. The preceding sections investigate the production of suffering as serving, first, economic and, later, political and moral ends. The brutalization of the body for such purposes has, through Christianization, become "translated into the imaginative and psychical and adorned with such innocent names that even the tenderest and most hypocritical conscience is not suspicious of them" (*GM* II:7). Nietzsche suggests that Christianity took root so quickly and was so compelling precisely because it *intensified* rather than alleviated pain—enhancement of the meaning of human existence was tied to the endurance of pain, and then the screws were turned. Power became measured by the amount of suffering one could *endure* rather than the amount of suffering one could *inflict*. The production and escalation of suffering were required to make life seem even more desirable. Bred with the capacity to promise, the animal that became the human, striving to be an angel, became a grotesque creature that celebrates and craves its own torture, a being with a penchant for masochism.

It is in this light that Nietzsche's conjecture[35] about "Negroes" and animals as less susceptible to pain occurs. William A. Preston cites it as evidence of both Nietzsche's cruelty and his racism.[36] Considered in context, however, it clearly cannot be read as a justification for torture. The passage reads:

Perhaps in those days [when making suffer was pleasurable]— the delicate may be comforted by this thought—pain did not hurt as much as it does now; at least that is a conclusion a doctor may arrive at who has treated Negroes (taken as representative of prehistoric man—) for severe internal inflammations that would drive even the best constituted European to distraction— in the case of Negroes they do *not* do so. The curve of human

susceptibility to pain seems in fact to take an extraordinary
and almost sudden drop as soon as one has passed the upper
ten thousand or ten million of the top stratum of culture; and
for my own part, I have no doubt that the combined suffering
of all the animals ever subjected to the knife for scientific ends
is utterly negligible compared with *one* painful night of a single hysterical bluestocking. (*GM* II:7, emphasis)

Preston reads this as justification for the torture of Negroes[37]—*why not
enslave and torment them—aren't they really as insensitive as animals,
anyway?* But that presumes that Nietzsche values the "hysterical bluestocking," that the hysteric's sensitivity is legitimate and worthy of
consideration. But that does not seem to be the case at all in this passage.
The bluestocking is *hysterical*, and he is so precisely because of his
bizarre susceptibility to pain; he is pathetic, not morally superior. Hence,
that with which he is contrasted—animals and "Negroes"—avoid such
condemnation. Animals and Negroes are less *dis*-eased, not less worthy;
they fare better, from a Nietzschean perspective, than the miserable
bluestocking who is nearly undone in a single night of pain. Nietzsche's
characterization of "Negroes" as primitive and exemplary of "prehistoric"
man no doubt betrays a kind of ignorance and pernicious prejudice
that others would use in the justification of slavery, but his discussion of
suffering here is not part of an attempt to justify racially based slavery
or the torture of others.

Mindful of these concerns, one is better positioned to consider the
production of meaning through the "interpret[ation] of a whole mysterious machinery of salvation into suffering" (*GM* II:7). In the grips of the
logic of suffering, exemplars of struggle shift from heroes who accomplish great deeds—whose actions are considered to extend the range of
human meaning—to paragons of excruciating suffering, the suffering
Christ, the turning of the other cheek. As the second essay of the
Genealogy tells the story, early human beings sought the *aisthesis* of
power and freedom in the infliction of pain and suffering. Hurting others
was pleasurable, because it gave one a sense of one's power and oneself
as free. Morality, particularly Christian morality, gained its hold through
a reversal of the process: *accepting harm* and *enduring suffering* provided the measure of one's power and freedom. One compelled by such
a worldview could conceivably be led to the extraordinarily perverse
conclusion that domination and torture are actually *morally enriching*,
in short, that slavery would not be something to resist but rather
would provide opportunities to be savored.[38] Nietzsche imagines what
might constitute the next stage of development of humanity. Would it

be yet another reversal back to preferring the *infliction* of suffering, which would seem to constitute a regression, or would it seek the *aisthesis* of power and freedom creatively, thereby breaking from the two prior destructive models? Nietzsche's notion of self-overcoming is an experimental effort to go beyond those paradigms.

When, in his later philosophy, Nietzsche turns his attention to spiritualized struggles he rejects ascetic forms of internalized contest, because he thinks they are essentially *self*-destructive insofar as they draw us into harmful and crippling activities of pushing down (drawing on the model of destructive contest elaborated earlier). The alternative that Nietzsche develops, the practice of self-overcoming, is supposed to enact a productive, creative mode of rising above, similar in its structure, although potentially different in its content, to Homer's revaluation of human existence as contest. The model of self-overcoming that emerges out of Nietzsche's middle and later writings utilizes the language of biology to describe the dynamic. In the process of self-overcoming, what one has been is incorporated and appropriated in the course of the *Kampf* that one is: "Thus the body goes through history, a becoming [*ein Werdender*] and a fighting [*ein Kämpfender*]. And the spirit—what is that to the body? The herald of its fights and victories, companion and echo" (*Z* 1: "Gift-Giving"; my translation).[39] It is true that the social benefits of this process are not the *central* concern in Nietzsche's later thought, but that does not mean that Nietzsche's later agonism is void of communal transformative applications. Speaking from a community that does not struggle in any way other than what is violent and destructive, Nietzsche attempts—perhaps feebly so—to envision a community of free spirits of which his fighting spirit will be properly a part. The solitude he laments and attempts to appropriate is not a goal but rather a consequence of the spiritual lethargy of those around him.

IV.

In conclusion, I suggest that the transgressive spirit that Nietzsche's work describes resonates with remarkable similarity to that which Douglass's work bears witness. Each seeks the overcoming of an aesthetic of agency that finds its ecstasies in sadism and masochism. Both demand that we ignite what we might call the eristic-erotic, or what I elsewhere designate the "erisotic"[40] in our pursuit of a life-enhancing and an enabling form of spirit, developed through resistance and agonistic engagement. Conceptualizing social relations in terms of the *erisotic* would reflect an understanding of both how loving and striving are inextricably bound and how both *bind us together*. Although I think that we would be right to claim that Douglass's work better exemplifies the significance the Other plays in this process,[41] I think Nietzsche has more to contribute to the discussion than some would allow. By tracing Nietzsche's interest in what he identifies as the agonistic form of striving, by connecting it to a particular mode of being and a specific type of approach to obstacles and challenges, we can take steps toward answering what I believe are some of the most serious charges against Nietzsche—that he is an *advocate* of war, violence, and cruelty—without watering down Nietzsche's claim that serious and significant struggles inform the kinds of lives we lead and the kinds of persons we become.

Finally, I wish to emphasize the positive aspects of Nietzsche's work that he also intends his readers to emulate. Despite his frequently gloomy disposition toward contemporary culture, Nietzsche understands himself as an advocate of love, as well as joy, and as one who strives to diminish the prevalence of cruelty. Zarathustra tells us that "life is a well of joy," but so far we have enjoyed too little life, for "[A]s long as there have been men, man has felt too little joy: that alone, my brothers, is our original sin. And learning better to feel joy, we learn best not to hurt others or to plan hurts for them" (*Z* II:3). When we better learn to realize the joy that is available in life, Nietzsche claims, we also will learn to diminish the role we play in inflicting and perpetuation harm and cruelty on others.

Still, my generous reading of Nietzsche alongside Douglass does not completely exonerate Nietzsche of the charges thus described. Nietzsche can and should be criticized for not taking seriously the real problems of suffering as they are experienced by persons who are physically and emotionally exploited, those who are starving, and those who live in communities devastated by war. I believe the qualifications I have made to what counts as agonistic and what does not help us recognize that those sufferings clearly do not fit the category of that which increases our health and strength; they are not examples of "going(s) under" that prepare us for overcomings. But Nietzsche was not as careful as he might have been in making those distinctions, and I do not mean to suggest that his work does not leave him vulnerable for other attacks.

Both Douglass and Nietzsche envision a subject who exercises freedom in creative appropriation of the meaning of human being. The agonized spirit is not simply hostile and aggressive. It does not seek the expression of power unbound. Indeed, the agonized spirit comes to appreciate that the *aisthesis* of powerful freedom is relational, and Douglass, particularly, is ever mindful of the ways in which real life struggles against the most oppressive forces afford us opportunities not only to forge an image of ourselves as individuals but also to give shape to our humanity. Neither Douglass nor Nietzsche adequately develops an ethos of agonism, although I hope these *unlikely illuminations* have shed light on the ways in which both provide us with resources to take up that task for ourselves.

Notes

1. Friedrich Nietzsche, *The Gay Science* (*GS*), trans. Walter Kaufmann (New York: Vintage Books, 1974), section 377. I return to this concern in the penultimate section of this chapter.

2. This particular charge against Nietzsche is levied by William A. Preston in his "Nietzsche on Blacks," in *Existence in Black: An Anthology of Black Existential Philosophy*, edited and with an introduction by Lewis R. Gordon (New York: Routledge, 1997), 169. I address Preston's article in greater detail in this chapter.

3. I am not the first to attempt such an interpretive exercise. Cynthia Willett's *Maternal Ethics and Other Slave Moralities* (New York: Routledge, 1995) precedes my account here. The material for this chapter began ten years ago as a commentary on that book, and I am grateful to Willett for her comments on a much different earlier draft. (Subsequently, she reiterated many of her claims about Douglass and a few of those about Nietzsche, with some slight modifications in her *The Soul of Justice: Social Bonds and Racial Hubris* [Ithaca, NY: Cornell University Press, 2001].) Willett's project is quite different from mine. She makes other points of comparison, and I take issue with the conclusions she draws. Where relevant, I shall engage Willett's interesting work in the notes that follow. For now, I shall simply mention her ultimate claims. Willett compares Douglass to Nietzsche in order to show how Douglass similarly shares Nietzsche's critique of the "stoic rational" tradition of ethics in Western culture, and how their anti-asceticism is related to their conceptions of ("phallic") "will to power" and the importance of the body. But Willett argues that their views diverge on their conceptions of freedom and community. While Nietzsche seeks sovereign, dominating individuality, Willett claims, Douglass holds a conception of will that is interested in power but has a "prosocial" goal. As I argue in what follows, I have found in Nietzsche a sustained and somewhat detailed account of distinctions between destructive violence and creative agonism, which I find in Douglass, too. This distinction is relevant to how each conceives freedom, which I discuss later.

4. Frederick Douglass, *My Bondage and My Freedom* (New York: Dover, 1969). This work is hereafter cited in the text as *MB*, followed by the page number; emphasis is in the original unless otherwise indicated.

5. For a discussion of the masculine character of Douglass's reflections, see Richard Yarborough, "Race, Violence, and Manhood: The Masculine Ideal in Frederick Douglass's 'The Heroic Slave'," in *Haunted Bodies: Gender and Southern Texts*, ed. Anne Goodwyn Jones and Susan V. Donaldson (Charlottesville: University of Virginia Press, 1997), 159–84.

6. I think this distinction is *somewhat* missed by Willett. For Douglass, it seems, what he describes as the *spirit* this encounter ignited welled up from the particular kind of power he managed to exercise, and not just its goal or end. Douglass's account of the fight with Covey and the role it played in his moral development are indicative for Willett of the fact that Douglass has a notion of "a certain will to power" (Willett, *Maternal Ethics*, 163). Precisely what is "will to power" for Douglass or for Nietzsche remains relatively unclear in Willett's work, although this reader gets the sense that it is supposed to be (self-evidently?) bad, masculinist, possibly misogynistic, "hybristic" (163), "repressive," and bound up with an "escapist fantasy" (167). Willett associates "will to power" with what she characterizes as the "mythos of the sovereign individual" (165), which is possibly a throwback to the Western emphasis on autonomy in the case of Nietzsche, but which is superceded by Douglass. I return to the figure of the sovereign individual later, since this characterization of power and the figure of its ideal expression are relevant to the conception of freedom Willett ascribes to Nietzsche and uses as a foil for Douglass's view.

7. As mentioned earlier, Willett's comparison of Douglass and Nietzsche is organized, in part, around discussion of how both aim to revalue the meaning of the body. Willett links this in both Nietzsche and Douglass, at least in part, to a renewed emphasis on the animality of humanity. But animality has very different connotations for each, as Willett portrays their views: Douglass awakens "animal sprits," while Nietzsche celebrates anti-social and violent *bestiality*. The claim concerning Nietzsche's celebration of bestiality revolves around his supposed reverie in violence. I return to this issue later.

8. Drucilla Cornell, *At the Heart of Freedom: Feminism, Sex and Equality* (Princeton: Princeton University Press, 1998), x. Also see her *The Imaginary Domain: Abortion, Pornography, and Sexual Harassment* (New York: Routledge, 1995).

9. Cornell, *At the Heart*, 10.

10. Cornell, *At the Heart*, 8.

11. I discuss these ideas in the context of analysis of works by Toni Morrison and by Ntozake Shange in my "Authorizing Desire Erotic Poetics and the *Aisthesis* of Freedom," in *(Un)Making Race, Re-Making Soul: Transformative Aesthetics and the Practice of Freedom*, ed. Christa Davis Acampora and Angela Cotten (Albany: State University of New York Press, 2007).

12. Cornell, *At the Heart*, 62.

13. This is apparently the view of Robert Levine, *Martin Delany, Frederick Douglass, and the Political of Representative Identity* (Chapel Hill: University of North Carolina Press, 1997), with which Frank M. Kirkland takes issue in his "Enslavement, Moral Suasion, and Struggles for Recognition: Frederick Douglass's Answer to the Question—'What is Enlightenment?'" in *Frederick Douglass:A Critical Reader*, ed. Bill E. Lawson and Frank M. Kirkland (Malden, MA: Blackwell, 1999). Kirkland criticizes emphases on self-legislation as the most significant feature of the fight with Covey for Douglass, since it follows from such an account that *"the action Douglass takes on himself takes precedent over the action he takes against Covey"* (298, emphasis in original). In such a case, "Douglass's freedom is [. . .] placed *outside* the interaction-context or the struggle with Covey" (298, emphasis in original). I also wish to emphasize the significance of the action taken within the context of the struggle and the way in which it created a particular experience that produced the sensations and insights described earlier. What is significant for my view is that the fight provided Douglass with a unique experience, the felt quality of which gave Douglass a new sense of his freedom. It was not simply an occasion of learning something that he had not recognized before or an opportunity for solidifying his moral principles through concrete action. My interpretation differs from those of others in its emphasis on the aesthetic significance as it relates to agency. Other interesting and highly noteworthy readings of the fight with Covey include Bernard R. Boxill's "The Fight with Covey," in *Existence in Black*, 273–90. Boxill sees the fight understood by Douglass as demonstrating "a willingness to stand up for the principles of morality," and that this is what Douglass means by "force (or power)" (287). He further claims that power is "a capacity to arouse the fear of others" (290). Also see Lewis R. Gordon, "Douglass as an Existentialist" in *Existentia Africana: Understanding Africana Existential Thought* (New York: Routledge, 2000), 41–61. Gordon claims that the fight with Covey is chiefly an account of Douglass's realization of his agency: "He speaks of force, but force here is ambiguous since he also contrasts it with helplessness. Force here refers to will, to agency, to the human being as active. At the very heart of the tale, then, is a statement on agency" (59–60).

14. See Simone de Beauvoir, *The Ethics of Ambiguity* (New York: Citadel, 1991), 35–40.

15. The idea of "loving perception" is discussed by numerous writers. It is initially defined in Marilyn Frye's *The Politics of Reality: Essays in Feminist Theory* (Trumansburg, NY: The Crossing Press, 1983). Also see María Lugones, "Playfulness, 'World'-Travelling, and Loving Perception," (Hypatia 2:2 [Summer 1987] pp. 3–19), who specifically objects to an agonistic conception of the self and relations to others, and Lewis R. Gordon, "Existential Dynamics of Theorizing Black Invisibility," in *Existence in Black*.

16. I am less concerned with this particular problem, but the connection to Nietzsche is found here too, albeit with a different twist. Nietzsche never

professes pacifism, of course, but he is accused of being an advocate of violence. Douglass's willingness to physically resist Covey appears to some to be more compatible with his writings after 1850, when he breaks with pacifist abolitionists and begins to publicly support violent resistance by slaves against slaveholders. Although Douglass was no doubt, in his words, "resolved to fight," I do not see his actions as violent in this particular encounter with Covey. If anything, he exhibits remarkable restraint for a man whose life is quite literally at stake. I think Nietzsche's conception of different kinds of contests and modes of actions, which aims to distinguish creative from destructive or violent activities, further supports the idea that Douglass was not committing violence in his fight with Covey, and so the conflict with his pacifist views is less significant.

17. This is precisely what Nietzsche thinks happened to ancient Greek *agon* following its co-option in Platonic philosophy and Christian morality. I develop these ideas at greater length in several articles, which were published after this text was written but was still awaiting publication, including "*Demos Agonistes Redux*: Reflections on the *Streit* of Political Agonism," *Nietzsche-Studien* 32 (2003): 373–89; "Nietzsche's Agonal Wisdom," *International Studies in Philosophy* 35:3 (Fall 2003): 205–25; and "Of Dangerous Games and Dastardly Deeds: A Typology of Nietzsche's Contests," *International Studies in Philosophy* 34:3 (Fall 2002): 135–51. Most of the ideas raised in this section appear in some form in these articles.

18. See Friedrich Nietzsche, "Homer's Contest" trans. Christa Davis Acampora, *Nietzscheana* V: 1996 pp. i–iv and 1–8. Thus I find a *qualitative* distinction in Nietzsche's conception of power, and not merely a *quantitative* one, as Willett describes (*Maternal Ethics*, 165).

19. Friedrich Nietzsche, *Human, All-Too-Human,* trans. R. J. Hollingdale (New York: Cambridge University Press, 1986).

20. The closest he comes to providing an affirmative answer to this question might be through his *Thus Spoke Zarathustra*, which might account for why he admired it so greatly.

21. See "Homer's Contest" and Nietzsche's notebooks from the 1870s.

22. These two features make Nietzsche's work particularly appealing to political philosophers working on radical democratic theory. See for example, Alan Schrift's "Nietzsche *for* Democracy?," *Nietzsche-Studien* 29 (2000): 220–33; Herman Siemens, "Nietzsche and Agonistic Politics: A Review of Recent Literature," *Nietzsche-Studien* 30 (2001): 509–26; Acampora, "*Demos Agonistes Redux*: Reflections on the *Streit* of Political Agonism," *Nietzsche-Studien* 32 (2003): 373–89.

23. This system of indebtedness, its multiple layers and circuits, is playfully treated by Pindar in his ode for Hagesidamos, the boys' boxing victor in 476 B.C.E., *Olympian X*; it also is where Pindar recounts the founding of the Olympic games.

24. In "Homer's Contest," Nietzsche offers the *hybris* of Miltiades as evidence that the Greeks were waning in their capacity to properly cultivate the agonistic spirit. Similar comments can be found in his notes for the unfinished "untimely meditation" on philology.

25. In *Maternal Ethics*, Willett repeatedly describes Nietzsche's conception of power as hubristic. In her later book, *The Soul of Justice*, more extensive discussions of hybris are found. There Willett draws interesting and illuminating comparisons between the tragedy of Toni Morrison's *Beloved* and the conception of tragedy in ancient Greek culture (see especially chapters 7 and 9). Willett emphasizes that Morrison's tragic story reveals *hybris* striking against "the libidinal core of the soul," and she contrasts this view with what she takes to be *hybris* as conceived by "the Greeks." The chief distinction is supposed to be the fact that boundaries drawn by Greek *hybris* are meant to protect the economy of glory and honor circulating among individuals through contests, whereas in Morrison's narrative, there is an erotic core, which is essentially social, that suffers the insult of arrogance. I do not think we have a rigid distinction between individual and social interest in these examples. Although the ancient Greek conception of *hybris* is tied to the commission of impropriety in contest, its assault is not against the honor of the individual with whom one engages. Rather, *hybris* is a failure to understand and/or respect the (human) relational nature of contest and its *social* rather than merely *egoistic* priority. The outrage is shared communally, and the community does not simply take on the insult vicariously through the contestant with whom the guilty party was engaged. One way of reading the whither and wherefore of *agon* in ancient Greek culture is that such contests constituted particular manifestations of an erotic channel in the social libidinal economy. I have argued earlier that such a view is consistent with Nietzsche's considerations of productive contest and its perversions.

26. Nietzsche tells this fable of Greek history in several different contexts: in "Homer's Contest," in his notebooks from the 1870s, particularly in the notes for an untimely meditation on philology, and in *The Birth of Tragedy*, when he tries to account for the influence of Socratism and its relation to the end of tragedy. See Friedrich Nietzsche, *The Birth of Tragedy* (*BT*), in *The Birth of Tragedy and The Case of Wagner*, trans. Walter Kaufmann (New York: Viking, 1967), section 15.

27. Nietzsche tells this part of the story twice, and a comparison is interesting. See (the early) *BT* 15 and (the late) in *Twilight of the Idols*, "The Problem of Socrates."

28. This account stands in contrast to Willett's characterization of Nietzsche's view of the Dionysian and the tragic in her *Maternal Ethics*, 172–73, but it resonates in interesting ways with her conclusions about Douglass's sense of the dynamic of sameness and difference (or what Willett later calls "hyphenated duality, or the correspondence of Self and Other" [173]).

29. Willett's characterization of Nietzsche's views is largely drawn from *GM*, and her conception of *will to power* is drawn from her readings of the first essay's account of the birth of slave morality and the second essay's reference to the "sovereign individual." I treat the latter issue in the section that follows, and I further elaborate Nietzsche's critique of violence and his views on suffering. Since I do not discuss the first essay of *GM* in this chapter, I shall just briefly comment on Willett's interpretation of that part of the text here as it runs counter to the view I am advancing. Willett claims that Nietzsche "celebrates a kind of predatory violence in those of strong will" and "applauds criminality" (164), but the passage she cites in support of the former claim (*GM* I:13, the (in)famous section on lambs and birds of prey) is not normative; in fact, it highlights the absurdity of moralizing the situation—that birds of prey *eat* lambs. It is no more praised and celebrated than it is denigrated. And the passage she cites in support of the claim about criminality (*GM* I:11) also is supposed to be *descriptive*, characterizing how the so-called nobles might think about themselves (and not how we *should* or *should not* evaluate them or whether we should try to be like them). I think Nietzsche's purpose for *describing* things in this way is to encourage his readers to consider the possibility that much of what we hold and value as "good" has a *brutal* basis and not that we should strive to be *more violent* or that violence is thereby justified.

For Willett, "Nietzsche's hero [which she apparently takes to be the "noble" of *GM* I] revels in the freedom from social constraint" (164). And she claims that Nietzsche's conception of animality and the human share in animality consists specifically in the possibility of committing violence (165). But in characterizing things in this way, Willett already judges the kinds of activities that might constitute expressions of animal vitality as morally suspect (which is precisely what moralities rooted in cruelty do). Moreover, she fails to appreciate how elsewhere in Nietzsche's works he specifically distinguishes creative and destructive activities (which for him are related to, if not synonymous with, *life-enhancing* or *healthy* and *life-denying* or *decadent* activities). I have argued that Douglass's own account of his resort to violence and the particular way in which his spirit was enlivened in his fight with Covey bears a similar sense of this distinction I find in Nietzsche's works.

30. Friedrich Nietzsche, *On the Genealogy of Morals (GM)*, in *On the Genealogy of Morals and Ecce Homo*, trans. Walter Kaufmann (New York: Vintage Books, 1967); emphasis in the original unless otherwise indicated.

31. Kaufmann's translation renders this as "with the right to make promises." I argue against this translation and explain the consequences of failing to do so in my "On Sovereignty and Overhumanity: Why It Matters How We Read Nietzsche's *Genealogy* II:2," *International Studies in Philosophy* 36:3 (Fall 2004), 128–29.

32. I further discuss the significance of "forgetting" in Nietzsche's works, particularly in the context of *GM* in my unpublished manuscript "Forgetting the Subject."

Christa Davis Acampora

33. See my "On Sovereignty and Overhumanity," cited earlier.

34. See Lawrence J. Hatab, *A Nietzschean Defense of Democracy: An Experiment in Postmodern Politics* (Chicago: Open Court Press, 1995), 37–38.

35. Nietzsche reminds his readers that his discussion of suffering and cruelty and its motives is conjecture in *GM* II:6.

36. William A. Preston, "Nietzsche on Blacks," in *Existence in Black*.

37. "But on the issue of the humanity of black people, there is no equivocation in Nietzsche," Preston writes. He continues, "Nietzsche addressed black suffering—of that there should be no doubt—but his intent, it appears from his writings, was to *make blacks suffer more*" ("Nietzsche on Blacks," 168, emphasis in original). The passage cited from *GM* II:7 is offered as Preston's most substantial evidence that Nietzsche is a racist. He does not discuss the context of the passage at all, not even in terms of the book generally. He does not elaborate precisely *how* it is racist, except to draw the conclusion that Nietzsche thinks Africans are subhuman. The abhorrent nature of Nietzsche's philosophy is presumed self-evident. Nietzsche certainly conjectures that Christianized humanity suffers more, but why does Preston think their suffering *matters more* to Nietzsche? This portion of Preston's article is the most prominent prong in the three-pronged case for Nietzsche's racism, and I think it requires much more support; the other prongs might be more promising. Preston claims that Nietzsche is not merely (embarrassingly) an occasional racist, but rather that his philosophy is racist through and through. Preston emphasizes Nietzsche's largely European and Asiatic audience, claiming that it addresses itself only to whites, thereby (intentionally?) excluding blacks. Moreover, Nietzsche attacks the very philosophical frameworks that would extend equality to blacks— chiefly the progressive, egalitarian philosophies of the French and Russian revolutions. But there seems to be no evidence at all that Nietzsche attacks those philosophies *because* they would extend equality to blacks, or that egalitarian philosophies are the only ones that might provide a basis for black liberation. Nietzsche's critique of egalitarian political movements and theories is fruitfully explored and framed in terms of the agonistic model discussed earlier, in Lawrence J. Hatab's *A Nietzschean Defense of Democracy*, especially 28–39, 94–107.

38. To some extent, one might argue, Nietzsche himself dangerously flirts with this very conclusion. He claims that growth can be fostered through a type of spiritualized slavery that instructs as it teaches what it means to hold uncompromisingly values and perspectives. Slavery thereby teaches "the *narrowing of our perspective*, and thus in a certain sense stupidity, as a condition of life and growth. 'You shall obey—someone and for a long time: *else* you will perish and lose the last respect for yourself'—this appears to me to be the moral imperative of nature which, to be sure, is neither 'categorical' as the old Kant would have it (hence the 'else') nor addressed to the individual (what do individuals matter to her?), but to peoples, races, ages, classes—but above all

to the whole human animal, to *man*" (Friedrich Nietzsche, *Beyond Good and Evil* [*BGE*], trans. Walter Kaufmann [New York: Vintage Books, 1966], section 188). Nietzsche does not intend the enslavement of groups or races of people but all of humanity, if it is humanity that is meant to pursue a higher form of existence. He tells us, "Becoming a philosopher is not something that one can learn; one must 'know' it, from experience" (*BGE* 213). Again, recalling the language that he uses to describe the higher self, Nietzsche claims that "[f]or every high world one must be born or to speak clearly, one must be *cultivated* [*gezüchtet*] for it" (*BGE* 213). The passages on slavery in *Beyond Good and Evil* should be compared to those in *The Gay Science*, where Nietzsche declares how he and "children of the future," those who are "homeless" because they do not hold the same values as their contemporaries, view their tasks: "We simply do not consider it desirable that a realm of justice and concord should be established on earth (because it would certainly be the realm of the deepest leveling and *chinoiserie*); we are delighted with all who love, as we do, danger, war, and adventures, who refuse to compromise, to be captured, reconciled, and castrated; we count ourselves among conquerors; we think about the necessity for new orders, also for a new slavery—for every strengthening and enhancement of the human type also involves a new kind of enslavement " (*GS* 377). Slavery cultivates, on Nietzsche's view, and although we might prefer that he had chosen another way to describe how one acquires the kinds of experiences that enhance one's development, it is clear that Nietzsche does not have in mind a return to slavery as it has been experienced in the past. The kind of slavery he envisions is not for the weak, whose values he critiques in the *Genealogy*; Nietzsche's new form of slavery is meant for the strong. Throughout *The Gay Science*, Nietzsche uses the first-person plural "we." He is addressing a community of free spirits, of which he believes himself to be a part. He strives to describe both their experiences as "untimely" and their tasks for the future. Nietzsche does not imagine himself and his company to establish any sort of rule or social order. Quite the opposite is true. Nietzsche writes, "We prefer to live on mountains, apart, 'untimely' " (*GS* 377). It is this group of free spirits who must assume the burdens of humanity as the "overly obligated heirs of thousands of years of European spirit" (*GS* 377). It is they who must take on the "new struggles" (*GS* 108), who must experience the "great pain" that "compels us philosophers to descend into our ultimate depths" (*GS* P 2:3), for those experiences make them "more profound" (ibid.). From these incredible challenges and "dangerous exercises of self-mastery one emerges as a different person" (ibid.) and "returns *newborn*; having shed one's skin ... with a more delicate taste for joy, with a tenderer tongue for all good things, ... with a second dangerous innocence in joy, more childlike, and yet a hundred times subtler than one has ever been before" (*GS* P 2:4). Slavery, in Nietzsche's view, is meant to serve this purpose.

39. Friedrich Nietzsche, *Also Sprach Zarathustra* (*Z*). Subsequent citation of *Z* is drawn from *Thus Spoke Zarathustra*, trans. Walter Kaufmann (New York: Penguin Books, 1966).

40. Christa Davis Acampora, "Beyond Altruism and Cruelty: Nietzsche on the Perversions of Power and Struggle," unpublished manuscript.

41. See Cynthia Willett's account of this feature of Douglass's work in her *Maternal Ethics and Other Slave Moralities*, chapter 7, and in her *The Soul of Justice: Social Bonds and Racial Hubris*, chapter 8.

9

Masculinity and Existential Freedom:
Wright, Ellison, Morrison,
and Nietzsche

CYNTHIA WILLETT

What does Nietzsche mean to provoke with the enigmatic ideal of the will to power? He portrays the will to power as a lust for danger, adventure, and risk, and he does not shy away from linking this lust to the pleasure of war, or even rape. He argues that ancient warriors and heroes were driven by the lust for danger, and that this lust accounts for their vitality and creative force. While he does not aim for us to emulate these mythic characters, he does draw upon these characters to trace the roots of our fantasies and desires. But then how do we interpret the will to power as a measure of health and, in this sense, an ideal?

We can gain some sense of the will to power by thinking about the appropriate limits for cultivating and restraining its strength. Nietzsche addresses the question of limits from different perspectives throughout his writings. I shall examine these different approaches and argue that the richest notion of a limit comes from Nietzsche's study of the contest in Greek culture. While the ancient societies cultivated the will to power through contests, these contests were not without socially imposed rules or restraints. The democratic Greek populace (*demos*) condemned the unbound will as a major source of social crime and tragic error. They named this crime hubris, and they forewarned the elites of the terrible consequences of the abuse of power.

Only once does Nietzsche endorse the democratic sentiments of the Greek populace, and this is in an early unpublished essay, "Homer's Contest."[1] In the unpublished essay, Nietzsche argues that friendships impose important curbs against hubris, and that these curbs promote the health and freedom of both the individual and society. The individual does not thrive apart from these social bonds. Nietzsche contributes a great deal to our appreciation of social bonds and the dangers of excessive power in this unpublished essay. Flights of hubristic fancy elsewhere in his writings illustrate his own and perhaps also a conventionally male difficulty in coming to terms with these vital insights. Throughout his published works, Nietzsche fails to recall the wisdom of the Greek people and valorizes acts of hubristic excess as a sign of strength. The valorization of hubris is, I think, a regression in Nietzsche's more fundamental project of enlarging and healing the psyche.

The project of enlarging and healing the psyche re-emerges among a prominent group of African American writers spanning the nineteenth and twentieth centuries. Richard Wright, Ralph Ellison, and Toni Morrison return to the same themes of male (sometimes also female) vitality and destructive arrogance that we find in Nietzsche's texts. Along with Nietzsche, these authors reflect upon fantasies that sustain male-centered cultures and valorize a freedom of spirit that might be called will to power. These American writers are less tempted however than is Nietzsche to pose hubristic excess as a sign of health. Heeding the ancient democratic call for limits against unrestrained power, these writers propose instead what we might call a will to power with what once was without irony called soul. This will to power thrives amidst the communal bonds that hubris threatens to tear apart.

Section I: Nietzsche: Active Arrogance and Reactive Slave

The major texts for understanding will to power are Nietzsche's later writings, including the literary text, *Thus Spoke Zarathustra*.[2] Clearly, literary texts, and especially fiction, cannot be read as direct statements about the world, but it is also useful to reflect upon the danger of interpreting the doctrine of the will to power, even in Nietzsche's philosophical texts, in a literal way. *In The Birth of Tragedy*, Nietzsche tells us that the ideals of individuals and cultures first appear as dreams (*BT* 1).[3] Keeping this in mind, I will interpret Nietzsche's imaginative account of the will to power, not as a literal doctrine but as a fantasy and I will read his statements on the will to power as I would read a dream. This does not mean that I think the will to power is not real. In *The Birth of Tragedy*, Nietzsche argues that our fantasies are woven into the fabric of reality. Even if social norms prevent us from acting out our fantasies directly, these fantasies shape our conscious decisions and actions indirectly. As Nietzsche claims, the sheer intensity of some of our fantasies guarantees their hold on our psychic and social lives. Nietzsche interprets the will to power primarily through the dreamlike fantasy of the warrior. He does not mean to pose this fantasy as a model that we are to imitate in everyday life. He does not think that we should aim in our actions to conquer, destroy, and rape. However, the fantasy of the warrior does guide Nietzsche's critique of modern Europe as well as his call for new values based on the will to power. But, then, what does the fantasy of the warrior reveal about the will to power?

As I understand it, the will to power names for Nietzsche a drive that functions something like, but distinct from, what Freud will later describe in terms of the sexual drives. Will to power exposes, as does sexual libido for Freud, hidden impulses and unspeakable desires of the seemingly moral person. Freud draws upon the Greek myth of Oedipus to trace the ideals of art, morality, science, and religion back to primitive sexual urges. Nietzsche draws upon Greek myths of pre-Hellenic warriors and heroes to expose social ideals as indirect expressions of will to power. Both of these men raise questions about our conventional reliance on either self-interest or altruism, or any other conscious mechanism, to explain human behavior. The ego and the conscience may deny, repress, or control the corporeal drives for sex and power, but our conscious actions are inevitably overdetermined by these same drives.

We might question the universal relevance of the particular myths that Nietzsche and Freud use to explore these drives. Nonetheless, their claims reflect certain patterns of social difference. While erotic drives explain in part our interest in lovers, intimate friends, and family, the will to power explains our interest in hunting and combat (mental or physical) and, as I will argue more extensively later, in the friendships that emerge through contests in general. Erotic drives thrive on feelings of intimacy and enduring emotional connection, and when fully (and I would think artificially) separated from will to power, erotic drives may seek out what is secure and uneventful. Will to power is a facilitator of risk, adventure, and contest and readily trades off quantity of life and, when fully separated from eros, even human relationships for intensity of experience.

Writer Andrew Sullivan claims that this kind of "trade-off is a deeply male one," and he traces the sexual difference to testosterone.[4] He recommends testosterone in the appropriate doses for "women who simply want to rev up their will to power." He claims to have amassed scientific data to prove that black men have more of this stuff than white men, and that the working class and strong political leaders have more of it than the white middle class. It is clear that the data are partly manufactured by fantasies. These fantasies are experienced, produced, and enacted differently by different groups and individuals and can develop regressive or progressive ways. But I think it is fair to say that Nietzsche's philosophical writings help us understand a drive to power that may operate with, and at times distinct from, sexuality (or eros more generally). The drive to power may prevail in some cultures as the more telling of the two drives. Nietzsche explains the drive to power by distinguishing healthy and unhealthy forms. I shall argue that a critical examination of Nietzsche's claims sheds light on the obscure motivations that often lurk behind our moral decisions and poses the need for social limits on the expression of basic human drives.

There are similarities between Freud's analysis of the erotic drive and the will to power. These similarities may reflect in part the historical time period in which these men lived. Freud and Nietzsche wrote in an era of expansionistic capitalism, accelerating industrialization, and urbanization. European cities severed the realm of family, love, and sexuality from production, politics, and civil society. Although the drives of eros and power may develop in some cultures (or individuals) in ways that make it impossible to distinguish one from another, a comparison of the writings of Freud and Nietzsche suggests ways in which the drives can diverge.

Both thinkers claim that the drive that he has discovered accounts for the basic structure of the psyche. Freud explains the moral and rational components of the soul in terms of the repression, deferral, or sublimation of erotic drives. Nietzsche interprets these same components of the soul in terms of the "introversion" of a will to dominate an external enemy. For both thinkers, men (they have little to say about women) adapt to living in a society by imposing limits on themselves. And for both thinkers, the sublimation (or restraint and indirect expression) of the basic drives explains major features of families, cultures, and political societies. While Freud uses the injunction against incest to explain the nature of these limits, Nietzsche focuses on laws or moral codes that restrain the will to dominate. Social constraints threaten the individual with real or symbolic emasculation, and both thinkers exhibit a preoccupation with this theme. Freud symbolizes the fear that social constraints induce through images of castration. Nietzsche symbolizes the effects of social constraints through images of the cage, the social straightjacket, and the prison system.

For the later Nietzsche the story of limits begins with the warrior represented in ancient Greek myths. According to the *Genealogy*, the concept of law (or moral limit) originated with the creative warrior-poet who, himself unbound by any law, invented Western civilization's first moral terms and imposed social order on those whom he conquered. After the rise of stable societies, social codes restrained the will of all men. In these societies, the instincts were no longer allowed free play. They were forced to turn inward, where they produced what, according to Nietzsche, we call the soul (*GM* II: 24).

There are, according to Nietzsche, two types of souls. The first type develops when external constraints (like bars on a cage) impose limits on the self, and this is called bad conscience. The second type of soul develops when one breaks free from social conventions and becomes a law onto oneself. Nietzsche calls this type of soul the sovereign individual (*GM* II: 2). The sovereign individual is unlike the mythic warrior in that he guides his action according to self-imposed limits. The sovereign individual retains the warrior's capacity to bestow meaning (limits, forms) upon the world. He experiences his act as generosity, and as the highest type of love. It is important to understand that this act of love represents the pure expression of the creative will to power. Even if erotic and power drives cannot be fully separated, the act of bestowing meaning on the world is not, for Nietzsche, primarily libidinal in content. The will to power manifests an artistic drive to give form and shape to the world. This is a drive that Freud too quickly reduces to a form of sexuality. For Nietzsche, the soul is fundamentally a formation of will to power.

While the notion of "will to power" does not emerge until Nietzsche's later work, this notion does bear a kinship to the creative and destructive life forces that Nietzsche discusses in the early work, *The Birth of Tragedy*. The notion of the will to power in the later work combines form-bestowing and destructive forces in a single drive. *The Birth of Tragedy* separates these forces through the distinct mythological figures of Dionysus and Apollo. As a consequence, earlier and later works have a somewhat different view on the role of limits, or restraints, to power. *Genealogy* valorizes the sovereign individual who restrains and orders the impulsive forces of his or her own soul. The primary interest is in a type of self-mastery, or self-control. *The Birth of Tragedy* calls for the Apollonian drive to give aesthetic form to the Dionysian forces of nature. The primary interest is in the aesthetic experience of life. Both early and later Nietzsche emphasize the importance of introducing limits that bring meaning to the individual. Although there are passing

references to friendships throughout his writings, the major published
works never elaborate on the importance of establishing limits to maintain friendships or other vital social bonds.

Nietzsche explains that the Dionysian force dissolves all boundaries
or restraints between things, including man and man. For the Greeks,
Dionysus is associated with excess, and sexual excess in particular.
While Nietzsche appropriates various Greek meanings of Dionysus, he
does not define the "transport" of Dionysian ritual primarily through
sexual ecstasy. For Nietzsche, if we are "to apprehend the essence of
Dionsyiac rapture," we must look to its "closest analogy [which] is fur-
nished by physical intoxication" (*BT* 1).[5] The intoxicating pleasure
of transgressing social conventions, ordinary habits, and embedded
categories is not libidinal; it is the pleasure of unbound power. Nietzsche
explains that "the peculiar blending of emotions in the heart of the
Dionysiac reveler . . . seems to hark back (as the medicinal drug harks
back to the deadly poison) to the days when the infliction of pain was
experienced as joy" (*BT* 2). The ancient Greeks understood this violent
pleasure of transgressing boundaries as "hubris," which we translate
as wanton aggression, outrage, or arrogance. In *The Birth of Tragedy*,
Nietzsche suggests that the Apollonian force restrains and balances
the horrifying excesses of Dionysus, not for social flourishing but to
secure for the lone individual the illusion of form, beauty, and meaning.

The mythic figure of Apollo allows Nietzsche to associate the need
for setting limits on Dionysus's hubristic force with the aesthetic qualities of art and the therapeutic effects of medicine. He argues that
arts inspired by Apollo allow us to recover from the "deadly poisons"
of Dionysus or nature's violence and pathos. He explains that just as
intoxication is the natural expression of Dionysus, so sleep and dream are
the natural expressions of Apollo: "Our profound awareness of nature's
healing powers during the interval of sleep and dream . . . furnishes
a symbolic analogue to the soothsaying faculty and quite generally to
the arts, which make life possible and worth living" (*BT* 1). Like the
dream, exemplary art gives form and meaning to the flux of life through
visual images that bring calm and peace to the individual. The visual
image accounts for the cathartic power of both art and dreams that
save the soul from fragmenting in the face of terrible violence through
illusions of beauty and wholeness.

While allowing for the fact that Nietzsche changes some of his views
on art, we can apply the conception of art's cathartic power to Nietzsche's
own texts. In fact, I would argue that the import of Nietzsche's philosophical works stems less from the literal content than from the visual,
and sometimes dreamlike, force of his style. This force of style lends

the text a kind of cathartic power. The effect of this force is to enlarge and heal the psyche through visual or dreamlike images that give meaning to the pathos of life. But what is health for Nietzsche, and for us?

In earlier and later published works, Nietzsche traces the robust will to power back to the hubristic protagonist in ancient epic or tragedy. In the *Genealogy*, he champions the active will of the warrior or other natural elite over the reactive psychology of the resentful slave. Nietzsche justifies what he views as the natural right of the master to commit acts of hubristic violence in contrast with the passive aggression of the resentful slave. Both master and slave respond to hubristic insult with violence, but the master, who by nature enjoys a kind of naive hubristic frame of mind, is also, paradoxically, more moderate. Nietzsche explains: "It is generally true of even the most decent people that a small dose of insult, malice, insinuation is enough to send the blood to their eyes. ... [But] [t]he active man, the attacker and overreacher, is still a hundred steps closer to justice than the reactive one" (*GM* II: 11). The overreacher, like Oedipus, is hubristic, but he does not dwell on his resentment of the offender; instead, he acts immediately though ruthlessly.

Nietzsche cautions that the slave should not experience the power of the master as an act of violation, or at least not primarily so; he should experience the power of the master to create meaning as a form of gift giving, and as love. Of course, what the master experiences as a peculiar source of pleasure in the assertion of his will might be experienced by the slave as an act of domination, or moral outrage. Nietzsche's reply to the slave is that "No act of violence, rape, exploitation, destruction, is intrinsically unjust, since life itself is violent" (*GM* II: 11). Nietzsche makes it clear that the natural right of the master, or the man who is of higher rank, is the "glorious feeling of treating another human being as lower than himself," and he describes this feeling as being akin to the pleasure of rape (*GM* II: 5). Only on rare occasion does Nietzsche invoke the metaphor of rape to describe the will to power, but he often depicts its power in terms of a sense of superiority over those who are less worthy. The exceptional human being is expected to respond to the lower type (the natural slave) with polite disdain or indifference, and the lower type is expected to exhibit fear and respect. Nietzsche accuses the Judaic-Christian tradition of fueling the slave's unhealthy hatred and resentment of this natural state by masking weakness as a virtue and strength as a vice.

Nietzsche supports his critique of the Judaic-Christian tradition with an appeal to Greek norms. He does not mention that those same ancient Greek people who viewed resentment as the typical vice of the masses viewed hubris as the corresponding vice of the elite. For these

Greeks, an act of hubris does not testify to the health but to the perversion of the social self. Much of the force of Nietzsche's philosophy stems from its cathartic power to liberate the angst-ridden modern reader from the conventional values and bad conscience that weaken the spirit. Nietzsche's style reinvigorates the fantasy through images of proud defiance and unbound creative power. However, the fantasy of hubris that Nietzsche employs does not speak to our more healthy needs. My contention is that Nietzsche confuses healthy and unhealthy types of creative sovereignty because he forgets what he had once characterized as the moderating wisdom of the Greeks. Without this wisdom we cannot distinguish the genuine cathartic force that Nietzsche seeks in his philosophical prose from the mock catharsis that comes from feelings of superiority and contempt for others.

Nietzsche does not only use the warrior image to portray creative sovereignty, he also uses images of birds, flying, or lightness. Like the warrior image, these images do not clearly separate the experience of breaking free from repressive social constraints and the feeling of superiority over others. Perhaps these experiences are always difficult to separate. The images of flight place the free spirit at some distance above the average person. Nietzsche, on occasion, introduces other images to counterbalance, or moderate, the feeling of superior status that is so easily conjoined with the feeling of freedom. In *Thus Spoke Zarathustra*, an eagle with a snake coiled around its neck leads the prophet Zarathustra to defeat the spirit of gravity and to a vision of the superman. The Prologue explains that the eagle represents Zarathustra's sense of pride, and that the snake represents his wisdom (*Z*, "Zarathustra's Prologue": 10). Nietzsche uses the figure of Zarathustra to warn that social constraints can destroy the spirit that the image of flight represents, and he is right to do so. Then what sense of wisdom might properly restrain the excesses of pride?

Nietzsche does not address the nature of this kind of wisdom in any of his major published works. In *Genealogy of Morals*, he portrays the will to power in terms of the parable of the bird of prey and the lamb (*GM* I: 13). In this parable, he describes the bird of prey as a "quantum of strength," and he mocks those who would "expect that strength will not manifest itself as strength, as the desire to overcome, to appropriate, to have enemies." The lamb, he observes, is the natural victim of this strength. This parable sets Nietzsche up for interpreting the will to power in terms of the pleasure of rape, or what the Greeks understood as a paradigmatic case of hubris (*GM* II: 5, 11, and 24; see also *BT*, "A Critical Backward Glance": 7). In fact, for the Greeks, one of the many meanings of hubris is rape. In *Beyond Good and Evil*, Nietzsche explains will to power as the discharge of excess and energy, which, as with Dionysian excess, sounds like male sexual release but is not primarily about male sex but male power.[6] These various texts stimulate the fantasy of a will that seeks not sexual pleasure per se but power—power is unbound, transgressive, and indifferent to limits on giving and receiving and, especially, giving and receiving pain. The redeeming quality of the will to self-mastery is that it is creative, vital, and fully alive. It bestows meaning to the world. Nietzsche does not aim for his reader to commit acts of violence and moral outrage in the name of the highest kind of love and deepest type of soul. But still some bit of wisdom is missing in what I think is after all a variation on a traditional, if not all-too-conventional, fantasy of male vitality and power.

Throughout his published works, Nietzsche celebrates hubris as a sign of health. *The Birth of Tragedy* distinguishes the active Greek crime of arrogance from the reactive and feminine notion of Christian sin (*BT* 9). The hubris of such tragic figures as Oedipus leads to self-destruction but also, Nietzsche claims, to glorious transformation. This transformation requires the wisdom stolen from nature's dark secrets, Nietzsche explains, using language that recalls the violation of rape (*BT* 12). Neither *The Birth of Tragedy* nor *Genealogy* interprets the concept of limit as a restraint on hubris, and neither dwells on the significance of these restraints for social friendships. For the Greeks, however, the concepts of limit and hubris were intimately connected in their drama. Nietzsche deemphasizes the importance of this connection in *The Birth of Tragedy*. He contrasts his Dionysian reading of tragedy with what he scornfully calls the "democratic" view of tragedy (*BT* 7). As he observes, the democratic view does not find wisdom, redeeming beauty, or therapeutic relief in crimes of hubris. The latter and I think more sanguine view emerges from the perspective of the chorus in Greek theater. The chorus was composed of actors drawn not from the elite, who were often portrayed as having committed the horrible act of hubris on stage, but from the masses (*demos*). Moreover, these choruses (composed of the poorer citizens) represented the voices of women, foreigners, and slaves, groups vulnerable to crimes of hubris. Given the composition of the chorus, it is not surprising to find that its primary if democratic function was to warn the elites of the destructive impact of hubris on the social fabric of the community (*polis*). What Nietzsche celebrates in The *Birth of Tragedy* as Dionysian wisdom the chorus of Greek tragedies portrays as blind arrogance, or careless pride, and tragic error.[7]

Interestingly, in "Homer's Contest," written just after *The Birth of Tragedy*, Nietzsche returns to the tragic theme of hubris and fully condemns it. Nietzsche begins this essay by contrasting the "emasculated concept of modern humanity" with the Greek virtues of struggle and competition (*HC*, p. 187). While this valorization of struggle charac- terizes all of his published and unpublished writings, this early unpub- lished essay carefully separates the wanton cruelty (or hubris) of the mythic pre-Homeric world from the friendly combat that characterizes Hellenic culture. Nietzsche elaborates on this difference in terms of two kinds of Eris (or struggle). According to the essay, the primitive Eris (associated in his mind with the Orient, and the cult of Dionysus) leads "into night and horror, into the products of a fantasy used to ghastly things" (*HC*, p. 188). The properly Hellenic Eris "acknowledged the [primitive Eris], terrible as it is." This Eris did not drive the wise and virtuous men in Hellenic times to struggle to the death. Eris drove these men to develop skills and work hard in competition for greater wealth and glory. The Greeks sent into exile those whose excessive power (or what Nietzsche glosses as unrivaled excellence) threatened this friendly competition. Nietzsche explains: "[E]very Athenian was to develop himself, through competition, to the degree to which this self was of most use to Athens and would cause least damage. It was not a boundless and indeterminate ambition like most modern ambition. . . .[S]elfishness was lit, as well as curbed and restricted" (*HC*, p. 192).

The ancient Greeks celebrated the risk, danger, and adventure of struggle but not without care for ethical codes against hubris. Excesses were thought to be unwise, for it was known that certain excesses, the excess of arrogance in particular, would threaten the bonds that sustain the soul. The older but I think not wiser Nietzsche, who develops the doctrine of the will to power from the eagle's view some "6,000 feet beyond man and time," has lost sight of these vital friendships.[8] For there is, as Nietzsche explains, the type of soul that defines itself through social constraints and conventional norms. There also is the type of soul that enjoys the solitary pleasures of self-mastery and perhaps also creative flights of fancy. But there also is a third type of soul that Nietzsche too often overlooks in his published writings. This type strengthens its vital powers through spirited relationships with others. The Nietzsche who tempts his reader with the parable of the bird of prey has forgotten the bonds that make us free.

Section II: Wright, Ellison, and Morrison

Major African American writers share with Nietzsche a concern for the ways in which social conventions demean the soul and destroy the spirit. Like Nietzsche, these American writers represent the spirit that breaks free from social conventions through images of flight, and sometimes through transgression, including theft or even rape and murder. These writers, however, are more wary in their published works than is Nietzsche of the soul that lacks the moderating wisdom of ancient cultures. In "Unspeakable Things Unspoken," Morrison explains the major features of African American literature through its similarities with Greek tragedy: "A large part of the satisfaction I have always received from reading Greek tragedy . . . is in its similarity to Afro-American communal structures (the function of song and chorus, the heroic struggle between the claims of the community and individual hubris) and African religion and philosophy. . . . I feel intellectually at home there."[9] While earlier writers, Wright and Ellison, focus on the importance of existential freedom for the black man in white America, and sometimes portray the free spirit as brutally transgressive against demeaning social norms, these writers return repeatedly in their novels to an ancient vision of social bonds. These bonds curb the excesses of the unbound will and preserve the friendships that make men and women, black and white, free when they are free together.

Wright's novel *Native Son* (hereinafter *NS*) explores the transgressive claims of a black man who resists the degradation of a white supremacy through the murder of a white woman.[10] What the later Nietzsche portrays as a restorative myth of the brutal, simple-minded, but creative Homeric hero for the "degenerate" European, Wright recontextualizes in terms of the primitive dreams and fantasies of his simple-minded, black protagonist in a white racist society. Perhaps less character than allegory, the protagonist (in his one moment of achievement in the novel) represents the valorization of the will to power as strength, hardness, and proud defiance. As is typical for Wright, the erotic interests of the protagonist are underdeveloped, and female characters function as targets of the protagonist's hostility toward Christianity or unrestrained sexual aggression. In this novel, Bigger Thomas, an impoverished black man who accidentally murders a white woman, manages through that transgressive act to exercise the only freedom he will ever know. Bigger does not in any way represent the sovereign individual Nietzsche praises. He does not commit this act through understanding the past or imagining a future, and he is certainly not capable of self-rule. Once we understand the circumstances of his life, however, we come to see Bigger's crime as bold, daring, and even (as his lawyer will explain) "creative". At this one moment, Bigger manifests what Nietzsche portrays as will to power in its most primitive, uncultivated, and brutal phase.

We learn about the cramped conditions of Bigger's life from the beginning of the novel, where Bigger and his friend Gus look up and gaze upon a plane in the sky. For a moment, they imagine themselves as the pilot, but this fantasy is destroyed by the brutal realization that in the 1930s black men from ghettoes cannot fly. For men like Bigger who are trapped, the exhilaration of freedom cannot come from soaring high above the limits that define their lives. These men, however, do find release through more realistic dreams of transgression. Bigger and his friends plan to rob the local white-owned deli. More daring yet is Bigger's transgression against the ultimate symbol of white power and property, the young white woman, Mary. As his lawyer argues in court, the murder of Mary was "the first full act of his life" (*NS*, p. 461); only by taking ownership over this act of violence does Bigger manage to break out of the reactive psychology of fear and shame. This "was an act of creation" (*NS*, p. 466). As Nietzsche portrays the mythic warrior, Bigger does not think, and he does not hold his anger inward and allow it to poison his mind (cf. *GM* I: 10). He seeks immediate and cathartic release. At the novel's close, the tragic Bigger utters the words that reveal who he is: "What I killed for, I am" (*NS*, p. 501). Bigger's metamorphosis into the warrior reclaims some partial but primitive sense of what it means to be a man.

Bigger's lawyer begins to respond to him with pity and compassion but then pulls back. His eyes fill with terror as he contemplates the meaning of Bigger's claim. Could such unbound acts of transgression as rape or murder symbolize the deepest and most original craving for freedom? Does Bigger's tale of revenge against white domination represent the cathartic violence of the repressed? Or is this fantasy lacking the wisdom and healing power that the early Nietzsche attempts, but finally fails to grasp, through the figure of Apollo?

As a tragic allegory of the will to power, *Native Son* pulls us back from the fantasy that Nietzsche encourages. The response of Bigger's defender to his final statement expresses the appropriate horror. Transgression that is not guided by ethical wisdom does not strengthen our spirit; it perverts and destroys it. Wright shows the problem both in black and white America. The life of the ghetto leaves Bigger feeling trapped like a rat in a cage. Reactive emotions of fear and shame debilitate his psyche and paralyze his action. As Wright warns, the reactive will turned inward constantly threatens to turn back outward and to become an active force of anger and revenge.

Wright describes this metamorphosis in Bigger most clearly in a scene that immediately follows his capture. With his capture, the murderous Bigger yields to a "mood of renunciation," which Wright characterizes, much as would Nietzsche, in terms of the internalization of a will to power: "There sprang up in him again the will to kill. But this time it was not directed outward toward people, but inward, upon himself. Why not kill that wayward yearning within" (*NS*, p. 317). Then something clicks within him. He sees that the whites are not going to execute him immediately, and that they will defer and postpone the act with glee as they treat him to a spectacle of mockery and humiliation: "When he felt his life again threatened in a way [that made him] . . . a helpless spectacle of sport for others, he sprang back into action, alive, contending" (*NS*, p. 319). Shame and fear give way to active hate. The lawyer Max explains to the judge, "Bigger Thomas and that mob are strangers yet they hate. They hate because they fear, and they fear because they feel that the deepest feelings of their lives are being assaulted and outraged" (*NS*, p. 454). Through this passage Wright exposes the racial arrogance that underlies violence and social pathology in the United States. No doubt because of the experience of slavery and racial hubris, African American writers are less likely than is Nietzsche to be tempted by the dream of unbound power. The fantasy of the unbound will to power does not create free spirits; it spreads hatred and terror and unravels erotic and other social bonds. The pathos does not stop with the target of the violence, for as the Greek tragedians understood, the pathos returns to haunt the perpetrators of the crime. This is what tragedy means.

In the United States, this crime does not begin or end with the white or black Bigger Thomases. This crime is woven into the expansionist dreams of our country. It defines the hubristic quality of the American will to power. This hubristic will defines our capitalist and imperialist spirit and our conventional social mores. Recall once again the plane that Bigger and his friend see at the beginning of the novel. This plane traces a message in the sky that reads: "Use Speed Gasoline." Through this message Wright signals to the reader how the dreams of white men (fueled by will to power) are weighed down by the blind vanity of a materialist culture. The hubris of this blind vanity takes its tow on the wealthy and liberal banker and his blind wife, whose daughter Bigger murders. Power in this country does not manifest superiority in strength or vitality of spirit; ignorant of its arrogance, unbound power enacts a cycle of violence that threatens to not stop. As the Bigger Thomases recognize the hubris, the reactive emotion of resentment, alongside fear and shame, threatens to metamorphose into the active emotions of hate and defiance. These men carry the seeds of revenge.

Like Nietzsche, Wright shows little interest in the erotic drives and focuses his attention on the creative and competitive spirit that drives men to excel. Without the cultivation of this spirit, men are left with a void in the place where the soul ought to be. Bigger Thomas feels this void when he surrenders to whites who seem unable to understand why he killed the white girl. These white men, however, suffer from the same void. Men "live amid the greatest possible plenty, on earth," and yet all the more do they hunger for emotional meaning, cultural rituals, and the common bonds that make them men apart only when they stand together (*NS*, "How 'Bigger' was Born," p. 522). The drive to excel cannot thrive apart from these social bonds.

Ralph Ellison carries forward the message of his mentor, Richard Wright, but in a more self-conscious form. Ellison's major novel, *Invisible Man* (hereafter *IM*), "erupted out of what had been conceived as a war novel."[11] Ellison's intended war novel becomes a novel about a black man who searches for an identity in a white-dominated political group called the "Brotherhood." Before Ellison begins the story of the Invisible Man, he publishes a short story that announces the novel's major themes. This story is about a black pilot in World War II who "experiences difficulty in seeing himself" (*IM*, p. xiii). The Invisible Man (the reader never learns the name of the protagonist) discovers that he cannot fully establish a strong sense of his own identity without some sense of recognition from a common humanity established across racial boundaries. Unlike *Native Son*, Ellison's *Invisible Man* takes on an edgy, comic tone. While Bigger Thomas manages at his highest moment to transform his fear and shame into the active emotion of rage, the Invisible Man claims to go one step farther. Ellison describes the voice he sought as one that "had been forged in the underground of American experience and yet managed to emerge less angry than ironic. That . . . would be a blues-toned laughter-at-wounds who included himself in his indictment of the human condition" (*IM*, p. xviii).

The laughter of the Invisible Man grows out of the fact that he, unlike others, is able "to snatch the victory of conscious perception from the forces that overwhelm them" (*IM*, xxi). His laughter is "blues-toned" because no one can exist as a man without the "more or less natural recognition of the reality of black and white fraternity" (*IM*, p. xxii). The laughter gives him some distance, allowing him to externalize some of the pain he feels as a result of this lack of recognition. Within limits, the externalization of threatening socio-psychic forces can be a significant, cathartic force of comedy. The comic stance, however, is about more than the externalization of pain. This stance results also in part from the protagonist's enlarged perspective on racial violence and other forms of dehumanization. By the novel's end, he views the dehumanization that he encounters as a "crude joke" (*IM*, p. 573). How can he see the process of dehumanization, a process that involves literal or figurative castration of men like himself, as a joke?

The comic stance serves as a shield against the hubristic insults of white men, but it also reflects the black man's recognition of the folly of the hubristic assaults that he encounters. The white men who would use their superior power in order to assault him act as though they are blind. In the Prologue, the Invisible Man (who is also the narrator) explains the mix of blindness and hubris in the white man with the following incident. One night, the narrator tells the reader, he bumped (quite accidentally) into a white man who responds by insulting him. The Invisible Man demands an apology, and instead the white man hurls out more insults. The black man then pulls out a knife, not as a murderous attempt on the white man's life but to reassert his threatened dignity. Then it occurs to the black man that the white man had not even "seen" him, not, at least, as a man, and certainly not as a "brother" (*IM*, p. 4). The black man is at first "disgusted and ashamed" but then, upon reflection, "amused." The white man had not meant to harm the black man. He simply did not see him as an equal. The "poor blind fool" misinterprets the Invisible Man's ethical demand for recognition as a criminal assault, indeed as a mugging, and he is scared out of his wits. The white man cannot see that the black man is a man no different from himself. Indeed, he cannot see beyond the phantoms of his own nightmarish imagination, for as it turns out, this powerful white man is afraid of his own shadow. The black protagonist's rage yields to amusement. He enjoys his own superior stance.

Toward the end of the novel, the Invisible Man reflects one more time upon the "arrogant absurdity" of the powerful men who act as though they do not see him (*IM*, p. 508). Throughout the novel, he portrays men, both black and white, who misinterpret fraternal appeals for recognition and social equality as criminal rebellion or simple treachery. The mysterious words of his dying grandfather echo back to him: "After I am gone I want you to keep up the good fight. I never told you, but our life is a war and I have been a traitor, . . . a spy in the enemy's country. . . . Live with your head in the lion's mouth. I want you to overcome 'em with yeses, undermine 'em with grins, agree 'em to death and destruction, let 'em swoller you till they vomit" (*IM*, p. 16).

Does the grandfather believe that the only chance for the powerless is to stand back and allow the arrogance and blindness of the powerful to grow monstrous and self-defeating? Arrogance is an old crime, well known to the audiences of ancient drama. The tragic pattern of hubris leads us to expect that the blindness and arrogance of the powerful will bring about their own demise. Like Oedipus, the hubristic white man may not recognize that the stranger whom he destroys is in fact bound in intimate connection with himself. The identity of the individual will exist through a nexus of social relationships that will define who he is. If he assaults these relationships, he defiles not only the target of his hubris, he pollutes the community as well as himself.

Men define themselves through their actions. The invisible narrator of Ellison's novel warns the arrogant white reader: "There's your universe[:] the drip-drop upon the water you hear [the blood of the castrated black man] is all the history you've made" (*IM*, p. 570). The whites have defined themselves through the crimes that they have committed.

Simple laughter at the tragic folly of the white man, however, does not suffice to give strength to the black man. This ironic stance threatens instead to leave the Invisible Man alone and detached, and unseen by his fellow men. His grandfather cannot have meant for his sons and grandsons to say yes to the white man without also saying yes to "the principle" that binds black and white men together in this country as equals: "We should affirm the principle because we . . . were linked to all the others in the loud, clamoring semi-visible world" (*IM*, p. 574). The principle of social equality has to be affirmed against the "exploitation" and "condescension" of those men who threaten to destroy each other and themselves. "'Agree 'em to death and destruction', grandfather had advised. Hell, weren't they their own death and their own destruction except as the principle lived in them and in us? And here's the cream of the joke: Weren't we part of them as well as apart from them and subject to die when they died?" (*IM*, p. 575). The Invisible Man finally learns that he must act in the name of the principle, despite "certain defeat." His identity is caught up in the identity of those who would harm him without even knowing what they have done, and it is this tragic humanist wisdom that casts a blue tone on his laughter. The black man is condemned by paradox to a life that is absurd.

No writer presents the themes of broken spirit, tragedy, and male freedom more wisely than does Morrison in her *Song of Solomon*. Along with Nietzsche, Wright, and Ellison, Morrison portrays the dream of a spirit that is set free in terms of images of airplanes, birds, or pilots, or what she describes as the "dream of flight."[12] In a central chapter of *Song of Solomon* (*SS*), the narrator mourns for those "landlocked people . . . [who] seldom dream of flight" (*SS*, p. 162). The novel portrays its central protagonist, Milkman Dead, as a tragic figure who, like Oedipus, suffers from a wound to the foot and who has trouble knowing who he is: "When the little boy discovered at four . . . that only birds and airplanes could fly—he lost all interest in himself. To have to live without that single gift saddened him and left his imagination . . . bereft" (SS, p. 9). Milkman, however, does not only need the capacity to dream in order to be free; as Morrison makes resoundingly clear, he also needs wisdom. In Morrison's novel, this wisdom is represented by Milkman's Aunt Pilate (also Pilot), who is described by the boy's father (for the wrong reasons) as a snake. Milkman finally learns what authentic freedom means from Pilate.

Like the Invisible Man the tragic protagonist of *Song of Solomon*, Milkman Dead, begins his quest to fill the void in his life by turning to the mysterious words from his dead grandfather. The dead grandfather's words are passed down to him from Aunt Pilate, who hears these words from the grandfather's ghost: "'You just can't fly off and leave a body.'" (SS, p. 208). At first Milkman searches these words' meaning for clues that will lead him to a missing bag of gold. He is able to piece together their meaning only at the end of the novel, after a hunting expedition with untrustworthy companions that strips away the ignorance and vanity that weighs him down. During the expedition, the ill-prepared Milkman experiences his vulnerability through his dependence on his companions. From this sense of vulnerability, he realizes that vanity and ignorance have led him to take part in the hunt, and that his quest for the bag of gold is just as foolish.

Milkman was foolish to believe that the gold would give him the sense of power that is lacking in his life. It is not simply the material wealth of the gold that he had mistakenly sought. He had thought that with the gold he would no longer "owe" his father or anyone else for who he is. The adventure promised to rekindle the sense of fear and danger that he had on occasion experienced with his friend Guitar, and that had given him some partial sense of what it was like to be a man: "Taking risks together the way they did when Milkman was twelve and Guitar was a teen-ager and they swaggered, haunched, leaned, straddled, ran all over town trying to pick fights or at least scare somebody. . . . When they succeeded they rode the wind" (SS, p. 177). Now, however, he sees in the gold the carelessness and arrogance with which he has wrecked the lives of others since he was a four-year-old boy. It was at age four when he could no longer dream of flying that he accidentally peed on his sister Lena, and as she tells the story, he has "pee[d] on people" ever since (SS, p. 214).

Milkman's Aunt Pilate had already warned the women who loved Milkman that this man's own ignorance would destroy him. In this respect, Morrison's tragic tale of Milkman repeats themes from Sophocles' tale of Oedipus. Like Oedipus, Milkman's fatal ignorance is of the social bonds that make him who he is. When Milkman assaults these bonds, his people, like the ancient Greek people, would expect the action to yield a violent outcome. The novel portrays tragic violence in terms that recall classic themes of hubris and revenge: "Southside people . . . believed firmly that members of their own race killed one another for good reasons: violation of another's turf (a man is found with somebody else's wife); refusal to observe the laws of hospitality; . . . or verbal insults. More important they believed the crimes they committed were legitimate because they were committed in the heat of passion: anger, jealously, loss of face, and so on" (*SS*, p. 100). Transgressions against proper sexual relationships, laws of hospitality, and verbal insults were among the primary meanings of hubris for the ancient Greeks. And it was expected that the target of the attack would experience not only the "reactive" emotion of resentment but also the active emotions of rage and revenge.

While the black people in Morrison's novel understand the cycles of violence among their own people, they do not understand the violence of the whites. From the black perspective, the white people live as though written or unwritten laws against hubris do not exist. They commit acts of violence for fun or adventure. It is as though they dwell with Nietzsche's godlike men. Milkman's friend Guitar observes that whites try to excuse their race from crimes against the colored man as foolish ignorance, but this cannot be: for castrating or lynching is "the kind of thing you never get too drunk or ignorant to do" (*SS*, p. 156).

But this is, I think, also "the kind of thing" that Milkman does to those around him. In any case, the focus of Morrison's tragic tale is not the tragic arrogance that separates black men from white men as it is for Wright and Ellison. Morrison's focus is on the arrogance that separates black people from each other. One of the casualties of Milkman's vain detachment is Pilate's granddaughter, Hagar. He causally breaks up their relationship without acknowledging her desperate need for him. Hagar dies, it seems, from a broken heart, and Pilate knows that it is Milkman's fault. In Pilate's case, however, rage does not lead to revenge, at least not when she recognizes that Milkman has returned from his search for gold to make amends for what he has done. While Pilate may not fully understand the needs of others, she is a natural healer. In many respects she bears a kinship to the barefoot Greek sage Socrates. Just as Socrates claims positive knowledge, namely, "eros," so Pilate claims to have only one concern, and that is "human relationships." From this special kind of wisdom, she teaches Milkman that a detached sense of one's own power does not lead to glory—not when this power is severed from the bonds that make one strong.

As Milkman puzzles through his grandfather's words, he learns more about these connections. He learns that his grandfather's father, Solomon, could fly, but he also learns that this was not enough for bringing either peace or happiness to his life. In the black folklore tradition, the story of slaves flying to freedom was entangled with the stories of their suicides, and the myth of Solomon's flight plays upon this same ambiguity. Morrison's retelling of this myth in the *Song of Solomon* reinvokes the dual themes of freedom and death but brings forward as well the pain of those who are left behind. When Solomon flies away, he drops his son, Milkman's grandfather. The grandfather's message, "You can't just fly and leave a body behind," grounds freedom in the links of love and friendship that form a people.

Pilate may not have understood the words that she relays from her dead father, but she understood the importance of these bonds for her life. The image of a snake symbolizes the chthonic wisdom that she possesses: "Now he knew why he loved her so. Without ever leaving the ground, she could fly. . . . 'There's got to be at least one more woman like you'" (*SS*, p. 336). Pilate is a kind of free spirit. But if the women in Morrison's novel center bonds of connection around erotic relationships of family, confessional friendship, and communal spirituality, then the male characters in her novels do not. In the end, Milkman does not finally seek to find himself in the arms of his mother, father, sisters, or even Pilate. In the final scene, after Pilate has been shot and falls alone into her grave, Milkman stands up and calls out for his male companion, Guitar. It is to this male friend that Milkman says at the end of the novel, "Here I am". When Guitar tries to shoot him, Milkman responds: "'My man.' . . . 'My main man,' . . . 'You want my life? . . . Here." And without tears he leaps into the "killing arms of his brother. For now he knew what Shalimar [Solomon, his great grandfather] knew: If you surrendered to the air, you could ride it" (*SS*, p. 337).

Along with Wright and Ellison, Morrison portrays the existence of the black man in white America as a paradox. For Morrison, the flight to freedom of the black man is bound up with forces that pull him back down. After the hunting expedition, Milkman joins the other men for the disembowelment of the bobcat that they have killed. Words from his cat-eyed friend Guitar come back to him: "'Everybody wants a black man's life.' . . . 'It's the condition our condition is in.' . . . 'What good is a man's life if he can't even choose what to die for?' . . . 'Fair is one more thing I've given up.' . . . 'It is about love.'" (*SS*, pp. 281–82) From Milkman's perspective, "life is," as Nietzsche writes, "intrinsically violent." But if life is not fair, then Milkman chooses to risk everything for the embrace of his friend. This is what it means for these men to have will to power, with soul.

Notes

I am very grateful to Jacqueline Scott and A. Todd Franklin for their wise editorial comments on this chapter. I am also grateful to Christa Davis Acampora, Harvey Cormier, Robert Gooding-Williams, Larry Hatab, and James Winchester for helpful questions they raised at our panel on "Nietzsche and African American Thought" for the International Association of Philosophy and Literature at Spelman College in May, 2001.

1. Except for the title of the essay, I will use the translation of this essay in Friedrich Nietzsche, *On the Genealogy of Morality*, ed. Keith Ansell-Pearson (Cambridge: Cambridge University Press, 1999), where it appears as "Homer on Competition," 187–94. For the translation of the title, I prefer Walter Kaufmann, *The Portable Nietzsche* (New York: Viking Press, 1968), 32.

2. Friedrich Nietzsche, *Thus Spoke Zarathustra*, trans. R. J. Hollingdale (Baltimore, MD: Penguin, 1971).

3. For references to the English translation of *The Birth of Tragedy* or *The Genealogy of Morals,* see Friedrich Nietzsche, *The Birth of Tragedy and The Genealogy of Morals*, trans. Francis Golffing (New York: Anchor Books, 1956).

4. Andrew Sullivan, "The He Hormone," *New York Times Magazine*, April 2, 2000, pp. 46–51 ff.

5. However, some scholars do regard the sexual dimension of the Nietzschean Dionysian transport and will to power as central. See Debra Bergoffen's "Oedipus and Dionysus," presented at the International Association of Philosophy and Literature, Spelman College, May 2001.

6. Friedrich Nietzsche, *Beyond Good and Evil*, trans. Walter Kaufmann (New York: Random House, 1967).

7. On the significance of hubris for the ancient Greeks, see "Prologue" to Cynthia Willett's, *The Soul of Justice* (Ithaca, NY: Cornell University Press, 2001).

8. Friedrich Nietzsche, *Ecce Homo*, trans. R. J. Hollingdale (New York: Penguin, 1979), "Zarathustra": 1.

9. Toni Morrison, "Unspeakable Things Unspoken: The Afro-American Presence in American Literature," *The Black Feminist Reader*, ed. Joy James and T. Denean Sharpley-Whiting (Oxford: Blackwell, 2000), 25.

10. Richard Wright, *Native Son* (New York: HarperCollins, 1991).

11. See "Author's Introduction," in Ralph Ellison, *Invisible Man* (New York: Random House, 1980), vii.

12. Toni Morrison, *Song of Solomon* (New York: Penguin, 1977).

10

—

Why Nietzsche (Sometimes) Can't Sing the Blues, or Davis, Nietzsche, and the Social Embeddedness of Aesthetic Judgments

JAMES WINCHESTER

We should not underestimate the racial divide in the United States today, but I believe it is possible for whites and blacks to understand each others' art and aesthetic judgments. Art is an important way of understanding our world, but it is also a difficult thing to understand across cultural borders because it lacks the clarity and repeatability of scientific knowledge. Talking to each other and most importantly listening to each other, we can often understand what others feel, even if we do not feel as they do. My optimism about our ability to understand the aesthetic judgments of others is grounded in the belief that art and aesthetic judgments are the products of social realities, and if we try it is possible to understand a great deal about another person's social reality. If we study the social realities out of which art works and aesthetic judgments come then we can understand much about the artwork or the judgment. If, however, we were to argue that art is the product of enigmatic genius or a gift of the gods then it would be much more difficult to understand art and aesthetic judgments across cultural borders.

I will not tackle the question of whether or not white people, in general, can sing the blues.[1] The problem that addressed here is rather the nature of artistic creation. The young Nietzsche claims that artists are mere mediums for primordial forces. In his later works he sometimes flirts with an updated version of this solipsism by arguing that

art is the product of the lonely genius—cut off from society and therefore
almost inevitably misunderstood.² At one point in his later writings,
Nietzsche claims that a great artist forces himself on objects enriching
them "out of his (the artist's) *own* fullness" (emphasis added). (I do not
use gender-inclusive language here, because for Nietzsche great artists
always seem to be male.) In other places in the later work, Nietzsche
argues that art is the product of the artist's biology.³ To the extent that
Nietzsche believes art is the product of primordial drives, only the artist's
fullness, or the artist's biology, then Nietzsche cannot sing the blues.
Blues singers have a more sophisticated understanding of the relationship between art and life. They recognize that their art is embedded
in their social reality. As Angela Davis writes "The social circumstances
of black people's lives produce an endless series of calamities."⁴ These
calamities as well as the joys of love, food, and travel make up an
important part of the inspiration for the blues. Davis argues that the
greatness of Ma Rainey, Bessie Smith, and Billie Holiday, for example,
can only be understood within the context of their times.

> Art never achieves greatness through transcendence of social-
> historical reality. On the contrary, even as it transcends spe-
> cific circumstances and conventions, it is deeply rooted in
> social realities.⁵

Amiri Baraka makes a very similar point. "Each phase of the Negro's music
issued from the dictates of his social and psychological environment."⁶
   At times, Nietzsche does recognize the social embeddedness of art.
There are places where Nietzsche acknowledges that he is a product
of time and claims that artists and artworks—even if they challenge
their times—are products of their times and can only be understood
as such. Nietzsche writes that both he and Wagner are decadent, but
he fights against his decadence. This is the bluesy Nietzsche. This Nietzsche recognizes that one understands art not through the analysis of
enigmatic primordial drives nor through a study of physiology but
rather through a detailed analysis of the artists and the times of both
the artists and the interpreters. If art is the product of inspiration and
inspiration comes from the gods—or for that matter from an enigmatic
artistic genius—then I am not sure how any of us who have not been
touched by the Gods can understand very much of art. But, if, as the
later Nietzsche sometimes suggests—and blues singers never forget—
art is deeply embedded in our social realities, then understanding of
art comes through intensive analyses of the life and times of both the
creators of art and the observers.

Nietzsche is not as Eurocentric as most Western philosophers, but he is a strange person to discuss in connection with the blues, and in particular with the female blues singers that Davis discusses. It is not just that he was born in the wrong place and the wrong time. He also was deeply sexist and classist. Keeping all of this in view, I will use Nietzsche's analyses of late nineteenth century art to explore how aesthetics judgments are tied to social life—even as art often challenges the social order. Nietzsche's importance to twentieth-century moral thinking has long been recognized. It was Nietzsche who proclaimed most forcefully and compelling the death of God. He announced that it was naive to think that ethics could be based on rationality and instead suggested that we should investigate the evolution of moral systems. Nietzsche proclaimed the death of metaphysics and argued that science is only an interpretation and never an explanation of the world. He plays a similar role for aesthetics, and writes that the notion of "art for art's sake," like the notions of "objectivity," "scientific," and "pure willless knowledge," is really a sign of paralysis of the will (*BGE* 208). The bluesy Nietzsche announces the death of divine inspiration and Godly art and bases aesthetics on an investigation of the culture that produced the aesthetic values. The bluesy Nietzsche relentlessly analyzes the relationship between artists, aesthetic judgments, and the social world.

Aesthetic understanding is born from an investigation of social reality, but there is no easy transition from the understanding of social reality to the understanding of art and aesthetic judgments. As bell hooks writes, "There can never be one critical paradigm for the evaluation of artistic work."[7] hooks calls for a radical aesthetic that would link art and revolutionary practice, but at the same time she envisions an aesthetics of blackness that would be "strange and oppositional." For hooks, Davis, and the bluesy Nietzsche art, is understood by placing it in its social context, but to paraphrase hooks, the relationship between social reality and aesthetic judgment will more often than not be strange and oppositional. Davis admires how Rainey, Smith, and Holiday are able to articulate "a new valuation of individual emotional needs and desires."[8] By comparing and contrasting Davis and Nietzsche, we will see how art both challenges its time and yet can only be understood within the context of its time.

This chapter is divided into three sections. The first traces the change in Nietzsche's thought about art from the early work *The Birth of Tragedy* to his later work. The early Nietzsche believed that life was so terrible that one needed Apollonian illusions in order to survive. The later Nietzsche, however, believes it is possible to embrace life without calling upon Apollo. Given the later Nietzsche's desire to live for this world as opposed to sacrificing our life in this world for rewards in the next, one might think that Nietzsche would be a particularly good candidate to sing the blues. The blues unambiguously acknowledges the importance of the social world in the creation and understanding of art. But the second section will show how Nietzsche vacillates in his later thought between understanding art as the creation of solitary individuals, as the creation of an individual's biology or as the creation of an individual acting within a social realm. To the extent that Nietzsche claims that art is the product of a solitary individual or the product of one's physiology, then Nietzsche cannot, I argue, sing the blues. The third section shows that blues singers unambiguously maintain that their art grows out of an individual and the time and place in which that individual lives. Nietzsche sometimes recognizes, but blues singers never forget, that art and aesthetic understanding take place within a social context.

Saying "Yes" to Life

It has recently been argued that much of Nietzsche's later philosophy of art is already present in *The Birth of Tragedy*, but there are decisive differences between this early work and the later Nietzsche's thought.[9] In *The Birth of Tragedy,* great artists serve as mediums for the Apollonian and Dionysian drives. The paradigmatic sign of a great artist, for the later Nietzsche, is the one who forsakes herd mentality and creates new values. In 1871, Nietzsche writes that the Apollonian and Dionysian are "artistic powers" (*Mächte*) or "artistic drives" (*Treibe*) that come out of nature without the mediation (*Vermittlung*) of human artists (*BT* 2).[10] The whole contrast between the "subjective" and the "objective" artist fails to appreciate that true artists are dissolved from their individual wills and become a medium (*Medium*) whereby "the one true subject celebrates its dissolution into appearance" (*das eine wahrhaft seiende Subject seine Erlösung im Scheine feiert*) (*BT* 5). In other words, artists do not create these drives, but rather they serve as mediums or conduits for these naturally occurring forces (*BT* 5). To be an artist is to be dissolved from one's own will into Apollonian *Schein.*[11] These drives always remain in conflict with one another. The summit of their strife is Athenian tragedy—an equally Dionysian and Apollonian artwork (*BT* 2).[12] The relevancy of these forces is not reserved for Greek culture, although Nietzsche does claim that it is only from the Greeks that one can learn what the sudden rebirth of culture means for the inner life of a people (*BT* 21).[13] But Nietzsche also writes that the further development of art, even in his own time, depends on the opposition of these two drives.[14]

The later Nietzsche rarely writes about Apollo. Neither Apollo nor the sense of *Schein* as shimmering that is associated with Apollo in the first edition of *The Birth of Tragedy* is mentioned in "Attempt at a Self-Criticism," the new preface to *The Birth of Tragedy* that was published in 1886. Apollo recedes from the later work, in part because existence is no longer seen as being so terrible that its full experience requires the mediation of the dream world. The later Nietzsche believes that he can embrace Dionysus without calling upon Apollo. The Dionysus that the later Nietzsche embraces is also different from the Dionysus of *The Birth of Tragedy*. Near the very end of his productive life, he interprets the Dionysian drive as the "yes-saying to life in its strangest and most difficult problems" (*TI*, "What I Owe to the Ancients," 5). He envisions a "psychology of the orgiastic" in which there is an overwhelming feeling of life and power and in which pain works as a stimulus" (*TI*, "What I Owe to the Ancients," 5). Here Dionysus is no longer one of the fundamental forces of life, but rather Dionysian becomes the adjective to describe all of those who say "yes to life." Whereas in *The Birth of Tragedy* Nietzsche used the name "Dionysian" for those artists, like Archilochus, who serve as a conduit for a primordial force, now Nietzsche calls himself "Dionysian" because he affirms life in all of its struggles.[15] In this beautiful passage from *Twilight of the Idols*, Nietzsche revels in his ability to sing of this world—and all of its heartbreaks and adventures. This is the bluesy Nietzsche.

Rainey and Smith sing of lovers who have left or have been thrown out, and they sing of jail time served and the joy of the road. They sing of the joys and challenges that face black people in general and black women in particular. The blues is an art form that sings of *this* world; in particular, it embraces the joys of sexuality. Davis notes that many of the blues singers saw a fundamental contradiction between the blues and Christianity. Both Rainey and Smith believed this and gave up the blues at the end of their lives and turned to Christianity. As Davis notes, the sexual ethic that emphasized the freedom to pursue autonomously chosen sexual relationships was not compatible with Christian beliefs about sexual abstinence: "In contrast to the condemnatory and censuring character of Christianity, it (the blues) knows few taboos."[16]

Davis notes that emancipation brought, in many ways, a profound disappointment for recently freed slaves, but in three respects the lives of blacks were changed. African Americans were no longer prohibited from traveling, education was now possible, and there was freedom to explore sexuality within autonomously chosen relationships. To the extent that the church inhibited the right to explore one's sexuality it was taking away, in Davis's view, one of the most important newly found rights of black people. Travel—another of these newly won freedoms— was also an important theme for the blues, and Davis believes that a link exists between travel and sexuality. The freedom to travel is "frequently associated with the exercise of autonomy in their (black women's) sexual lives."[17] In "Farewell Daddy Blues," for example, Rainey tells her "daddy" that she is wild about him and wants him all the time, but she does not want him if she cannot "call you mine." She sings that her bags are packed and that she is ready to go. Davis obviously admires the commitment to sing of this world. Given the later Nietzsche's criticism of the otherworldliness of Platonism and Christianity, one would think that Nietzsche would embrace art that finds its meaning and indeed revels in the joys of this world, but, as we will see, even the later Nietzsche sometimes loses track of his own commitment to be of this world.

"The Blues Come from Black People"

Nietzsche writes in the 1886 preface to *The Birth of Tragedy* that the sentence "only as an aesthetic phenomenon is life justified" recurs several times (*kehrt mehrfach wieder*) in the text. In the work from 1871, Nietzsche suggests that the artist is not really the creator of the art-work. It is, rather, that art is created by the primordial drives acting through the artist. Nietzsche writes that we are not the real creators of the art worlds,

> but we can assume that we are already pictures and artistic projections for the true creator of the art worlds—for only as an aesthetic phenomenon is the existence and the world eternally justified. (*BT* 5)

In other words, for the early Nietzsche, we are aesthetically justified because we are phenomena created by the Apollonian and Dionysian forces.[18] He finds little value in the distinction between the objective and subjective artist, because to be a subjective artist is synonymous with being a bad artist. Every art first and foremost demands the conquering of the subjective, salvation from the "I," and the stilling of every individual will and desire (*BT* 5). There is no art without pure contemplation devoid of all interest (ibid.).

In "Attempt at a Self-Criticism" (again, this is the new preface added to *The Birth of Tragedy* in 1886), Nietzsche explains the phrase "justified as an aesthetic phenomenon" as meaning that his book "knows only an artist-meaning and a hidden meaning behind all occurrences" (*BT* "Attempt at a Self-Criticism," 5). That is, there is no definitive objective meaning behind events. These artistic metaphors in the later Nietzsche underline the way in which creative individuals question traditional values and create their own values. As independent "free spirits," these creators of values are often despised by society. Nietzsche admires those who stand apart from others, who refuse to accept "time-honored truths" and create their own highest values. For the later Nietzsche, artistic endeavor becomes the paradigmatic case of the effort of an individual to create his or her values. In short, the later Nietzsche is clearly distancing himself from *The Birth of Tragedy*'s contention that there is no such thing as a subjective artist. The later Nietzsche often refers to himself as an artist precisely in order to emphasize, as he writes in "Attempt at a Self-Criticism," that he is offering us a "purely aesthetic world interpretation and world justification" that no longer attempts to judge things by absolute values (*BT*, "Attempt at a Self-Criticism," 5).[19] "Purely aesthetic" here means roughly that there is no recourse to absolutes in the justification of the world interpretation.

The later Nietzsche calls himself an artist and allies himself with artists to stress that he no longer believes in truths that exist outside of social reality.[20] In the fifth book of *The Gay Science*—composed at about the same time as "Attempt at a Self-Criticism"—Nietzsche writes that it is impossible to know the extent to which existence is more than perspective (*GS* 374). "We" are beyond the point where we can claim that there should only be one perspective. The world has become infinite, because we cannot exclude the possibility that it contains an infinite number of interpretations. Nietzsche ends this aphorism by discussing how one should react to this state of affairs. He asks who would want to deify, in the old way, this monstrosity of the unknown world. Rather than deify the unending perspective, Nietzsche's later philosophy uses the undermining of absolutes to prepare the way for the construction of new perspectives. The artist becomes the prototype of the creator of these perspectives.[21]

Artists, for the later Nietzsche, are all those who enrich things out of their own power (*TI*, "Raids of an Untimely One," 9). Like philosophers

who no longer seek to uncover immutable truths, Nietzsche admires
artists who

> metamorphose things until they mirror their power—until
> they are reflections of their perfection. This need to metamor-
> phose into perfection is art. Even everything that he is not,
> becomes for him an occasion for joy in himself. In art man enjoys
> himself as perfection. (*TI*, "Raids of an Untimely One," 9)

Nietzsche must, it seems to me, walk a fine line. What is the perfection
of which Nietzsche writes here? In contrast to his earlier rejection of
the role of individual creativity, the later Nietzsche wants to underline
the importance of the individual in artistic creation. The risk is that
Nietzsche will forget the extent to which art is the result of an interaction between the individual and the world. Nietzsche is opposed to
those who would impoverish the things of this world by fleeing into
an otherworldliness, but if he overemphasizes the notion of the artist
as a solitary great individual, he risks needlessly impoverishing his
notion of art as well. As *Twilight of the Idols* demonstrates, Nietzsche
does not write his philosophy of the future by ignoring the philosophers
of the present and past. Both philosophic creation and artistic creation
come about through a reworking of the past and present.

The later Nietzsche often seems intoxicated by his ability to
deflate the icons of the modern age. At times this sense of intoxication
leads him to lose sight of what he has actually accomplished. He writes
that the prototype of the great artist/philosopher is the architect.[22] For
the architect

> represents (*darstellen* this could also be translated "presents")
> neither an Apollonian nor a Dionysian condition. Here is the great
> act of the will, the will that moves mountains, the intoxication
> of great will that arrives at art (*TI* "Raids of an Untimely One," 11).

Here Nietzsche clearly distances himself from his earlier position,
that great artists are the medium through which the Apollonian and
Dionysian forces express themselves. Now the architect is named as
the model for the great artist, and the architect does *not* serve as the
medium for either the Dionysian or the Apollonian. But is Nietzsche
moving mountains? He is deflating the idols of modernity and endorsing
art that is more life affirming. Unlike Descartes, who claims to have
torn down the edifices of all prior philosophers, Nietzsche constantly
revisits and reworks the ideas of those who have gone before him.

Art is, for Nietzsche, an antidote to morality; in particular, art is an antidote to the morality that sacrifices this life for the promise of an otherworldly paradise. Against those who claim that art serves only art, Nietzsche argues that art does indeed serve a purpose. It is " the greatest stimulus for life" (*TI*, "Raids of an Untimely One," 24). Nietzsche quickly adds that life often brings forth much that is ugly, hard, and questionable. But the tragic artist—that is, the great artist—has the courage to confront the terrible and frightening things that he (again, for Nietzsche great artists always seem to be male) uncovers. Many of Nietzsche's critiques of nineteenth-century morality and culture still ring very true. Nietzsche has a sharp eye for some of the moral hypocrisy of his day. His problem is his uncertainty about what to erect in its place. He offers us deconstructed modernity, not a new city on the hill.

Rainey and Smith are quite good at challenging society's pretensions and offering new perspectives, and they do this by forcing us to reexamine that which we thought we understood. Davis analyzes artistic production in its societal context, arguing that the artistic accomplishments of Rainey, Smith, and Holiday cannot be understood apart from the society in which they lived. Clearly these singers also embodied something like Nietzsche's creation of value, but it is not creativity for creativity's sake. The threat they face is much more concrete than the flight into otherworldliness. Their lack of political rights deeply affected their ability to live their lives.

It took a "great act of the will" for these women to produce their art. Davis relates that Smith confronted the Ku Klux Klan in July 1927 when it tried to disrupt one of her performances.[23] Davis also notes that Rainey and Smith sing about the problem of male violence, but they fail to name or analyze the social forces responsible for this violence. Davis writes, "The blues accomplish what they can within the confines of their form. The political analysis must be developed elsewhere."[24] In other words, artistic creation comes out of a certain context, and that context limits its possibilities. Davis notes that sexual assault is not referred to in either Rainey's or Smith's music. She argues that this is to be expected, given that rape was not at this time an acknowledged problem of domestic relationships. In addition, this was the time when many middle-class black women were campaigning against the false charges of rape that were used to justify the lynching of black men. Given this context, it is not surprising that we find no reference to sexual assault in these women's songs. Clearly Rainey and Smith were pushing the limits. The sexual freedom and the freedom to travel of which they sang were typically freedoms reserved for men. Through their music "they forged and memorialized images of tough, resilient, and

James Winchester

independent women who were afraid neither of their own vulnerability nor of defending their right to be respected as autonomous human beings."[25]

Artistic creation takes place within a context. This is true of the blues, abstract expressionism, impressionism, and rock and roll. There is very often something like a Nietzschean great act of the will, but that will plays itself out within a social realm. Patricia Hill Collins writes that the blues is a part of African-inspired communication patterns that "maintain the integrity of the individual and his or her personal voice, but do so in the context of group activity."[26] The later Nietzsche goes back and forth—sometimes acknowledging the ways in which society shapes art, and at other times he does not. Davis writes:

> Blues singers, regardless of their ethnic backgrounds, recognize the historical connection between blues music and black experience. As blues man Houston Stackhouse put it, "Hardworking people, been half mistreated and done around—I believe that's where the blues come from . . . well the blues come from Black people."[27]

The blues takes its inspiration from individual as well as collective experience of African Americans. The problem I am highlighting here is not that Nietzsche does not understand African American experience, but that he sometimes fails to acknowledge the social origins of art. In particular, the later Nietzsche sometimes writes as though artistic creation is solely the act of an individual will. To the extent that the later Nietzsche sees art solely as the product of individual genius or one's biology, he cannot sing the blues.

Nietzsche borders on this when in the fifth book of *The Gay Science* he claims that artists are creative individuals who are often not conscious of what they are doing. Here Nietzsche refers to himself as an artist and asks this:

> Must we not admit, we artists, that we contain within ourselves an unbelievable difference? Our tastes and also our creative powers are, in a wonderful way, self sufficient and have their own rate of growth. (*GS* 369)

He illustrates what he means through an example of a musician. A musician can create things that will rub against the tastes of listeners. According to Nietzsche, the artist is often not even aware of the contradiction between his art and the tastes of the audience. Nietzsche adds that artists may not be able to keep pace with their own creations. In particular, very creative artists do not know their own works—just as parents often do not know their children. This was certainly true, according to Nietzsche, of Greek artists.[28] It is important to distinguish between this claim—that artists may not understand their own works—and the claim that an artist's work represents a complete rupture with its social surroundings. By claiming that his creative powers are self-sufficient, Nietzsche approaches the claim that he creates in a vacuum.

At times, Nietzsche goes even farther in this direction. At one point in the later work, he claims again that artistic creation arises out of intoxication (*Rausch*), but now he claims that sexual arousal is the "oldest and most original form of intoxication," and that the most essential part of intoxication is the feeling of elevation of power (*Kraftsteigerung*) and fullness (*TI*, "Raids of an Untimely One," 8). Great style is the result of power that no longer feels the need to prove itself (ibid.). It comes out of spirits who no longer even notice that there are those who contradict them. It is out of a state of intoxication that artists force themselves on things—"raping them." Make no mistake, Nietzsche writes, idealiza-tion consists in "a monstrous bringing out of the principal characteristics" (*TI*, "Raids of an Untimely One," 8). The source of idealization is the individual. The individual creates by idealizing phenomena. Although the reference to intoxication is reminiscent of *The Birth of Tragedy's* references to the Dionysian, there are important differences. In calling sexuality the oldest form of intoxication, Nietzsche is suggesting that aesthetic values are to be explained through reference to biology. This is the anti-blues Nietzsche.

The Case of Wagner underscores the separation of artistic creation from consciousness, but it goes a step farther. At times this work advances a biological explanation for artistic creation and as such is both anti-blues and undermines Nietzsche's own recognition of the social embeddedness of art. In the epilogue to *The Case of Wagner*, he writes that our aes-thetic values are biologically determined. All aesthetics can be divided into two categories: they are either the product of a declining life, or the product of an ascending life. He then uses morality to illustrate his point. Master morality is, for Nietzsche, a sign of ascending life, and Christian morality is a sign of the declining life. The spirits who belong to master morality judge things according to their own inner spirit. They explain, beautify, and even make the world reasonable out of the fullness of their spirits. Christian morality, on the other hand, impoverishes and vilifies the things of this world. There is a great deal of discussion of decadence and some discussion of physiology in the later Nietzsche, but this quasi-physiological aesthetic is never fully developed.

But even within *The Case of Wagner*, Nietzsche does not always hold to this anti-blues aesthetic. The later Nietzsche is disgusted with Bayreuth and in particular with what he saw as Wagner's attempt to court favor with the "masses." Much of *The Case of Wagner* is devoted to elucidating this criticism. In the preface to this work, Nietzsche asks what a philosopher demands of himself. He answers that the philosopher demands that he must overcome everything of his time that he carries around in himself (again, I do not use gender-inclusive language here because for Nietzsche only men can be philosophers). The philosopher's most difficult battle, Nietzsche continues, is with all that which marks him as a child of his time. Nietzsche then goes on to make an extraordinary confession:

> I am just like Wagner a child of this time, that is to say, a decadent, but I comprehended it but I fought against it. (*CW* "Preface")

This is what I call the bluesy Nietzsche. This is the Nietzsche who realizes that he is a child of his time—which is not to say that he cannot rebel. He is, to use Jacqueline Scott's term, a strong decadent who is a part of his time and yet challenges his time.[29] This Nietzsche sings of this world, not the next.

Art and Community

Much to the chagrin of the later Nietzsche, the first edition of *The Birth of Tragedy* contains a mix of ancient and modern things. That is, in the early work, Bach, Beethoven, Schopenhauer, and Wagner embody the possibility of a rebirth of German culture, and Nietzsche writes extensively about the communal nature of Greek tragedy. The overriding concern of the Nietzsche of 1886 is for the life of the individual. In 1871, Nietzsche hopes that his analysis of Greek culture will help lead the way for the rebirth of German culture—the ancients will supply the model for the moderns. Looking back, Nietzsche finds these youthful hopes for German culture to be one of the greatest embarrassments of this work. In "Attempt at a Self-Criticism," he reinterprets *The Birth of Tragedy* and suggests that it is primarily a book that offers artistic creation as a paradigm for a way of life for the individual. Greek tragedy is now seen as a model for how the *individual* can develop a pessimism of strength.

The later Nietzsche often writes as if nothing positive can come out of our interactions with others. But Nietzsche's anti-social rhetoric obscures the important role that others play in his later thought. As Nietzsche abandoned the notion that the artist is a medium for the Apollonian and Dionysian drives he relied, even though he did not always acknowledge it, upon the theater of human interactions to serve as the source for artistic and philosophic creations. At times it would seem that there is no positive role for a community to play in the later Nietzsche's thought. At odds with his extreme statements about community are, however, other texts where Nietzsche identifies himself as a member of a community of European artists and thinkers. Art and philosophic thought come to be judged by their ability to transcend narrow national boundaries.

Once Nietzsche moves away from the notion that the artist is a medium for primordial forces, it is not surprising that he turns to the theater of human culture to find both the sources for artistic inspiration as well as the criteria for evaluating art. If the old eternal truths have lost most of their credence—or at least their omnipotence—where can one find the source for philosophic writing, or artistic creation if not human culture? Even as he seems to glorify the lonely thinker and artist, Nietzsche's reliance on the cultural icons of his day, as well as figures of the past, becomes increasingly evident. His philosophic creations come through reexamination and reevaluation of concepts, values, and personalities in artistic and philosophic traditions. Nietzsche now judges artists according to their relationships with their times, as well as with the past and the future. They are no longer evaluated according to their relationship to primordial drives.[30]

Although the later Nietzsche seems to have little appreciation for the positive role that community can play, there is praise for the "good European" in both *Beyond Good and Evil* and *The Gay Science*. In *Beyond Good and Evil,* he writes that he has become a Southern European "by faith" and is now constantly on guard against Northern European music. He longs for a supra-European music that does not fade away at the sight of the voluptuousness of the Mediterranean sky and sea. This would be a music that no longer knows anything of good and evil (*BGE* 255).[31]

In another place he writes that "we" are fortunate that Mozart's music still appeals to us. At some point we will no longer appreciate his "gentle enthusiasms and his childlike delight in curlicues and chinaisms" (*BGE* 245). Appreciation of Beethoven will disappear even faster. Beethoven is only "the epilogue of a transitional and style break and not, like Mozart, the epilogue to a great, many centuries old, European taste" (ibid.). Mozart and Beethoven are greater than Schumann, in Nietzsche's estimation, for Schumann has only a limited sense of taste. Schumann, unlike Mozart and Beethoven who are European events, is only a German event. In Schumann, German music approaches its greatest danger—that is, "to lose its voice for the European soul and descend into a mere fatherlandishness" (ibid.). These artists are judged according to whether or not they have transcended their narrow nationalism and joined the community of European artists. Nietzsche no longer believes that atemporal objective criteria can be used to evaluate art. Art is judged by its ability to transcend the narrowness of a national border and fit into a larger transnational and decidedly social context.

This line of thinking leads Nietzsche to a striking reinterpretation of Wagner. Nietzsche writes that all deep men of the nineteenth century—including Goethe, Beethoven, Stendhal, Heine, and even Wagner—were preparing the way for the European of the future.[32] Wagner, too, is a European event. The greatness of these artists is judged according to their cosmopolitan appeal. In addition, the cultural relativity of artistic creation is discussed. It is not that Mozart or Beethoven will no longer be great, but future generations will be too far removed from them to appreciate them. In short, there is no independent standard for judging art. Our aesthetic judgments are inevitably the product of our times. Nietzsche states this belief in many other places as well. For example, in *The Case of Wagner,* Nietzsche admits that both he and Wagner are products of their times. The difference between them is that Nietzsche fights against this decadence (*CW*, "Foreword").

Nietzsche describes himself as a good European. He explains that it is his "homelessness" that makes him a good European.[33] He and other Europeans are "homeless," for they are "children of the future." They are somewhat jealous of those who feel at home in this time, but the homeless ones cannot believe in modern realities. He claims not to be a conservative seeking to return to some idyllic past, nor is he a liberal believing in progress.[34] More striking, he is not a liberal, because the ideas of equal rights, free society, and "no master and no servant" do not appeal to him—nor to the community of good Europeans.

We believe it is simply not desirable that the realm (*Reich*) of justice and harmony would be established in the world. (*GS* 377)

He writes that these homeless ones love danger, war, and adventure. They consider themselves conquerors and consider it necessary to establish a new order that will include slavery:

For to every strengthening and elevation of the prototype of man (*des Typus "Mensch"*) there belongs a new art of enslavement (*GS* 377)

His notion of slavery is not tied to nationalism and racism. As he wrote this twenty years after the abolition of serfdom in Russia and the Civil War in the United States, this call for the reintroduction of slavery—even if it is a new art of slavery—had to sound as brutal, shocking, untimely, and morally repugnant as it does to us today.[35] Even as we abhor his suggestion for the reintroduction of slavery, it is clear that one of the motivating factors for this outrageous suggestion is its untimeliness. Nietzsche's philosophic project is now tied to the creation of new values. These values will be formed in dialogue with other thinkers and artists—many of them will be Nietzsche's contemporaries. They will be life affirming—at least they will be life affirming for a select few.

It is difficult to see how Nietzsche's homeless ones would participate in civil society—not to mention a system of slavery. They prefer to live—according to Nietzsche—alone on mountaintops. These homeless ones are too multifarious and mixed for the tastes of the Germans of his day. This metaphor of the ideal humans living on the tops of mountains underlines the extremely attenuated ties that the later Nietzsche's philosophy sometimes seems to envision between individuals in his ideal artistic-philosophic communities. His extreme distrust of collective actions, along with his glorification of the lonely individual, would seem to leave little place for artists or philosophers to exchange ideas or to inspire one another.[36] Yet at other points he makes it clear that even these homeless ones have connections with others. They live in society, for they are good Europeans—the inheritance of thousands of years of European history. In short, Nietzsche's goal is the production of the elite, homeless, good European.

Davis, on the other hand, sees in Billy Holiday's work

> a symbiosis drawing from and contributing to an African American social and musical history in which women's political agency is nurtured by, and in turn nurtures, aesthetic agency.[37]

Art opens up new ways of thinking about our social reality that defy traditional modes of understanding. Davis sees in this great emancipatory possibilities. Nietzsche prizes art because it can lead to the flourishing of the great individual. Davis prizes it for its emancipatory possibilities for the many. Furthermore, for Davis, political and aesthetic agency nurture one another. Part of what makes Billie Holiday great, for Davis, is her ability to transform Tin Pan Alley love songs that were contrived and formulaic.[38] If she wanted to have a musical career, Holiday was forced to record such material. Davis argues that, for example, Holiday transforms "You Let Me Down" through her style of singing.

The song tells of a woman who was told that she was an angel and put on a pedestal. She was told that she would wear diamonds:

> I was even looking for a cottage I was measured for a wedding
>   gown
> That's how I got cynical
> You put me on a pinnacle
> And then you let me down, let me down
> How you let me down

Through her style of singing, this becomes not merely a song about a woman who is "let down" by a man. It also becomes a complaint protesting the myriad of ways that African Americans had been let down as well as an invitation for the listeners to reflect upon how to move beyond the loss that they have experienced. The last phrase, "How you let me down," seems to reach out and encompass a host of grievances, personal and political, inviting listeners to reflect on loss and on the possibilities of moving beyond that loss.[39]

The later Nietzsche writes that there is no greater difference than the one between art made in front of the eyes of witnesses and art that has forgotten the world (*GS* 367). It is not entirely clear where he places his own art, but he seems, in this passage, to value the artists who forget the world. Nietzsche never really forgets the world. In practice, if not in his rhetoric, Nietzsche's later philosophy is an extended engagement in debates with other thinkers and artists. One of the greatest changes from the early to the later Nietzsche is that he no longer claims that others (i.e., Bach, Beethoven, Wagner, Kant, or Schopenhauer) are at the crest of the rejuvenation of culture. Now it is Nietzsche himself (and his Zarathustra) who represents the great challenge to his time as well as the harbinger of the next stage of European culture.

He can only challenge his time because he studies it. His writings are full of analyses of European thinkers (and some Asian thinkers), past and present. Even as Nietzsche speaks of the solitary life of great individuals, in practice his philosophy was the result of a conversation with the leading thinkers and artists of European tradition. The later Nietzsche is more reliant upon others than his extreme anti-communal rhetoric suggests. Having abandoned the notion of the artist as purveyor of the primordial drives, the later Nietzsche turns to others to find his artistic inspiration. Having given up on the search for eternal truths, his philosophy became, of necessity, based in social realities.

Nietzsche's reliance on social realities is underlined as one considers the titles of his later works. *Beyond Good and Evil, On the Genealogy of Morals, Twilight of the Idols, The Antichrist, The Case of Wagner,* and *Ecce Homo.* The titles of all of these works point toward social phenomena that Nietzsche dissects. Nietzsche never was and never tried to be a Faust shut away in some ivory tower. Yet in spite of his involvement with his times, Nietzsche's distrust of communal involvement ran so deep that the best he could envision from community life was a community of "higher individuals" that would occasionally band together in order to defend itself (*BGE* 262). Much more common in Nietzsche are sentiments such as "common good is a self-contradiction" (*BGE* 43). Although he castigates narrow nationalism, anti-Semitism, and the widespread anti-Slavic feelings of his day, at the same time his anti-liberalism is equally strong. The later Nietzsche abandoned not only the notion of a rebirth of German culture. His glorification of the lonely artist signals a disparagement of most, if not all, communal involvement in the production of art. The turn toward quasi-physiological explanations for artistic inspiration can be understood, in part, as a failure to acknowledge the role that others play in inspiring us. At times, Nietzsche writes very clearly about the role that social forces play in the production of art. At other times, in his anti-liberal rush to underline his untimeliness, he forgets his own conclusion, that we are primarily socially constructed creatures. As such, our artistic creations, like everything else about us, have their origins in our social environment.

Lovers left or leaving, the joys and sorrows of the road, jail, injustice, prejudice, lack of work, and/or lack of money, the pleasures and evils of drink—these are the recurrent themes of Bessie Smith and Ma Rainey. They sing of the joys, trials, and sorrows of their lives and of the lives of people like them. Their genius is, in part, their ability to open up the world of black, working-class people. Even if Nietzsche has little or no appreciation for the plight of people of African descent in the Americas, in so many other ways he seems like such a good candidate to sing the blues. His love troubles are the stuff of legend, as are the wanderings of his adult life. He lived, in some ways, a privileged life. He never suffered from racism, but he did suffer from numerous professional and personal rejections.[40] Most important, Nietzsche emphatically writes of embracing this world rather than the next. But it must be through the embrace of some part of our social being that we embrace this world. Nietzsche would have to say that not only is hell made out of our relationships with others, but our yes saying to this world is a yes saying to some sort of social reality. If this is the case, then, at some level Davis and Nietzsche agree, because both find that great human potential comes about through the affirmation of some parts of our social being. But unlike Nietzsche, Davis, given that she has studied the blues, unambiguously acknowledges that the stage upon which this struggle is presented is the theater of social life.

Notes

1. On the question of whether or not white people can sing the blues, see Amiri Baraka, *Blues People: Negro Music in White America* (New York: Quill, 1963). For another point of view, see Joel Rudinow, "Race, Ethnicity, Expressive Authenticity: Can White People Sing the Blues?," *The Journal of Aesthetics and Art Criticism* 52:1 (Winter 1994): A longer version of this chapter can be found in my *Aesthetics across the Color Line: Why Nietzsche (Sometimes) Can't Sing the Blues* (Lanham, MD: Rowman & Littlefield, 2002), 45–72.

2. Many have divided Nietzsche's work into an early, middle, and late period. See, for example, Walter Kaufmann's *Nietzsche: Philosopher, Psychologist, Anti-Christ* (Princeton, NJ: Princeton University Press, 1974). In what follows, what is commonly referred to as Nietzsche's middle period will not be discussed. *The Birth of Tragedy* will be contrasted with Nietzsche's later works that were written from 1885 to 1888. Here the "early Nietzsche" means the Nietzsche of *The Birth of Tragedy*. The "later Nietzsche" means the works Nietzsche wrote from 1885 to 1888.

3. See, for example, the epilogue to *The Case of Wagner*. In *Twilight of the Idols*, "Raids of an Untimely Man," 20, Nietzsche writes that ugliness and beauty have physiological effects on us.

4. Angela Y. Davis, *Blues Legacies and Black Feminism* (New York: Pantheon, 1998), 117.

5. Davis, *Blues Legacies*, 183.

6. Baraka, *Blues People*, 65.

7. bell hooks, *Yearning: Race, Gender, and Cultural Politics* (Boston: South End Press, 1989), 111.

8. Davis, *Blues Legaces*, 5.

9. Julian Young argues that there is a pessimism inherited from Schopenhauer in both *The Birth of Tragedy* and the later work. See Julian Young, *Nietzsche's Philosophy of Art* (Cambridge: Cambridge University Press, 1993).

10. Several texts were written around the time of *The Birth of Tragedy* that Nietzsche himself never published. For a discussion of these texts, see John Sallis, *Crossings: Nietzsche and the Space of Tragedy* (Chicago: University

of Chicago Press, 1991), 7. See also M. S. Silk and J. P. Stern, *Nietzsche on Tragedy* (Cambridge: Cambridge University Press, 1981).

11. There are at least three different ways in which the words *Schein* and *Erscheinung* are used in *The Birth of Tragedy*. Two of these usages occur within a few lines of each other in "Attempt at a Self-Criticism." The Nietzsche of 1886 claims that *The Birth of Tragedy* places morality in the world of *Erscheinungen*. Even in this early work, morality is

> placed in the world of appearance (*Erscheinung*) and not only in "appearance" (in the sense of the idealistic technical term), but rather (morality) is classified as pretense (*Schein*), delusion, error, interpretation, contrivance, art. (*BT*, "Attempt at a Self-Criticism," 5)

Here I translate the word *Schein* as "pretense," for Nietzsche is claiming that morality is a delusion, and that even this early work recognized it as such. Moreover, Christian morality is an unnecessary illusion or a contrivance that at least some people do without.

A few lines later, while contrasting his view of art with Christianity's view of art, the word *Schein* appears again. Christianity, he writes, is anti-artistic, for it assigns art to the realm of lies and therefore condemns it. Such an attitude is actually hostile to life, according to Nietzsche, for life depends upon *Schein*, art, deception, optic, necessity of perspective, and error (*BT*, "Attempt at a Self-Criticism," 5). Unlike the deception associated with Christianity, this time the word *Schein* is used to describe something that is necessary for life. Along with deception, perspective, and error, all human beings need *Schein* in order to survive.

Neither of these usages of the word *Schein* is equivalent to the shining of Apollo, as it is described in the original work.

12. Sallis claims that "there can be no doubt that tragedy surpasses the Apollonian: Apollo speaks finally the language of Dionysus. . . . Even its Apollonian images are images of Dionysus, and to this extent, it is, in the end, a double mimesis of the Dionysian (Sallis, *Crossings*, 91). What Sallis does not mention at this point is how this section of *The Birth of Tragedy* ends. Nietzsche writes that this "difficult" relationship between the two gods should be thought of as a "brotherhood." I interpret Section 21 as suggesting a reciprocal relationship between the two gods rather than a predominance of Dionysus. Sallis's interpretation is colored, I think, by the importance he places in *das Masslose*.

13. This is a point upon which there is general agreement in the secondary literature. For example, Julian Young also makes this point but goes somewhat farther than I would. He claims that

> Nietzsche's first thesis is not, in its most fundamental intention, a genetic thesis about Greek tragedy at all but rather an analytic and valuative thesis about great art in general. (Young, *Nietzsche's Philosophy*, 31).

I question the claim that Nietzsche's "first thesis" is a thesis about great art. It is hard to say whether Nietzsche is more concerned about Greek tragedy or great art in general. He is clearly concerned about both in *The Birth of Tragedy*.

14. Nietzsche begins the first section of *The Birth of Tragedy* with the claim that there is considerable progress to be made in the science of aesthetics.

15. My appreciation for the richness of this passage stems in large measure from my conversations with and the writings of Louis A. Ruprecht Jr. See his *Tragic Posture and Tragic Vision: Against the Modern Failure of Nerve* (New York: Continuum, 1994), 137 ff.

16. Davis, *Blues Legacies*, 133.

17. Davis, *Blues Legacies*, 66–67.

18. Nietzsche also makes this claim in the original work (*BT* 24) to explain how the ugliness and disharmony of the Greek myths can produce an aesthetic effect. Here Nietzsche argues that ugliness and disharmony are found in the will, that is, they are a part of the Dionysian and therefore inherent in art.

19. In a sense, the early Nietzsche linked the artist and the philosopher, but less directly. In *The Birth of Tragedy*, citing Schopenhauer, Nietzsche writes in Section 1 that the philosophical man has a premonition (*Vorgefuhl*) that beneath the reality in which we live there lies a second that is covered. The Apollonian dream world where all things appear as phantoms is the sign of philosophical capability. "As the philosopher stands in relationship to the reality of Dasein, so the artistically aroused man relates to the reality of dream" (*BT* 1).

20. For example, he writes in *The Case of Wagner* that one is more of a philosopher when one is more of a musician (*CW* 1).

21. In *Beyond Good and Evil* (10), Nietzsche says that there are very few who really possess the will to truth. And those who would prefer a "certain nothing to an uncertain something" are nihilists and possess despairing, mortally weary souls.

22. Note that this is in contrast to Schopenhauer, who believes architecture to be one of the lowest forms of art. For Schopenhauer's discussion of architecture, see *The World as Will and Representation*, vol. 1 § 43.

23. Davis, *Blues Legacies*, 37.

24. Davis, *Blues Legacies*, 33.

25. Davis, *Blues Legacies*, 41.

26. Patricia Hill Collins, *Black Feminist Thought*, 2d ed. (New York: Routledge, 2000), 105.

27. Davis, *Blues Legacies*, 114

28. Nietzsche also makes this claim that great artists are usually not able to understand the significance of their own work, in *Beyond Good and*

Evil (256). Here he writes about Wagner that "Geniuses of his type [Wagner] seldom have the right to understand themselves."

29. Jacqueline Scott, "Nietzsche and Decadence: The Revaluation of Morality," *Continental Philosophy Review* 31 (1998): 66.

30. Adrian Piper claims that the contemporary argument that art should be apolitical has been fueled by Greensburg's formalism—a movement that gained currency under the McCarthyism of the 1950s. She suggests that there is a long-standing European tradition of seeing art as "a medium of social engagement." She sees it as particularly unfortunate for European art that it should eschew political content at the very moment Europe's "turbulent social, political, and demographic changes offer such fertile conditions for social engagement." See Piper, "The Logic of Modernism," in *Out of Order, Out of Sight,* vol. 2 (Cambridge: MIT Press, 1996), 209–14.

31. In *The Case of Wagner* (3) Nietzsche also makes the distinction between Northern and Southern music and praises Southern music. He even refers back to this aphorism (*Beyond Good and Evil* 255).

32. Note that Nietzsche's estimations of people are constantly changing. In *The Case of Wagner*, he writes that it is blasphemy to group Wagner and Beethoven together. Wagner is not really a musician. His genius really lay in his capabilities as an actor (*CW* 8). In *Ecce Homo*, "Why I Am So Clever," he repeats his claim that Wagner was a great artist and an European.

33. In *Beyond Good and Evil* Nietzsche also writes about the provincialism of those who are tied to a single nation in Europe. He writes that although the sickness of nationalism sometimes hides it, in fact, "Europe wants to become one" (*BG* 256).

34. In *The Antichrist* 4 he also disavows the notion that civilization is progressing.

35. In *Beyond Good and Evil* (258) Nietzsche writes that a "healthy aristocracy" accepts not only slavery but the sacrifice of a mass of people as well. In some places in the *Nachlass* he goes even farther. For a further discussion of the issue, see my *Nietzsche's Aesthetic Turn: Reading Nietzsche after Heidegger, Deleuze and Derrida* (Albany: State University of New York Press, 1994), 153–55.

36. In *Twilight of the Idols* Nietzsche writes that "To live alone one must be either an animal or a God—according to Aristotle. The third case is missing: one must be both—a philosopher. . . .

37. Davis, *Blues Legacies*, 164.

38. Holiday is a jazz singer, but Davis argues that she also sings of the concerns of black, working-class people, and she was clearly influenced by the blues.

39. Davis, *Blues Legacies*, 170.

40. For an excellent study of Nietzsche's conception of race, see Gerd Schank, *Rasse and Züchtung bei Nietzsche* (Berlin: Walter de Gruyter, 2000). See also "'The Great Play and Flight of Forces': Nietzsche on Race," in *Philosophers on Race: Critical Essays*, ed. Julie K. Ward and Tommy Lott (Oxford: Blackwell, 2002). See also my "Nietzsche's Racial Profiling" in *Race and Racism in Modern Philosophy* edited by Andrew Valls (Ithaca, NY: Cornell University Press, 2005).

Contributors

Christa Davis Acampora is an associate professor of philosophy at Hunter College and the Graduate Center of the City University
of New York. She is the co-editor of *A Nietzschean Bestiary* (State
University of New York Press, 2004) and has published numerous articles
on Nietzsche. She is currently completing a manuscript on Nietzsche's
conception of contest and a two-volume project on aesthetics and the
cultural productions of women of color (also for SUNY Press).

Daniel W. Conway is a professor of philosophy at Pennsyl-
vania State University. He has published numerous articles on Nietzsche,
nineteenth-century philosophy, political theory, and ethics. He is the
author of *Nietzsche and the Political (Thinking the Political)* (Routledge,
1997) and *Nietzsche's Dangerous Game: Philosophy in the Twilight of
the Idols* (Cambridge, 1997). He is the editor of *Søren Kierkegaard:
Critical Assessments of Leading Philosophers* (Routledge, 2002) and
Nietzsche: Critical Assessments (Routledge, 1998), and he is the co-editor
of *Nietzsche, Philosophy, and the Arts* (Cambridge, 1998), and *The Politics of Irony: Essays in Self-Betrayal* (Palgrave Macmillan, 1992).

A. Todd Franklin is an associate professor of philosophy at
Hamilton College. He has authored several scholarly works on Nietzsche,
the social and political import of various forms of existential enlightenment, and philosophical conceptions of the self. His current work
focuses on issues of race and the pedagogical project of promoting critical consciousness.

Robert Gooding-Williams is a professor of philosophy, adjunct
professor of African American Studies, and director of the Alice Berline
Kaplan Center for the Humanities at Northwestern University. He
was the Jean Gimbel Lane Professor of the Humanities for 2000–2001.
He is the author of *Zarathustra's Dionysian Modernism* (Stanford,

2001), the co-editor of the Bedford Books edition of *The Souls of Black Folk* (pub. 1997), and the editor of *Reading Rodney King / Reading Urban Uprising* (Routledge, 1993). He has published articles on Nietzsche, DuBois, multiculturalism, and the representation of race in film. He also has been the recipient of numerous academic honors, including two NEH College Teachers Fellowships and a Laurance A. Rockefeller Fellowship, awarded by Princeton's University Center for Human Values.

Lewis R. Gordon is the Laura Carnell University professor of philosophy and religion and director of the Institute for the Study of Race and Social Thought and the Center for Afro-Jewish Studies at Temple University. He also is an ongoing visiting professor of government and philosophy at the University of the West Indies at Mona, Jamaica, and president of the Caribbean Philosophical Association. He is the author of several influential books, including *Her Majesty's Other Children: Sketches of Racism from a Neocolonial Age* (Rowman & Littlefield, 1997), which won the Gustavus Myer Award for Outstanding Book on Human Rights, *Existentia Africana: Understanding Africana Existential Thought* (Routledge, 2000), and his latest book, *Disciplinary Decadence: Living Thought in Trying Times* (Paradigm, 2006).

Kathleen Marie Higgins is a professor of philosophy at the University of Texas at Austin. She has written, edited, and co-edited many books, including *Nietzsche's Zarathustra* (Temple, 1987), *Reading Nietzsche* (with Robert C. Solomon, Oxford, 1996), *The Cambridge Companion to Nietzsche* (with Bernd Magnus, Cambridge, 1996), *Comic Relief: Nietzsche's Gay Science* (Oxford, 2000), and *What Nietzsche Really Said* (with Robert C. Solomon, Schocken, 2000). In addition, she has published many articles on Nietzsche and aesthetics, and she has conducted a series of audio and video lectures on Nietzsche with Robert C. Solomon, *The Will to Power: The Philosophy of Friedrich Nietzsche* (The Teaching Company, 1999).

John Pittman teaches philosophy and humanities at John Jay College of Criminal Justice. He edited *African-American Perspectives and Philosophical Traditions* (Routledge, 1997) and is co-editor, with Tommy Lott, of *The Blackwell Companion to African-American Philosophy* (2003).

Jacqueline Scott is an assistant professor of philosophy at Loyola University of Chicago. She has published several articles on Nietzsche and critical race theory, and she is currently working on a manuscript, *Nietzsche's Worthy Opponents: Socrates, Wagner, the Ascetic Priest, and Women*.

Paul C. Taylor is an associate professor of philosophy at Temple University and a fellow of the Jamestown Project at Yale Law School. He is the author of *Race: A Philosophical Introduction* (Polity-Blackwell, 2004) and several articles on aesthetics, critical race theory, and pragmatism.

Cynthia Willett is a professor of philosophy at Emory University. Her books include *Maternal Ethics and Other Slave Moralities* (Routledge, 1995), *Theorizing Multiculturalism* (Blackwell, 1998), and *The Soul of Justice: Social Bonds and Racial Hubris* (Cornell, 2001). Her articles focus on nineteenth- and twentieth-century philosophy, social theory, race and gender studies, and philosophy and literature. She is currently writing on empire and comedy.

James Winchester is an assistant professor of philosophy at Georgia College and State University. He has published *Nietzsche's Aesthetic Turn: Reading Nietzsche after Heidegger, Deleuze and Derrida* (State University of New York Press, 1994). His selection in this volume is from his book *Aesthetics across the Color Line: Why Nietzsche (Sometimes) Can't Sing the Blues* (Rowman and Littlefield, 2002), which explores the understanding of art across the white and black racial divide in the United States. He is currently working on a book about the ethics of global poverty.

Index

Aaron, Hank, 80
Absolutism: philosophical rejection of, 22; promotion of authoritarian conformity and, 28; religious, 22; scientific, 22; value, 28
Acampora, Christa Davis, 10, 175–194
Action: possibilities of, 24
Adell, Sandra, 52
Africa(n): as active Subject, 103; cultural practices, xi, 103; names, 109; as self-defining subject, 108
African American(s): achievements, 89; assimilation, xi, 78; awareness of views of white world, 57; consigned to Dionysiac world, 76; creativity in survival of, 78; as cultural healers, 4; double consciousness of, xi, xii, 51–70; experience of modernity, xi; implied inferiority and, 26; musical expression, 75–89; need for self-respect and self-assertion in, 56; problem status of, 77; reinforcement of inferiority taught to, 55; resistance, 7; resolution of inner turmoil of, 56; seeing self through eyes of others, 4; as source of distress for white America, 78; spiritual advantage of, 56; struggle with tyranny of social intimidation, 26; treated as problems, 77, 78; violence against, 80
African Cultural System, 107

Afrocentrism, 101, 102. *See also* Centrism; abuse of, 102–110; closing self to future, 107; constricted perspectives of, 109; and efforts to recover history of African culture, 107; empowerment and, 107; projecting African agency in, 103, 108; provision of resources for individual self-creation and, 107; race theory and, 105–110; rejection of biological determinism in, 105; understanding from African standpoint, 103; use of African names and, 109; uses of, 102–110
Agency: aisthesis of, 176, 180–183; in imaginary domain, 180; transformative possibilities of, 10
Agon, 10, 183, 187
Aisthesis: of freedom, 175–194
Alcoff, Linda, 153, 154, 163
Alienation: axiological, 8; intellectual, 8
Allan, Lewis, 82
American Body Politic: as white body politic, 78
Anti-foundationalism, 101, 102
Appiah, Anthony, 9, 111, 114, 117, 118, 121, 133, 134, 140, 141, 145*n32*; *Color Conscious,* 111, 115, 116; cosmopolitan ideal and, 111, 119; dismissal of race as unscientific, 139; eliminativism

Appiah, Anthony, *continued*
of, 111, 115; on the *human* race,
111, 112; *In My Father's House,*
111; on race talk, 116; and use of
identity in everyday life, 114, 115;
use of irony, 113
Armstrong, Louis, 85, 87
Arnold, Mathew, 21, 116, 146*n38*
Art: African American, 8; as antidote
to morality, 233; and artist's biology,
226; cathartic power of, 208;
challenge to social order and, 227;
community and, 236–242; contextual understanding of, 226, 228;
of cultural physician, 1–11; decay
of, 8; emancipatory possibilities of,
10; form and meaning of, 208;
impedance of development of, 24,
25; of inquiry, 81; interracial
quality to processes of decay, 85;
intoxication and, 235; Negro, 24,
25; race and, 128, 129; revolutionary practice and, 227; social
context for, 10, 11; social reality
and, 226; tragic, 187; understanding across cultural borders, 225; of
Wagner's music, xii; will to power
and, 207
Asante, Molefi, 9, 102, 105, 107, 108,
109, 121; on Africalogy, 122*n4*
Asceticism: functions of, 34
Assimilation, 78; as eradication, 78
Atlanta Compromise, 55

Baldwin, James, 77, 150, 165
Baraka, Amiri, 77, 94*n27,* 226
Beauvoir, Simone de, 182
Bellow, Saul, 21
Berlin Conference (1884), 113
Beyond Good and Evil (Nietzsche),
21, 67, 112, 113, 118, 119, 125,
129, 134, 157, 158, 184, 210, 211,
240, 241
Bigotry: of Western culture, 24
Biracialism, 108
The Birth of Tragedy (Nietzsche), xi,

76, 78, 184, 203, 207, 208, 210,
211, 228, 229, 230, 235, 236
Black. *See also* African American(s):
achievements, 80; allegiance to
values embedded in logic of
victimization, 90*n8*; attribution of
failure to, 80; creativity, 83; creolization, 92*n12*; duplicity, xi; existentialism, viii; freedom through
music, 82; identity, viii, xiv; illegitimate existence, 84; location with
music and dance, 82; myopia of, 5,
6; myth of rapist, 47; opposition
to, 81; politics, viii; suffering,
200*n37*; threats to "Southern
white womanhood" by, 48
Black Boy (Wright), 77
Black Skin, White Masks (Fanon),
84
Blues, 75–89, 225–242; admired by
the oppressors, 94*n28*; Apolline-
Dionysiac synthesis of, 77; as art
form, 229; black experience and,
234; contradiction to Christianity
in, 229; dependence on racism
and oppression, 94*n28*; embrace
of sexuality in, 229; as impulse to
keep pain alive in consciousness,
77; relations between art and life
in, 10; sexuality and, 233, 234
Blues People (Bakara), 77
Body: complexity of, 138;
contextuality of, 138; education of,
135, 136, 137; as facilitator of
development of people into races,
135; invisible, 138; prereflective
racialization of, 145*n30*;
racialized, 127; reality of race
and, 134–138; soul and, 135, 136
Byerman, Keith, 52, 54

Calhoun, John, 79
Capitalism, 206
Castes: knightly-aristocratic, 37;
master, 37; priestly, 37
Castration, 206

Cavell, Stanley, 106
Centrism, 102; acceptance of, 103; rejection of biological race in, 102; understanding culture in, 103
Change: affecting, 70; pedagogues of, 23–25; social, 83; value, 29
Christianity: blues music and, 229, 230; hypocrisy of, 3; intensification of pain in, 190, "of Christ," 3, 4; slavery and, 3
Collins, Patricia Hill, 234
Colonialism, viii–xi
Color Conscious (Appiah), 111, 115, 116
Conrad, Joseph, x
Conscience: bad, 37, 38, 207; call to, 57; good, 22, 23; guilt and, 189; requirement of memory for, 189
Consciousness: critical, 18; development of, 18; dominating, 20; as a law, 20; liberating, 18; mass, 96n38; meaning of existence and, 1; racial, 30; raising, 63; social, 46
Consciousness, critical: axiological liberation and, 30; counter-hegemonic force of, 25–27; development of, 27; effort to effect human liberation and, 26; importance of, 26; pedagogies of, 27–29; recognition of oppression in, 26
Consciousness, double, 8, 51–70; accompanied by threatening stance, 53; adoption of self-disparaging judgments, 53; of African Americans, xi, xii; aspects of, 52; awareness of being invisible in, 53; awareness of self as mixed being, 53; awareness of white world's surveillance in, 53; as basis for distance from judgment of others, 57; black identity and, xiv; development of second sight through, 68; energy draining in, 53; failure of others to confer genuine recognition and, 52; as form of mental illness, 52;

Hegelian roots of, 52; identification by single trait in, 53; and illumination of concrete experiences of African Americans, 62; influence of James on, 71n6; inner tension created in, 53; internalization of mechanisms of surveillance in, 53; self-alienation and, 52; sense of surveillance by unsympathetic others, 53; of spiritual person in modernity, 61
Conway, Daniel, 9, 125–142
Cornell, Drucilla, 180, 181
Cosmopolitanism, 113, 119
Creditor-debtor relationship: punishment and, 42; relationship to ancestors and, 42
Critical race theory, 8, 110, 111, 149; health/liberation and, 9; role of biology in, 9
Cultural: autonomy, xiii; bigotry, 24; contexts, 102; decline, 1; distinctiveness, xiv; diversity, 29; dominance, 45; form, 128, 131, 134; forms of repression, 7; health, 2, 154; identity, 25, 154; imperialism, 21; independence, 112; mainstream, 58; moderation, 10; movements, xii; nationalism, 107; orientations, xiv; pluralism, 18; predispositions, 107; prejudices, 113; production, 85; racialism, 108; renewal, 144n18; subordination, 17, 23; superiority, 96n34; transformation, 7
Culture: African, xi, 102, 103; alternative, 23; contextualization of, 28; defining, 28; degeneration of, 126; Dionysian, xii; diseased aspects of, 6, 7; domination of by ascetic ideals, 38; essence of, 22; European, 17, 102, 129, 130; fixed ideals in, 1; foreign, xiii; German, 170n36; Greek, 203; health of, 149; individual's relationship to, 61; interpretation of, 28; mass,

Culture, *continued*
93*n18*; meaning of, 33; modern,
xii; nature of, 17; New World
black, 92*n12*; non-Western, 23;
organic, 157; pathological, 77;
perspectival, 25; postmodern, xii;
of poverty, 77; science of, xii, 134;
self-definition of, 151, 152;
Socratic, xii, 88; transmissibility
of, 109; tyrannical forms of, 28;
understanding, 28, 103; Western,
21, 22, 24; and work of racial
transmission, 137

Davis, Angela, 10, 226, 227, 229,
233, 234
Daybreak (Nietzsche), 27
Decadence, 132, 155; art and, 8; in
black music, 95*n31*; causes of, 2;
contending with, 156; counter-
acting, 2; as decay of values, 155;
German, xv; music and, 85;
nihilism as symptom of, 95*n32*,
167n21; as part of normal life
span of living things, 95*n32*;
revaluation of, 167n21; symptoms
of, 167*n21*; of whiteness, 87
Derrida, Jacques, xi
Descartes, René, 232
Determinism, 152; biological, 105
Dewey, John, 101, 121
Discourse: on blackness, 80; of
dominance, 7; race, 116; religious,
3; of whiteness, 12*n15*; white
supremacist, 5
Dislocation, 104, 109
Diversity: cultural, 29; of human
types, 126
Dogmatism: axiological, 20;
destruction of, 1; moral, 21, 27, 28
Dominance: axiological forms of, 18;
cultural, 45; discourses of, 7
Douglass, Frederick, 175–194;
concepts of freedom, 175; concepts
of human power of, 10; as cultural
physician, 3, 4; *My Bondage and*

My Freedom, 176; narratives of
fight with slave-breaker, 176–183,
196*n16*; production of meaningful
freedom and, 10; on slavery, 3
Drives: artistic, 228; erotic, 205, 206
DuBois, W.E.B., xi, 12*n15*, 51–70,
113, 121, 139; on attitudes that
African Americans should
cultivate, 58; claims capitulation
of Atlanta Compromise, 55;
conceptions of race and, 4;
consciousness-raising of white
readers, 63; as cultural physician,
3; debates with Washington, 85;
description of police system, 53;
development of self-conscious
racial identity and, 4; double
consciousness and, 51–70;
rejection of classical racialism
by, 116; Emersonian roots of
reflections of, 71*n13*; on false lure
of wealth, 54, 55; historical
specificity of, 63; internalization
of pragmatism as method of
thinking by, 71*n6*; level of specificity in writing, 62; on obliga-
tions to reconstruct social policy
for benefit of all citizens, 57, 58;
on problem of color line, 150; on
psychological state provoked by
African American's social circumstances, 51; rejection of classical
racism and, 118; *The Souls of
Black Folk,* 77; veil of color line
separating whites and blacks, 53

Ecce Homo (Nietzsche), 18, 19, 58,
60, 101, 102, 110, 118, 120, 121,
241
Eliminativism, 111, 115
Ellington, Duke, 85
Ellison, Ralph, 10, 77, 78, 94*n27*,
204, 213; as cultural physician, 3,
5, 6; *Invisible Man,* 82, 216–218
Empowerment: Afrocentrism and,
107; by feeling of freedom, 181

Eris, 184
Essentialism, 105, 108; biological, 116, 152
Ethnicity, 134, 151
Evil: as form of valuation, 36; moralized projection of, 47; rechristening, 67
Existence: aimless, 132; meaning of, 1
Existentialism: black, viii
Experience: of active engagement in struggle, 10; aesthetic, 207; centrism and, 102; dependence on context, 102; evaluation and, 56; imaginative, 181; of inner tension, 61; personal, 176; shared, 118; of slavery, 3, 175

Fanon, Frantz, 79, 80, 83, 85, 94$n24$
Fantasy, 204, 205; colonialist, ix, x; of hubris, 210; intensity of, 205; of male power, 210, 211; variations in enactment of, 206; of the warrior, 205; will to power and, 205
Feminism, viii, 71$n10$
The Fire Next Time (Baldwin), 77
Forgetting, 188, 189
Form: cultural, 128, 134; imposition onto matter, 128; race and, 127–131
Förster, Elisabeth and Bernhard, ix, 129
Foucault, Michel, x, xi, xvii$n17$, 120
Franklin, A. Todd, 7, 17–30
Freedom: aisthesis of, 175–194; black, 82; Douglass and, 10, 175, 176; empowerment and, 181; existential, 203–222; masculinity and, 203–222; meaningful, 176; metaphors for, 95$n31$; Nietzsche and, 10, 182, 183–188; power and, 176; resistance and, 177–183; struggle for, 175–194; through music, 82
Freire, Paulo, 26, 27
Freud, Sigmund, 205, 206

Gaye, Marvin, 83
The Gay Science (Nietzsche), 22, 58, 65, 69, 139, 166, 184, 231, 234
Genealogy: advent of modern racism and, x, xi; as critical form of analysis, 13$n21$; development of, 28; and discourses of dominance, 7; Foucault's analysis of, xvii$n17$; psychologically/historically sensitive, 28; of race, 149–166; resemblance to critical relativism, 29
German(y): anti-Semitism, 170$n36$; culture, 170$n36$; decadence and, xv; emergence as colonial power, viii–ix; identity, xv; music, xii; nationalism, viii, xi–xv; racial mixture of, 129; Reformation, xii; spirit, xii
Gershwin, George, 76
Gilroy, Paul, xiv, 111, 113
Gobineau, Arthur de, 76
Going to the Territory (Ellison), 78
Goldberg, David Theo, 153, 154, 163
Gooding-Williams, Robert, vii
Gordon, Lewis, 8, 12$n15$, 75–89
Gramsci, Antonio, 93$n18$
Greeks, ancient: contests and, 203; cultural superiority of, 135; health of, 8, 78; insights for health from, 1; merging of Dionysian and Apollonian into art form by, 8; tragic drama of, 78; use of philosophy by, 1; valorization of, 76

Hacking, Ian, 119, 120
Harris, Leonard, 17
Hartmann, Nicolai, 20
Headley, Clevis, 95$n31$
Hegel, G.W.F., xvii$n12$, 4, 90$n4$
Hegemony: of discourses of dominance, 7
Heidegger, Martin, 138
Hemingway, Ernest, 81
Herder, Johann Gottfried, xiv, 127
Higgins, Kathleen Marie, 8, 51–70

Historians: antiquarian, 106, 107, 110; critical, 106, 109, 110; monumental, 105, 106

Holiday, Billie, 82, 226, 227, 233, 239

Hollingdale, R.J., 157

Holub, Robert, viii, ix, xvi*n10*

"Homer's Contest" (Nietzsche), 183, 184, 198*n24,* 203, 211, 212

hooks, bell, 26, 227

Hubris, 204; as arrogance, 208; condemnation of, 212; defining, 208; fantasy of, 210; of the master, 208; restraints on, 210, 211; as sign of health, 210, 211; valorization of, 204; of white supremacist discourse, 5

Hudlin, Reggie, 84

Hughes, Langston, 24, 25, 75–89

Human, All-Too-Human (Nietzsche), 158, 159, 184

Humanism: transcultural, 113

Identity: American, 81; assigned, 114; black, viii, xiv, xv; choosing, 114; collective, 176; communal, 8, 43, 150; complexity attending, 109; contemporary, 109; contingent on white supremacy, 108; creation, 161; cultural, 25, 154; damaging, 5; development, 55; diasporic, xv; dual, 4; embodied, 151; formation, 150; German, xv; healthy, 6, 7; idealizations of, 2; individual, 150, 154, 161; modern, xiv; play, 112; politics, 112; racial, 4, 5, 6, 7, 8, 25, 111, 112, 115, 127, 150, 171*n43*; reconception of, 150; self-conscious, 4; social, 61, 109; white, 4, 5, 94*n24*

Ideology: imperialist, x; of lynch law, 47; moral, 47; racist, x, xi

Imagination: agency and, 180; colonialist, ix, x, xvi*n10*; moral, 63; philosophical, ix; poetics of, 81; relevance for moral deliberation, 176

Imitation: psychology of, 26

Imperialism: alternative to, x; cultural, 21; demeaning forms of, 21; denigration of diversity and, 17; ethnoracialized, 22; of the future, ix; supranationalist, ix; threat of, 134; Western, 17

Impulse, mythical, 1

Incest, 206

Industrialism, 206

Inferiority: implied, 26

In My Father's House (Appiah), 111

Inpsychation, 188

Instinct, 23, 134; automatism of, 137; herd, 40

Invisible Man (Ellison), 82, 216–218

Irony, 121

Irrationalism, 142

James, C.L.R., 93*n18*

James, William, 52, 71*n6,* 101, 105, 121

Jaspers, Karl, 92*n11*

Jazz. *See* Music

Jefferson, Thomas, 116, 146*n38*

Jews: acculturation of, 129; negative characteristics of, 159; as purest race, 170*n36*; spiritual revenge and, 34; success in racial constitution, 129

Jones, Leroi. *See* Baraka, Amiri

Judgments, aesthetic, 10; products of social reality, 225; social embeddedness of, 225–242; social life and, 227

Kant, Immanuel, 32*n24,* 78, 143*n5*

Kaufmann, Walter, 78, 92*n11,* 169*n30*

Kierkegaard, Soren, xiv, 146*n34*

Kinds: human, 120; indifferent, 119, 120; interactive, 119, 120; of kinds, 120; natural, 120; as sets of things, 119

Knowledge: seekers of, 25

Language: American, 78; chauvinistic, xiii; of natural science, 119; of

Language, *continued*
pathology, 80; philosophy of, 119; of sight, 4; vernacular revolt and, 79
Law: abstract, xiii
Lewis, David Levering, 4, 5
Liberalism, viii
Lincoln, Abby, 82
Locke, Alain, 17–30; and acquiescence to ideals of prevailing systems of values, 25–27; aversion to absolute values, 30; axiological theories of, 7, 17–30; criticism of axiological hegemony, 18; cultural pluralism of, 18; demystification of tyrannical forms of culture and, 28; on nature of values, 17; problems of Western culture and, 21, 22; rejection of classical racism by, 116; value absolutes and, 20
Lukács, Georg, viii
Lust: for danger, 203; pleasures of war and, 203; for power, 203
Luther, Martin, xii
Lynch, Charles, 39
Lynching and lynch law, 33–48; as ceremony of catharsis, 40; class and power relations in, 41; community identity and, 8; cruelty and family dynamics in, 42, 43; development of, 39; documentation of, 48n3; evolution in practice of, 39; as expression of racial and class hostility from white Southerners, 48; ex-slave status as focus of mob fury, 44; extensive forms of atrocity in, 40; functionality of, 44; growth of, 33; herd instinct and, 40; historical reality of, 38; history of, 34, 38–42; ideology of, 47; myth of black rapist and, 47; quasi-theological rationales justifying, 41; racialization of, 39; rationalization of, 47; reassertion of solidarity of

Southern white community in post-Civil War era, 44; in relation to *ressentiment*, 7, 8, 33–48; rise in Post-Reconstruction America, 7, 8; ritualistic character of, 39, 40; role of Protestant fundamentalist ministers in, 41; self-justification in, 47; slide from "Negro" to "criminal" and, 44; spectator/participant in, 40; stages of, 39; value system and, 8; white wage labor and, 49n7

Marcuse, Herbert, 93n18
Marginalization, 8; of innovator, 67; Nietzsche's feelings of, 58, 59; as precondition for assumption of significant cultural role, 67; reassessment of situation in, 67; recognition of limitations of majority's viewpoint and, 66
Marxism, viii
Mason, Ernest, 17, 28, 30n1
McWhorter, John, 90n8
Meaning: of all culture, 33; assigning, 115; creating, 1, 155; of existence, 1; narratives of, 1; production of, 175, 191; values and, 155
Memory: compensation and, 189; conscience and, 189; morality requiring practices of, 189; necessity of, 188; production of, 189
Metaphysics: death of, 227; of presence, xi
Mills, Charles, 151, 152
Miscegenation, 127, 144n19
Modernity: African American experience of, xi; alternative, xiv; Socratic ethos of, xiii
Monumentalism, 106; goal of self-overcoming in, 107
Moral: corruption, 3; dogma, 21; dogmatism, 27, 28; enrichment, 191; habits, 24; hesitancy, 57; ideology, 47; ideology of priests, 37;

Moral, *continued*
  imagination, 63; indignation, 64;
  limits, 207; past of manking, 27;
  prejudices, 141; responsibility, 188;
  traditions, 21; values, 17, 149, 162
Morality: abstract, xiii; alternative,
  23; art as antidote to, 233;
  autonomy and, 189; Christian,
  154, 186; decadent, 156; defining,
  20; development of, 189; European, 21, 22; expression of opinion
  and, 27; herd, 21; Kantian, 189;
  need to obey and, 27; psychic
  evolution of, 188; secular, 61;
  slave, 34, 36, 37, 47, 175; slave
  revolt in, 33, 34, 43
Morrison, Toni, 10, 77, 204, 213;
  Song of Solomon, 218–222
Movements: cultural, xii; Negritude,
  xviii*n23*
Multiracialism, 108
Music: African American, xiv,
  225–242; black's location in, 82;
  blues, 10, 11, 75–89; decadence
  and, 85, 95*n31*; direct image of
  slave's will and, xv; disco, 85;
  eradication of black competition
  in, 83; expressive power in, xiv;
  freedom through, 82; German, xii;
  hip-hop, 76, 83, 85, 95*n31*; jazz,
  76, 77, 85; as leitmotif of African
  American expression, 76; metaphors for freedom in, 95*n31*;
  ragtime, 76; rap, 83; rhythm and
  blues, 76, 85; role of soloist, 85;
  soul, 76; spirituals, 76; status of,
  xv; unjust appropriation of wealth
  by whites in, 85
My Bondage and My Freedom (Douglass), 176

Narcissism, 80
Narratives: conforming to needs of
  the present, 106
Nationalism, 121, 133, 239; in *The
  Birth of Tragedy,* xi; cultural, 107;

German, viii, xi–sv; race theories
  and, 127
Native Son (Wright), 213–216
Naturalism: scientific, 142
Negritude, xviii*23*
Negrophobia, 85
New Negro Movement, 17
Nietzsche, Friedrich: abstract focus
  of, 62, 63; on absurdity of
  oppressing blacks, 91*n9*; account
  of criminals as debtors, 42, 43;
  accounts of morality by, 188; and
  acquiescence to ideals of
  prevailing systems of values,
  25–27; admiration for Jews, 129;
  advocacy of liberation of spirit,
  51; on anger at the past, 69, 70,
  73*n37*; appropriation of myth of
  Aryan conquest, 129, 130,
  144*n14,* 145*n28*; aristocratic
  radicalism of, 115; on artistic
  creation, 225–242; attention to
  bodily gesture, 135; aversion to
  absolute values, 30; axiological
  theories of, 7, 17–30; *Beyond
  Good and Evil,* 21, 67, 112, 113,
  118, 119, 125, 129, 134, 157, 158,
  184, 210, 211, 240, 241; *The Birth
  of Tragedy,* xi, 76, 78, 184, 203,
  207, 208, 210, 211, 228, 229, 230,
  235, 236; on black suffering,
  200*n37*; bluesy/nonbluesy, 226,
  227, 228, 234; call for recognition
  of *vis creativa,* 10; as champion of
  science, 126; character of values
  and, 17; comparison to DuBois,
  51–70; concepts of human power
  of, 10; concepts of illness and
  health, 92*n11*; criticism of
  axiological hegemony, 18; on
  cruelty, 35; cultural analysis of
  Greek forms of *agon,* 10; cultural
  elitism of, 18; as cultural physician,
  1, 149, 151, 154; cultural theories
  of, 157; *Daybreak,* 27; and death
  of God, 227; on decadence, 2, 155,

156; description of blacks as inferior, 91*n9*; dialectical period in thought of, 76; disconnection from others, 58, 59; distaste for nationalism, 121; on doing historical work, 105, 106; and Douglass, 175–194; and DuBois, 51–70; early dialectical thought, 90*n4*; *Ecce Homo,* 18, 19, 58, 60, 101, 102, 110, 118, 120, 121, 241; and emergence of values, 182, 183; evaluation of philosophers, 118; feeling of marginalization, 58, 59; focus on problems of modern European morality, 21, 22; *The Gay Science,* 22, 58, 65, 69, 139, 166, 184, 231, 234; genealogical diagnosis of dangers of traditional race purity, 9; genealogical method of, 13*n21*, 28, 102; *On the Genealogy of Morals,* xviii*n17*, 27, 33, 34, 37, 38, 42, 62, 69, 129, 131, 140, 154, 175, 184, 188–192, 207, 210, 240; genealogy of race and, 154–158; generalized theorization on integrated visions, 62; geopolitics of, ix; and German nationalism, viii, xi–xv; herd morality and, 21; "Homer's Contest," 183, 184, 203, 211, 212; hostility to egalitarianism, 51; and hubris, 204–212; *Human, All-Too-Human,* 158, 159, 184; on human development, 2; identification with priest caste, 37; on inner tensions in conflict, 58, 61; level of specificity in writing, 62; as "man of the Right," ix; on miscegenation, 127; misguided views on power, 10; model for struggle, 183–188; on morality engendering repression, 21; nature of culture and, 17; nomadic existence of, 125; "On the Uses and Abuses of History for Life," 105, 111; and origins of struggle, 182, 183–188; perfectionism of, 9; philosophy of art, 228–230; and postmodern philosophy, 126; pragmatic theory of truth and, 105; prereflective racialization of the body by, 145*n30*; and problem of decadence, 155; production of meaningful freedom and, 10; proposes revaluation of traditional philosophy, 149; proto-phenomenological approach to race, 125–142; and pursuit of freedom, 182, 183–188; on question of limits, 203; race theory and, 126, 139–142; racial formalism of, 128, 129, 131–134; and racism, viii–xi, xvii*n12*; references to breeding, 133, 188; reflections on historical inquiry, 105; relates travel to race, 125, 126, 143*n5*; on relativity of values, 19; *ressentiment* and, 33–48; on science of race, 139–142; on seeing self as having will, 70; seeking resolution to inner conflict, 70; self-analysis of, 58, 59, 61; self-description, 18; on "shadows of God," 61; skepticism of, 126, 127; status of truth in work of, 121; strategies for overcoming self-disparagement, 65; on suffering, 190; technique for provoking empathic moral indignation, 64; *Thus Spoke Zarathustra,* 31*n12*, 66, 67, 69, 210; traditional notions of race and gender, 121; *Twilight of the Idols,* 23, 229, 241; understanding of artistic creation, 10; understanding of health, 78; universalistic stance of, 62; *On the Use and Disadvantage of History for Life,* 106, 107; view of blacks as representatives of prehistoric man, xvii*n12*; view of struggle,

Nietzsche, *continued*
175–194; views of blacks, viii; *The
Will to Power,* 81, 88, 94n22; will
to power and, 10, 204–212;
writings on women, 65
Nihilism: active, 88, 167n21;
avoidance of, 2, 155; decadence
and, 167n21; passive, 88, 167n21;
rescue from, 1; suicide and, 156;
as symptom of decadence, 95n32
Norms: absolute, 21; social, 205;
universal, 21

Objectivity: philosophical preoccupation with, 17
Oedipus, 205, 210, 211
On the Genealogy of Morals
(Nietzsche), xviin17, 27, 33, 34, 37,
38, 42, 62, 69, 129, 131, 140, 154,
175, 184, 188–192, 207, 210, 240
*On the Use and Disadvantage of
History for Life* (Nietzsche), 106,
107
"On the Uses and Abuses of History
for Life" (Nietzsche), 105
Oppression: axiological forms of, 18;
mechanisms of, 58; psychology of,
4; psychology of axiological,
23–25; racial, 4; recognition of, 26;
stylized, 94n28; subversion of, 2
Ortega Y Gasset, José, 93n18, 96n38
the Other: formative role of, 4
Outlaw, Lucius, 151, 152, 154, 161,
162, 166n6

Patterson, Orlando, 90n8
Perfectionism, 106; Nietzschean, 9
Phenomenology: existential, 138; of
race, 125–142
Philosophy: analytic, 118, 119;
isolation of, 118; of language, 119;
as liberating tool of culture, 1; as
means of curbing mythical
impulse, 1; positive, 155; postmodern, 126; preoccupation with
objectivity, 17; science and,

139–142; significance of, 1;
Socratic, 186; traditional, 149
Physician, cultural, 1–11, 155;
aesthetic facet, 3; diagnostic
aspect, 7–8; prescriptive aspect,
8–9; recovery aspect, 9–11; revelatory facet, 3; theoretical facet, 3;
treating decadence and, 155
Pittman, John, 7, 8, 12n15, 33–48
Politics: black, viii; of fulfillment,
xiv; of transfiguration, xiv
Positivism: Cambridge, 119
Posnock, Ross, 111, 113
Powell, Colin, 80
Power: to affect change, 70; of art,
208; to be the author of one's life,
180; creative, 10; dynamics of, 63;
excessive, 204; institutional, 27;
intoxication and, 235; male, 210,
211; in marginalization, 8;
meaningful freedom and, 176;
perversions of, 175; political, 55;
realization of, 175; sensations of,
175; social reality of, 38; transfiguring possibilities of, 175
Pragmatism, 102; Deweyan, 9
Preston, William, viii, ix, 91n9, 190,
191
Priests: abstinence and, 36; ascetic,
34, 37; creation of, 36; customs of
personal hygiene, 37; as distinct
caste, 37; functions of, 37;
hybridity of, 36, 45; impact on
human culture, 36; moral ideology
of, 37; practices of purification
and, 36; slave morality and, 36;
value-creating, 38
Public Enemy, 83
Punishment: as core content of
concept of lynch law, 38; in
creditor-debtor relationship, 42;
practice of, 33; reconstitution of
community by, 43; relation of to
revenge and guilt, 33; for violations of community standards, 40
Putam, Hilary, 116

Race: as achievement, 128; art and, 128, 129; biological foundations of, 102, 134, 150, 151; bodily cultivation and, 134–138; color-coded, 113; complexity of, 110; conception of as problem by critical race theorists, 149, 150–154; conservation, 152; contribution to individual/cultural health, 151; as created ontology, 153; creation of meaning in life and, 152; defining traits of, 110; discourse, 116; distinctions of, 110; doing away with, 151; as fiction, xiv, 127, 153; fixed designations of, 126; genealogy of, 149–166; hierarchical rankings and, 110; historically pernicious concept of, 7; material component of, 127, 131, 133; metaphysical role of, 152; mixed, 108, 153; nationalist notion of, 158; one-drop rule and, 162; operation in culture, 8; overlapping contexts of discourse and, 139; as personal journey, 9; and priority of form, 127–131; psychical consequences of hierarchical conceptions of, 4; purity model of, 161, 162, 163; radical mixtures of, 125, 126; reality of, 134–138; recasting reality of, 9; reconstruction of, 9; rejection of, 102; revaluation of, 9, 149–166; science of, 108, 139–142; socially constructed, 115, 152; as subpopulation, 110; talk, 116; as "thick," 161, 162; transmission of, 127; values assigned to, 150, 151
Racelessness, 153
Race theory, 101–121, 126, 139–142; afrocentrism and, 105–110; classical, 110, 113; cosmopolitan prejudices and, 110–120; critical, 110, 111, 149; ending racial nightmare through, 150; nationalism and, 127; xenophobia and, 127

Race work, 101–121
Racial: acculturation, 134, 137, 144n19; categories, 153; classification, 138, 142; consciousness, 30; cultivation, 128, 129, 133, 138; decline, 144n19; divide, 225; embodiment, 134–138; etiquette, 137; as fissure plaguing American society, 6; formalism, 127, 128, 129, 131–134; forms of repression, 7; identity, 4, 5, 6, 7, 8, 25, 110, 111, 112, 115, 127, 150, 171n43; individuality, 24; inferiority, ix; oppression, 4; past, 109; prejudice, 53; purity, 9, 110, 126, 127, 153, 161, 162; "scripts," 112; self, 161; self-worth, 26; sense, 30; subordination, 17; superiority, 129; tradition, 30; violence, 33, 90n8
Racism: challenges to, 150; demands for blacks to fix themselves, 83; denial of existence of, 90n8; ideology of, x; overcoming, 7; pernicious effects of, 152; raising children to survive, 94n24; supposed scientific foundations of, 8
Radicalism, viii; aristocratic, 112, 115
Rainey, Ma, 226, 227, 229, 230, 233
Rationalism, 81
Reality: counterfeit, 120; debased, 120; of power, 38; ressentiment and, 34; social, 11, 47, 118; values and, 19
Relativism: critical, 29; in organic approach to systems of value, 29
Religion: as dogmatic moral tradition, 21; German, xii
Repression, 20–23; cultural/racial forms of, 7; ideological, 21; of rage, 93n19
Resistance: aesthetic, 83; African American, 7; black, 84; as ignition to struggle for freedom, 177–183; intrasystemic, 84; slavery and, 175; superior moral character

Resistance, *continued*
  and, 181; through struggle, 175;
  visibility and, 182
Ressentiment, 33–48; articulations
  of, 38; basic structure of, 38; as
  basis for action of a being of the
  noble type, 37; beings of, 35, 38; as
  component of spiritual achievement of humanity, 33; content
  preservation of, 35; creativity of,
  34; cultural dominance of, 45;
  deepening function of, 35;
  dynamic of, 34; dynamism of, 45;
  essential cruelty of, 35; expression
  of, 37; generation of more-than-
  bipolar social structure by, 45;
  holistic tendency of, 35; in hostile
  behavior aimed at one who has
  injured, 34; humiliation of the
  powerless and, 41; lynching in
  relation to, 7, 8, 33–48; as meaning
  of all culture, 33; metaphorical
  function of, 35; moral distinctions
  and hierarchy in, 45; precipitation
  of, 46; proper discharge of, 46; as
  psychic phenomenon, 33, 35; rank
  orderings in, 45; reactivity of, 35;
  reality and, 34; revenge and, 46;
  reversal of valuations in, 44; role
  of priests as organizers in, 41;
  slave morality and, 36; as space of
  hybrid forms of social relation, 38;
  thwarted intentions and, 35;
  unconscious structure of, 47; as
  way of being/seeing, 35
Revenge: desire for, 36; discharge of
  desire for, 37; ideological form, 34;
  imaginary, 34; of the Jews, 33;
  lynching and, 33; spiritual, 33, 38;
  sublimated, 34
"Richard Wright's Blues" (Ellison), 77
Roach, Max, 82
Roosevelt, Theodore, 81

Said, Edward, x
Schopenhauer, Arthur, xv, 90*n4*

Science: of culture, 134; folk, 142;
  gay, 140, 141; "hard," 119; natural,
  119; philosophy and, 139–142; of
  race, 139–142
Scott, Jacqueline, 9, 149–166
Selectivity, 106
Self: overcoming, 107; racial, 161; as
  worst enemy, 67
Self-actualization, 23
Self-consciousness, 57
Self-determination: possibilities of,
  24; repression of, 20
Self-esteem: bolstering, 69
Self-expression: distinctive forms of,
  20; repression of, 20
Self-perception, 4
Self-realization: collective, 10;
  individual, 9–10
Self-worth: positive sense of, 26;
  racial, 26
Senghor, Léopold Sédar, 76
Sexuality: blues and, 229, 230, 233,
  234; Christianity and, 229; inter-
  racial, 48; travel and, 230, 233
Sight: imagery of, 4; language of, 4
Sight, second, 4, 5, 8, 51–70; ability
  to *see* through other's judgments,
  56; as function of having perspective on everyday experience
  differing from other's, 56; as
  power of discernment, 56; through
  double consciousness, 68
Sin, 73*n37*
Skepticism, 126
Slavery. *See also* Morality, slave:
  Christianity and, 3; deconstruc-
  tion of, 3, 4; dehumanization
  through, 3; denouncement of, 4;
  divine sanction for, 3; experience
  of, 175; industrial, 56; moral
  reprehensibility of, 175; new
  kinds of, 176; provision of
  opportunities to be savored in,
  191; resistance to abuses of,
  176–183; spiritualized, 200*n38;*
  visibility and, 182

Smith, Bessie, 226, 227, 229, 233
Snead, James, xi
Social: access, 115; bonds, 204;
    change, 83; coercion, 30; con-
    sciousness, 46; constraints, 206;
    contract, 44; conventions, 212;
    critique, xvii*n21*; identity, 61, 109;
    injustice, 83; intimidation, 26;
    location, 115; mainstream, 8,
    misery, 84; norms, 205; order, 207;
    reality, 11, 47, 118; suffering, 85;
    thought, x; transformation, 8,
    11, 83
Socialism, viii
Society: civilized, 43, 48;
    complacency in, 87; inability to
    remain young, 88; internal
    divisions of, 22; judgment of
    individuals, 61; minority outlooks
    in as enhancement, 67; value of
    race to, 151
Song of Solomon (Morrison),
    218–222
Soul, 135, 136; bad conscience and,
    207; sovereign individual type,
    207
The Souls of Black Folk (DuBois), xi,
    xii, 51–70, 77; xiii, xi–xv
Spirit: folk, xi; German, xii; libera-
    tion of, 51; metamorphosis of,
    31*n12*; purification of, xii; in
    resistance to abuses of slavery,
    176–183; and struggle for freedom,
    176–183
Spirituals, 76, 85
Stackhouse, Houston, 234
Stereotypes: of female behavior, 65;
    rejection of, 26
Stoler, Ann Laura, x
Struggles: creative, 175, 184, 187;
    destructive, 175, 184; for freedom,
    177–183; freedom and, 175–194;
    value of, 177
Subjectivity: expressions of, 7;
    human, 7
Submission: rejection of, 58

Subordination, 20–23; cultural, 23;
    demeaning forms of, 21; political, 23
Suffering: ancient Greek, 92*n12*;
    balance of debts and guilt and,
    190; black, 200*n37*; blues music
    and, 78; communal, 87; confront-
    ing, 78; group, 96*n34*; infliction of,
    190; production of, 190; social, 85;
    struggle against, 8; of untested
    existence, 96*n34*
Sullivan, Andrew, 205
Sympathy, 64

Taylor, Paul, 9, 101–121
Thought, African American:
    analysis of psychology of racial
    oppression, 4; promotion of egali-
    tarian, cosmopolitan agendas, 2;
    subversion of human oppression
    in, 2
Thus Spoke Zarathustra (Nietzsche),
    31*n12*, 66, 67, 69, 210
Totalitarianism: ideological, 24
Toynbee, Arnold, 22
Tradition: allegiance to, 21; conser-
    vative, 21; Judeo-Christian,
    73*n37*, 208; moral, 21; racial, 30
Truth: acceptance of, 105; deflations
    of, 119; discovery of, 156; faith in,
    140, 141; inestimable, 140; "new,"
    140; objective, 162; pragmatic
    theory of, 105; seeking, 141;
    strengthening, 1; transcendental,
    154; universal, 162; will to,
    140, 141
Twilight of the Idols (Nietzsche), 23,
    229, 241
Tyranny, axiological, 20–23;
    repression, 20–23; subordination,
    20–23

Universalism, 111
Universality: alternatives to, 102;
    rejection of, 103
"Unspeakable Things Unspoken"
    (Morrison), 213

Value(s): absolute, 7, 17, 20, 21, 23, 25, 28, 30; adherence to, 21; aesthetic, 227; alternative systems of, 30; assigned to race, 150; attitudes and, 19; belief justification and, 19; change, 29; communal, 21; creation of one's own system of, 22; cultural context and, 19; decay of, 155; definitive, 19; denoting essence of culture by, 22; as derivative expressions of human subjectivity, 7; development, 29; dogmatic systems of, 18, 26, 29; dynamic nature of systems of, 30; emergence of, 18, 182, 183; European, 21, 102; evolution/emergence of systems of, 28; in flux, 150; healthy, 6, 7; historical/functional relativity of, 29; idealizations of, 2; imperatives of, 20; interpretation of, 28; Judeo-Christian moral, 17; life-world, 161; local, 102; locating, 119; lynching and, 8; moral, 17, 149, 162; naturalized conception of, 18–20; nature of, 17; as normative constructs, 19, 20; objective interpretation of, 29; organic, 28, 29; perspectival, 25; plebian origins of, 18; preferred, 20; prejudicial, 26; prevailing systems of, 25; production of, 175; proposing new, 70; rationalization of, 20; reality and, 19; reconceptualization of, 28; revaluation of, 47, 156; of struggle, 177; systems of, 29, 155; unassailable, 19; universal, 20, 21, 29

Veil: of color line separating whites and blacks, 53; dimming of acuity and, 53; penetration of, 65; perspectival, 65; reader awareness of, 63; two sides of, 64; wealth and, 55

Visibility, 182

Wagner, Richard, xii, 62, 82, 155, 238

Wald, Priscilla, 52, 56, 63, 71$n13$

Waller, Fats, 84

Washington, Booker T., 55, 56, 85

Washington, Johnny, 17

West, Cornel, x, xi, 26, 80, 90$n4$, 90$n8$; on critical consciousness, 27

White: capitalization of black creativity, 83; desire to be, 24; gatherings, 84; identity, 94$n24$; inadequacy, 79; mass appropriation of black creation by, 87; mediocrity, 80; myopia of, 5, 6; need to conquer, 81, 82; participation in music signaling start of decay, 85, 86, 87; performance of black music, 85; pride, 81; privilege, 53; racial identity, 5; rebellion through black music, 83; relations between wealthy and poor, 8; right to enjoyment, 84; role in lynchings, 38–42; supremacy, viii, 80, 88, 108; unjust appropriation of wealth, 85

Whiteman, Paul, 95$n33$

Whiteness: affirmation of American identity, 81; as Apolline rationalization of spirit, 76; baggage of, 87; decadence of, 87; degenerate manifestations of identity in, 5; desired by immigrants, 93$n20$; discourse of, 12$n15$; entitlements of, 88; as indication of divine selection, 94$n21$; megalomania and, 5; as powerful commodity, 81; premodern, 94$n21$; race toward, 24; role as that of domestication of chaotic forces, 76; technocratic, 81; as unconscious symbol of virtue, 24–25

Will: art as act of, 11; direct image of, xv; to know, 20; to self-mastery, 210, 211; to truth, 140, 141

Willett, Cynthia, xvii*n21*, 194*n3*,
195*n6*, 195*n7*, 198*n25*, 198*n28*,
203–222; on healing of psyche, 10;
199*n29*
Williams, Mary Lou, 77
Will to power, 10, 194*n3*, 203,
204–212; artistic drives and, 207;
emergence of, 207; fantasy and,
205; healing of psyche and, 10;
hidden impulses and, 205;
indirect expressions of, 205;
intensity of experience in, 205;

libido and, 205; masculinity and,
205, 206; metaphor of rape and,
208; origin of values and, 20
The Will to Power (Nietzsche), 81,
88, 94*n22*
Winchester, James, 10, 225–242
Woods, Tiger, 80, 93*n19*
Wright, Richard, 10, 76, 77, 113,
204, 213; *Native Son*, 213–216

Zack, Naomi, 111, 150, 151, 153, 163
Züchtung, 157, 158

Made in the USA
Lexington, KY
26 June 2011